Feltrinelli

Feltrinelli

———

Carlo Feltrinelli

Translated from the Italian by
Alastair McEwan

Harcourt, Inc.
New York   San Diego   London

Requests for permission to make copies of any part of the
work should be mailed to the following address:
Permissions Department, Harcourt, Inc., 6277 Sea Harbor Drive,
Orlando, Florida 32887-6777.

www.HarcourtBooks.com

Library of Congress Cataloging-in-Publication Data
Feltrinelli, Carlo, 1962–
[Senior service. English]
Feltrinelli: a story of riches, revolution, and violent death /
Carlo Feltrinelli; translated from the Italian
by Alastair McEwan.–1st U.S. ed.
p.   cm.
Includes index.
ISBN 0-15-100558-3
1. Feltrinelli, Giangiacomo. 2. Political activists–Italy–Biography.
3. Publishers and publishing–Italy–Biography.
4. Italy–Politics and government–1945–1976.
5. Radicalism–Italy–History–20th century. 6. Feltrinelli editore.
7. Italy–Intellectual life–20th century.   I. Title.
DG579.F45 F4513 2002
945.092'092–dc21   2002005346

Text set in Berthold Walbaum
Designed Kaelin Chappell

Printed in the United States of America

First U.S. edition
A C E G I K J H F D B

For Inge and Tomás

Feltrinelli

1

Austria, Christmas 1967. We came to the edge of the wood in Indian file, the man with the rifle in the lead, a long trail of foot-
steps in our wake. Mine spoiled the symmetry. Sometimes we
walked in the footprints left by those in front, to save effort. I remember the slow, hesitant, mechanical movement of boots sinking
too deep in the snow.

When we got to the barn, we had to open it, and it fell to me to
fill the bucket with oats and sesame. Carrying the bucket was my
job. The others loaded the hay.

Then came the turnips, gigantic turnips, so sweet-smelling that
you felt like peeling away the rind to the hard flesh beneath. The
turnips had to be scattered around. I hurled them as though I were
an Olympic shot putter. When I threw them at the tree, they burst
into mush.

Then we were all up in that tree, squatting down hidden and
silent, screened only by four pieces of wood nailed to the branches.
We were sitting on a creaky plank, forbidden to move. Even I, the
least experienced of the three, had brought along two pairs of thick
socks, remembered my gloves, and was wearing the right type of

pants. In the Thermos there was mulled wine, but only a mouthful
for me.

My father lit an unfiltered Virginia cigarette. Now it was a matter of waiting, the minutes stretching into quarter hours, waiting
for something to move up there on the crest of the hill: they usually came down into the gully from the left slope.

The herd never arrived in one group. First came a reconnaissance party of three or four that I never managed to spot. (I am
nearsighted like my father.) When I finally did see them, there
were already ten or twenty head, maybe more. They were almost
to our hiding place.

The man with the rifle (he did not need it that day, but he always carried it) was the forest ranger. That evening he seemed satisfied because lots of deer had come, even big Walter with ten kilos
of bony antler on his head. The season, announced the ranger, had
gone better than they thought: fewer head shot, no eye disease, no
animals fallen down the crevasse. And for the winter some new
arrivals had come from the neighboring valley.

Every so often, muzzles would be raised from the troughs to
observe our tree. They knew we were there, they smelled it and
sensed it. But it's all right, they seemed to say, we'll play along.

Watching the deer come down from the Fütterung, I associated
their movements with those of people. Where had I seen that face
before? The first were the courageous ones, smarter or prouder than
the rest, while the last were diffident, fearful, or perhaps simply
more prudent. I saw human expressions on their animal faces.

But now darkness was falling and the wind ruffled the waters of
the mountain stream. The big buck stationed on the left emitted a
throaty rumble; a dry branch snapped; all the vague gestures became a single movement: the herd was gone, having darted off for
no reason. We remained motionless.

After a few moments, my father nodded to me. We could get the
ladder, climb down, and go back the way we had come. Ingelein

would be waiting for us with dinner, wanting to hear in the local dialect what we'd been doing.

The man with the rifle watched over his mountains for another thirty years. One day, he surprised me by saying, "Your father had a real feeling for the mountains, just like Hemingway." I can't say he was right; he may not have really known Giangiacomo Feltrinelli, or Ernest Hemingway, for that matter.

My grandfather, who was called Carlo like me, may have seen and heard the same things on the summit of the Hochsitz, and one day, who knows, my children may want to don those heavy green jackets with the horn buttons. They were born more than a hundred years after him, but the heavy green jacket is still a good idea when going out after deer.

I believe that the person who chose the valley as the family's holiday home was Maria von Pretz, my Austrian great-grandmother. The twentieth century had barely begun when she bought the only hunting lodge in the area. It was built in 1880 for one of Queen Victoria's grandchildren. After the Great War, Maria's middle-aged children added a new wing to the residence, whose furnishings were inspired by the Wiener Werkstätten. The new wing was the work of thirty men who lived in the valley; my grandfather provided their sons with two pairs of shoes, complete summer outfits, and the necessary winter clothing.

Carlo Feltrinelli was of average height, with a prematurely bald but well-shaped head, an aquiline nose, and the slim mustaches in vogue at the time. He was an important man.

Left fatherless at the age of fifteen (Giovanni Feltrinelli died in 1896), Carlo was the eldest of four brothers. Maria, his mother, was helped by Giacomo Feltrinelli, Giovanni's uncle, who made the family leave Bolzano and move to central Milan. Uncle Giacomo, who had no children, acted as a father to the four boys, a task he carried out with generous and responsible affection. His wish was that the boys, once they reached adulthood, should maintain the place in society that their father had earned for himself.

German was spoken at home, and discipline was strict. A set of family rules accepted by adults and children alike prescribed standards of behavior, with a system of fines and incentives. Those who went into the kitchen for no reason were fined ten cents (article 3), and there was the same fine for those who dared to speak in Italian more than three times over lunch (article 5). There was a twenty-cent fine for anyone caught touching the maids (article 9), a two-cent fine for anyone who bit his fingernails (article 10), and a twenty-cent fine for anyone who did not switch off the light when he left the room. But there was more to life than punishment, so arriving at breakfast in the correct order (by age) meant a five-cent reward, a whole day without a reprimand was worth ten, and three As on the weekly school report brought in thirty cents.

All the boys were educated. Carlo, for example was sent to Rosmini College in Domodossola in 1895. It was a hard, spartan life, with few privileges. He was good at math, but found Latin difficult.

Shortly after Giovanni's death, Giacomo Feltrinelli took his nephew Carlo on a European tour. They spent time in a variety of places, including a two-week stay in Carlsbad, where Carlo's uncle took the waters once a year. During lunch in the hotel restaurant, Carlo was asked what he would like. "A chicken breast," he replied timidly. The waiters brought a whole chicken. After Giacomo served himself, he let Carlo do the same, saying only, "It's all paid for, so you must finish it." Carlo did not dare disobey, and the rest of the chicken was forced down with great difficulty, an episode he never forgot.

This brief educational trip included Munich, Zurich, and I don't know how many other places. Before returning to Milan, they stopped at the family villa on Lake Garda. Carlo's uncle taught him how to snare birds on Mount Gargnano, using all kinds of traps and decoys. During that period Giacomo sent a report on his young great-nephew to the boy's mother. "He is good company," he told her, "although shy and still very much a child. But if he learns to travel, for it is of paramount importance to know how to travel, then he may make something of himself."

A few years later, Giacomo came to appreciate Carlo's level-headed ways, his reserved intelligence, and his capacity for study and work. He saw in him the main hope for the continuation of the family's business enterprises.

According to Giannalisa (my paternal grandmother), the founder of the Feltrinelli family was a certain Piero da Feltre, who lived around 1500: because the town of Feltre has walls dating from the 1500s, they must have been built by him. This, at least, is grandmother's version.

At any rate, the people in the Garda area who earn a living from timber have always said they were Feltrinéi (hailing from Feltre), which may not be entirely true; tradition has it that these expert carpenters came to Garda to construct merchant vessels and warships as well as fortifications.

I know Giacomo Feltrinelli's face very well, because in the park at Gargnano there is a heavy life-size bust of him, mounted on a pedestal too tall for the bust. We stuck a basketball basket under his chin. Disrespectful, perhaps, but at least I know the face of my great-grandfather's uncle.

Giacomo was born in 1829, the youngest of thirteen. That the family was a poor one is clear from the fact that at the age of twelve he wandered the streets of Gargnano selling "three of a kind," a mixture of yellow flour, white flour, and rice. Later he went into the charcoal business.

In 1846, when Pius IX was elected pope and when the people of the Lombardy-Veneto region, still a part of the Hapsburg empire, were dreaming of a federal Italy, the first Feltrinelli timber yard was opened.

Initially the timber came from the woods behind the house and was transported down the lake to Desenzano, where the yard was situated. But soon wood was also coming in from the Trent area, and from there all the way up to Val Pusteria. When Giacomo joined the family firm full-time he gave the business a decided boost. Joking, my father used to say that the secret lay in selling "heavy" timber, that is to say lumber that had been soaked with water in order to increase the weight. A more plausible reason for Uncle Giacomo's great success in business was that those were boom years for both the construction industry and the railroads. Industrial expansion, especially around Milan, was leading to a growing demand for timber: wood for scaffolding, wood for cross ties, wood, wood, wood: it seemed as if all people wanted was wood, particularly deal, the specialty of the Feltrinelli firm.

By 1870, the national rail network was three times bigger than it had been a decade before. But because of the limited size of Italian forests (and their inaccessibility), the production of resiniferous trees was still insufficient.

The firm moved to Milan in 1857, and over the following decade its clientele grew remarkably, even though the business was still semi regional. From the early 1880s things changed radically: Feltrinelli timber expanded with the addition of fifteen branches in Italy, and various commercial agencies in the Austro-Hungarian Empire and in the Balkans were also opened. The strategy was to take direct control of the sources of supply and to have a hand in processing and installing timber. This was the reason for the purchase of whole forests in Carinthia and the firm's participation in the construction of railroads to Vienna and Salonika, and in Sicily and Calabria.

Things went so well that it became necessary to diversify further, and in 1889 Uncle Giacomo created the Banca Feltrinelli. One of the bank's first moves was to finance the work of the engineer Giuseppe Colombo, the founder of Italy's first electrical company.

This was the Milan-based Edison concern, named after Thomas Alva Edison, with whom Colombo had been in contact since 1881. With this operation (1896) the bank managed to ward off a takeover bid by German financiers, thereby welding the future of Edison to that of the Feltrinelli family.

In those years the business also branched out into textiles, with the establishment of the Feltrinelli & Co. Cotton Mill, and transport, with a stake in a company that ran the boat service on Lake Garda.

At the beginning of the twentieth century, while the timber company was supplying half the world with wood, the construction and real estate branch had attained at least equal importance. One of the early moves made by the real estate company was to purchase twenty-four lots with a total of 115 thousand square meters in the Testaccio, the working-class district of Rome. The Feltrinelli group held other properties in Rome as well, like the semicircle around Piazza Esedra. The entire block had been picked up for 271,000 lire following the failure of the Banca Tiberina.

One of the leading lights of the entrepreneurial bourgeoisie, Giacomo Feltrinelli apparently never lost the "horse sense" of a man who always knew where to find a good Bardolino and how to decant, transport, and drink it. The same held true for pressing olives and growing lemons.

Looking at him face to face before taking a foul shot, I would imagine him as authoritative, with a proud gaze and a wise frown. This was the image he left his great-nephews when he died in 1913. The newspapers, in their obituaries, spoke of him as a "singular example of a self-made man," and in defining him as "the wealthiest man in Milan," they estimated his personal assets at 60 million lire.

I imagine that Giannalisa also waited in silence for the herd of deer to come, getting her ration of cold up there in the tree. But maybe not; she was not partial to waiting, although she definitely loved to hunt.

One day, the story goes, Giannalisa had to wait at a grade crossing at the mouth of the valley. She was in her Rolls (she never went
out without a Rolls in all her life). The train was late. As she
waited, she noticed that a hundred meters away a roe had come
too far down the mountainside to graze. The animal was perfectly
visible, ten paces beyond the edge of the wood. She picked up the
brand-new rifle she had with her, steadied it against the copper-
colored window frame of the car door, and took aim. Three shots.
The chauffeur, terrified, nearly had his eardrums broken. She was
not the kind of woman you forgot.

As every good grandchild does, I felt a sincere and serene affection for my grandmother. She gave me strange presents, almost
always with no appeal for a young boy: one of the last was an umbrella stand; perhaps not devoid of value, but an umbrella stand
none the less. A more charming instance of her generosity was the
time I asked her to bring me the American edition of *Blonde on
Blonde* from New York. I wanted it because of the photo of Claudia
Cardinale on the inside cover: the European version of the album
did not have the photo. She made a note. And she made a visit to a
record store on Fifth Avenue just for me.

On the death of Giacomo Feltrinelli, of the four heirs it was
Carlo who understood the situation. Merely managing the assets
would not be enough. Much better to broaden the company's
prospects step by step, even within a Europe exhausted by the
Great War. Since international business was the most important
aspect of Carlo Feltrinelli's career as an industrialist and financier,
I would say he was a kind of pioneer, though the term is too frequently used to mean adventurer, something he definitely was not.

Little is known about my grandfather. He lived and had his personal offices on Via Andegari, next to the La Scala opera house.
There are no biographies or profiles of him, a few newspaper articles at most. In the economic yearbooks there are pieces on emi-

nent names who were perhaps less important at the time, but only a few terse lines on him. He was said to be a reserved and private man.

Eulogizing Carlo on his death (in 1935), the attorney Edoardo Majno described him as a man "of few words but having sound knowledge and profound experience, who was thoughtful and accustomed to approaching problems calmly in order to subject them to thorough examination." Aristocratic in spirit, he was definitely not eloquent when it came to expressing his thoughts, "but how pithy, how prudent, how profound!" Majno added: "He really was a man of sound counsel, in the full Latin sense of the word." And he defined Carlo as a "simple and melancholy" man, whose industriousness was felt and professed "as a technical activity, to which he devoted himself out of duty and a lofty awareness of its social function and importance." But, he concluded, "With that joyless temperament of his, he was left, as it were, on the outside of things, wrapped in the cloistered modesty of his life and in a constant and serene bitterness."

With Carlo the fame of the Società Fratelli Feltrinelli grew even more thanks to a massive importing program: deal, beech, and oak from Europe; pitch pine and Douglas fir from North America; teak from Asia; and costly mahogany from Africa. He also acquired Austria's biggest lumber company, and in 1932 he signed agreements of decisive importance with a Russian trade delegation (Feltrinelli became the exclusive importer for Italy). From the United States he obtained one of the first licenses granted by the Masonite Corporation for the production of hardboard panels.

The family's forestry company, the Società Forestale Feltrinelli, based in Fiume, invested heavily in Transylvania. Photos show factories, cableways, railroad networks, workers' houses, all specially built. The first Italian undertaking of this kind, it provided employment for about three thousand people. From Transylvania lumber was sent off to Bulgaria, Greece, Turkey, Egypt, and Syria.

In the thirties, warehouses, depots, and sawmills were also set up in numerous locations in East Africa, while European deal for urban construction work was sent to Eritrea and Ethiopia.

Some thought Carlo was overly involved in his work, forever driven by the idea of increasing the firm's assets. Others, less agreeably, thought him a miser, unresponsive to the promptings of the heart. To all he replied, "The management of our assets is a necessity. Should I diminish them, or make deals to lose money?"

From the early years of the twentieth century, through the Banca Feltrinelli my grandfather helped finance the Acciaierie Ferriere Lombarde, the steel concern run by the Falck family. He was a man to whom everyone listened with respect. Giorgio Falck described him as "eclectic and shrewd."

The list of companies in which he was involved was a long one. In Italy alone, there were dozens of companies in fields like construction, land reclamation, chemicals, textiles, and building. But he also ran companies in Calcutta, the Italian Far Eastern Company, the Bank of Italy and Egypt, and electrical companies in Latin America.

Toward the end of the twenties, at the peak of his career, he became chairman of the Edison Company, the most important in Italy, as well as of Italy's second largest bank, the Credito Italiano. The controlling shareholder in both institutions, through them he obtained the right to exploit the hydroelectric resources of the Styria region, thereby illuminating half of Austria. The *Times* estimated his personal fortune at eight hundred million lire.

Before her death, my grandmother set down her recollections; they were exclusively for family members. Only a few pages were devoted to her husband, Carlo; all the rest dealt with their first meeting and its immediate aftermath. The interesting thing about this document is what it *doesn't* say.

I came to know more about Carlo through Teresa, the trusty,

faithful, long-lived secretary I shared with him. Teresa first arrived in the office in Via Andegari when she was twenty and didn't retire until fifty years later, when I was nearly twenty.

By her account, Grandfather was a reserved gentleman and a tireless worker. He had little time for himself. He married when he was past forty, and nothing is known about the women in his life, except for a Russian noblewoman, Ljuba Aleksandrovna, with whom he shared a passion for classical music.

As for art, the family pictures (including an Antonello da Messina donated to the Brera Museum) are fine but somber. There was literature, certainly: what could be better than a good book after a frugal meal in his austere country house? But he was not a literary man. According to Giacinto Motta,* "he was devoid of lyricism." His only real love was music, and the piano was his favorite instrument.

He was a benefactor of the Scuola Industriale Giacomo Feltrinelli in Milan, a school still active today in the technical-scientific field. He had no inclination toward charitable works but, true to the family's public spirit, he contributed toward the foundation, on the Gargnano estate, of a hospital, a nursery school, and a retirement home.

"Grandfather Carlo had two brothers, Bepi and Tonino": Giannalisa's handwriting is recognizable on the envelope with some family photos inside. Come, Grandmother, weren't there three brothers? Pietro, born in 1885, committed suicide at twenty-eight for love of a Romanian dancer. He was in charge of the lumber reserves at Sibiu, and his life was so short that Giannalisa must have thought it wiser to have him disappear altogether.

For Bepi (Giuseppe), things did not go that much better, even though he lived through the last splendor of the Austro-Hungarian

*(1870–1943). Engineer, professor at the Milan Polytechnic, businessman, managing director and CEO of Edison during the Fascist period. (Footnotes are by the translator.)

Empire. The division of family labor assigned him the Eastern European side of the business, which is why he lived between Vienna and Villaco, and oversaw the importation of lumber into Italy.

He spent his free time hunting wolf, grouse, fox, roebuck, red deer, and mouflon. His hunting exploits are documented in a photo album in which he appears with all his trophies, including a group of zebras dispatched on an expedition to the African savanna. His career as an obsessive hunter is also documented by some hundreds of horns and a bizarre variety of stuffed animals: from an eagle shot just as it was sinking its talons into a white hare (both of them ended up stuffed) to the bust of an enormous wild boar felled on the Hungarian estate of Prince Andràzy, who my mother claims was Empress Sissy's lover.

Every time Bepi returned to Italy, he lived the glittering life of a wealthy man about town and made sure he was seen with the most beautiful women (including the celebrated Mazzolenis sisters), but he had no real interest in culture. Once, at the railway station in Rome, the conductor came puffing up, all excited, to ask him if he would be so good as to let the renowned poet Gabriele D'Annunzio have a seat in his compartment (or maybe it was in his personal car). "Don't know him," Bepi is said to have replied.

The life of Giuseppe Feltrinelli took a dramatic turn the day he decided to take care of a bear cub found in Valle dei Cervi. Perhaps the cub had lost its mother–who knows? The fact is that Bepi decided to keep it, in the garden of his home.

As the cub grew, it really became fond of Bepi. To the point that, one evening, on seeing its master return after a long trip, it greeted him with such exuberance that it gave him a bad wound on the shoulder. Bepi took morphine for the pain of the deep slashes left by the bear's claws, until he became addicted to it. He died in Rome in 1918 after an injection. He was thirty-five.

Antonio Feltrinelli, called Tonino, survived his three brothers and ended his life holed up on the shores of Lake Garda. Tonino enjoyed painting in oils. Married to the Countess Luisa Doria, he frequently clashed with Carlo's widow and, being childless, out of spite left a large part of his estate (including a majority stake in Fratelli Feltrinelli Lumber) to the Accademia dei Lincei.* The rich prize that bears his name is still awarded to outstanding international figures from the worlds of letters, the physical sciences, mathematics, history, and medicine.

Tonino died in 1942. He was hit by an army truck near Brescia and had a number of his ribs fractured. The doctors prescribed pepper poultices to ease the pain. Septicemia set in within the week. When Tonino was laid in his coffin, or so they say in Gargnano, his body burst in two, full of worms.

In early 1925, on behalf of the Italian government, Carlo Feltrinelli was nominated a board member of the Reichsbank, within the terms of the agreement between the Allies and Germany.

In Milan, it was rumored that he wanted to take a wife and start a family: it's a thought that tends to surface at a certain point in life.

One evening, when Carlo visited Mino Gianzana's box at La Scala (Gianzana had started out as a clerk with the Banca Commerciale, of which he became the chief executive officer), his eye fell on one of Gianzana's daughters, a faunlike twenty-two-year-old by the name of Giannalisa. Wasn't she the little girl who had gone swimming with them six years before, at Forte dei Marmi?† That summer, Carlo had rented Villa Hildebrandt for his mother, Maria. Giannalisa was still in high school then (she went to school with Dino Buzzati)‡ and her swimsuit was almost laughably chaste. How she had grown! Carlo felt she had become quite another person.

A reception during Carnival at the Esterle home served to

---

*Academia dei Lincei: an academy of science founded in 1603 by a small group of noblemen. Galileo was one of its earliest members.

†An upper-class seaside vacation resort in Tuscany.

‡The author of *Tartar Steppe,* one of the great Italian novels of the last century.

renew the acquaintance. The girl was enchanting. Then came the announcement to her parents, smelling salts, fainting fits, tears, and strings of pearls: then the wedding, forty days later.

At the mouth of Valle dei Cervi, a landau drawn by a pair of horses and two hunters wearing light-colored festive livery awaited the bride and groom for the first stop on their honeymoon journey.

Giannalisa entered the house on Via Andegari with a black pearl in her left earlobe and a white one in the right. Light-blue eyes, long neck, short hair, slim figure: a classic beauty with a hint of something odd about her. She had been undisciplined as a child. Her father, a very strict man, had struggled to tame this wild little creature, and her mother's last words on her deathbed were, "Giannalisa, I never understood you. Forgive me."

Her sister Josefa was the opposite: less effervescent, less attractive, and docile. The two of them were about as compatible as the devil and holy water. When Josefa found a husband in the person of Filippo Sacchi, a young teacher not devoid of charm, Giannalisa did all she could to oppose the marriage and sow discord between the respective relatives.

The first two years of Giannalisa's marriage to Carlo were punctuated by two forceps-assisted births: Giangiacomo Feltrinelli was born on 19 June 1926, Antonella on 13 November of the following year.

Then came the long vacations in all the right places for bringing up children, with many nannies and the husband often busy elsewhere. A serene and privileged life spent between Lake Garda, Villa Rosa (the Gianzanas' estate on Lake Como), the Baur du Lac in Zurich, the Excelsior at the Lido, and the Austria Hotel on Via Andegari. Sometimes Carlo took Giannalisa with him, and for her those trips were the beginning of a great adventure. From her book of memoirs:

> Life picked up again and in mid-January 1928 Carlo and I took great joy in going to the landing stage in Genoa to take up residence in our splendid cabin on board the *Esperia*. Carlo had to go to Cairo to

chair a meeting of the Banca Italo-Egiziana, of which he was chairman. Egypt was still a British protectorate, a system that inculcated
order and discipline. We lodged at the Hotel Semiramis, perfectly
kept red felt and not a white thread to be seen. On our arrival we
found an invitation to dine with King Fuad at the royal palace. The
king had great difficulty in talking, because of a bullet that had
lodged in his esophagus during an assassination attempt. Also in
Cairo at that time were His Royal Highness Prince Umberto and
Guidone Visconti di Modrone, who conducted the orchestra in the
theater of the royal palace. In all my various dinners at court, I will
never forget the incredibly wide staircase, on which, at each side of
every step, Arabs and Negroes in full dress uniform stood motionless with long, burning torches in their hands. The dinners were
served by enormous waiters in sumptuous uniforms. There were always about a hundred guests seated around a long, horseshoe-
shaped table. The local dignitaries wore frock coats and tails. Only
three ladies were invited, the Italian ambassadress, the lady in waiting to the queen, who never appeared in public, and I, who usually
sat opposite the Prince of Piedmont. He lived in the same hotel as
we. His room was above mine, and every morning at eight I would
hear his feet touching the floor when he got up. Our friendship dates
from then. Carlo and I invited the prince to lunch in the desert
under an immense Arab tent, with the elite of the Italian colony. An
Arab equestrian show was planned to enliven the lunch. I recall saying to the prince, "Your Royal Highness, we are eating more dust
than they can serve us." Another day, we invited him to visit the
three pyramids near the Mena House Hotel. I can still see His Royal
Highness climbing the one-meter high steps all the way to the top of
a pyramid. After this social whirl, Carlo had promised me we would
visit the royal tombs at Luxor, and a wagon-lit left us at the Hotel
Palace on the banks of the Nile. The mountains before us housed the
royal remains. We took a little boat to cross the Nile, and on the
other side a camel took us to the foot of the mountains. Our guide,
an Arab, warned me not to visit the tomb of Tutankhamen because
it would bring me bad luck. But I am not superstitious, even though
the pharaoh was still in his tomb all wrapped up, awaiting trans-
portation to London. He had been assassinated at twenty-one. The
tomb was small, the objects all packed in crates. We visited the treasure chamber, the first to be discovered by Carter, financed by Lord
Caernarvon. The other tombs were much larger because [their oc-
cupants] had lived longer. Luxor too came to an end, and on our

return to Cairo, fascinated by the Arabs and their abilities, I suggested to Carlo that we take one back to Milan, but with great sweetness Carlo had me understand that our house would soon be infested with little Arabs. I was enchanted by the work they could do. In Cairo I saw one with a clothes iron attached to his ankle pressing a most delicate blouse with an infinity of pleats on the front.

The prophecy of the Arab guide before the tomb to Tutankhamen was to come tragically true in the subsequent pages of her memoirs.

Carlo accepted an invitation to spend a few days hunting at Castello della Mandria, where the guests included the Duke and Duchess of Pistoia and the Prince of Piedmont. On 21 November 1928, with joy, we set off in the car for Mandria, which stands a few kilometers outside Turin. Not far from the castle was the cottage built for "la bella Rusin."* The next morning, we were going to stroll through the estate to try to take a few hares. It was a damp, drizzly day. I shot one and saw a hint of something tragic in its dying eyes. The pheasant shoot proper was scheduled for the afternoon, with the Duke and Duchess of Pistoia. It was just midday when another guest arrived from Milan. I refuse to write his name, in any case he was the managing director of the Credito Italiano, the Milan bank of which Carlo was the chairman and held 80 percent of the stock. A little later, Giacomo (our host) said, "Giannalisa, let's see if we can bag a partridge in the quarter hour before lunch." We came to a wide, asphalted road. The coach backed away from the point where it left us. Giacomo assigned a place to everyone. Carlo was in the meadow in front of me. I was on the edge of the road, and less than a hundred meters to my right stood the "jinx," also at the edge of the road. At a certain point I heard him call me, and as I turned toward him I saw his shotgun trained on a level with my eyes. He fired at my face. I felt an atrocious pain, and the blood gushed down my cheeks. I put the safety catch on my gun and put it down before making off as fast as I could to Carlo, who was running down the meadow toward me, as were Giacomo and Gigetto, who, protected by the trees, emerged in the meadow. They comforted me, Carlo put his handkerchief over my right eye, and I saw a flash of madness in his eyes. In the mean-

*Rosa Vercellana, called "la bella Rusin," was the mistress of King Victor Emanuel III.

time the guilty party was escaping in his car toward Milan and on the way his chauffeur ran over and seriously injured a man. The hunting party at Castello della Mandria was suspended.

"Child, did you shoot yourself for love?" "No, Sister, someone shot me." While in the hospital, Giannalisa received an affectionate letter from the queen.

We shall never know if the shot was fired in error or if the wretch, a certain Orsi, was inspired by a sudden fit of insane hatred. All we know is that a specialist summoned urgently from Switzerland to save her uninjured eye, had to remove the eye struck by the pellets, the right. A sad Christmas awaited the family.

The only alternative to a pirate's patch was a glass eye. Giannalisa took courage: to disguise the glass better, she used a monocle. Life was not allowed to change. She did not even want to give up hunting. She ordered the sight of her rifle to be realigned for her left eye. But her husband obliged her to accept one condition: hunting on family land only.

Despite their efforts, the incident at Mandria introduced a note of gloom into their marriage.

"Mister Carlo," already reserved by nature, began to close up like an oyster. But in the professional field, these were the years of his apotheosis as one of the leading lights of Italian capitalism. In 1922 he became vice president of Edison. In 1924 he was appointed to the board of the Credito Italiano; in that same year he was nominated Knight Grand Officer of the Crown of Italy, and the government appointed him to the board of the Reichsbank.

Between 1925 and 1926, together with Giovanni Agnelli, Riccardo Gualino, Piero Puricelli, Giovanni Lancia, Piero Pirelli, and Silvio Crespi, Feltrinelli was one of the promoters of the S. A. Austostrada Milano-Torino, at the time the longest highway in Italy (125.8 kilometers), and his name was linked more and more with the dynamic side of big business.

In 1928, with Mussolini already in power for six years, the appointment to the chairmanship of the Credito Italiano marked the peak of Carlo's career. The lumber business carried on without particular problems for the entire decade.

I have not managed to find out much about my grandfather. My father didn't have time to get to know him well, and I didn't have time with my father to learn about his father from him. In her flight from time, Giannalisa somehow managed to lose her husband's most private papers.

Only the reports of the Fascist police, found in the state archives, provide more information on Carlo. There is one interesting request from the chief of the political police to the chief of police in Milan (July 1927), in which the latter was asked to provide "highly confidential" information on Carlo Feltrinelli, suspected of having expressed "strong disapproval of the actions of the National Government." One of Carlo's employees, an informer, had caught him making ironical remarks to a colleague about Mussolini's government. The issue was the revaluation of the lira. "It may be that Mussolini and his gang of toadies are right, but I don't think so," Carlo is said to have remarked.

The following year, another black-shirted employee was fired for persistent lateness, and he inundated many desks—all the way up to those of Achille Starace* and Mussolini—with denunciations of "serious tax evasion on the part of the Feltrinelli company." The dossier was sent to the finance minister. But there the matter ended.

Another report concerned Giannalisa: "They say that, when Feltrinelli's wife was on vacation last summer, she not only talked freely of her husband's immense wealth but also added that he kept a large amount of Italian capital in England."

In many confidential reports on my grandfather, reference is

*A die-hard Fascist who rose to become secretary of the Fascist Party. He was known for his ferocity.

made to the "silk waste affair." He was arrested in 1918 (for one
night or perhaps a little more) because he was the managing director as well as a stockholder in the Società Anonima Cascami, a
firm dealing in silk waste. The other partners were arrested too.
During the war, the company had exported seven hundred thousand kilos of yarn and silk waste. The purchaser was a Swiss firm
with contacts in German industry. The bottom line was that the
consignment ended up in Germany, where it was used to make the
skin of Zeppelin airships.

Although the Italian producers were finally cleared of all direct
responsibility, the regime remained suspicious in the years that
followed. Numerous reports on the group's foreign business began
with "It is rumored that..." Carlo's nomination to the senate was
quashed and labeled an "infamous idea" by the highest echelons of
the military. His patriotism was not trusted.

But formally relations between Feltrinelli and the Fascist government were perfect: he was chairman of the Fascist Lumber Industry Federation, frequently called on the head of government,
and received awards. These canonical signs of respect were necessary to preserve the status quo. Being pro-government is a pre-
dictable option for great industrialists. Though Carlo's politics
might have been described as liberal, he was first and foremost
faithful to his work.

In 1930, Carlo Feltrinelli was almost fifty, not an old man but
sometimes feeling old, perhaps because of the continuous burden
of responsibility or because he was losing his teeth. The son of his
dentist recalls that Giannalisa (twenty-three years younger than
Carlo) never missed a chance to rub salt in the wound: "You're an
old man!" she would say to him.

In April, Carlo and Giannalisa took the *Orient Express* to Roma-
nia. They met with the managers of the local branch of the firm,
visited Bucharest, and, their work done, stopped over at Sibiu.

Such was Giannalisa's passion for the chase that Carlo could not avoid a hunting party near the mouth of the Danube. Before them lay the Black Sea: she shot at ibis but failed to hit any of them.

On his return, Carlo had other things to deal with. After the Wall Street crash, the banks were in crisis and everything was in turmoil. Although deposits with the Credito Italiano had slumped by 14 percent, this was a time of mergers, incorporations, and takeovers. But not every move met with success, like the attempt to gain control of the Bastogi group (which meant gaining control of a large part of the electrical sector). The government, the Bank of Italy, and Alberto Beneduce (the government's top man in the public finance sector and the chairman of Bastogi) all vetoed the bid of Feltrinelli's bank.

The developing crisis led to the restructuring of the great "mixed" banks (including the Credito and the Commerciale), which were saved by state intervention. In 1933, through the banks, the state came to hold a 40 percent share in Italy's joining stock companies. The Iri was created.*

Carlo's control of Edison began to weaken, because it was dependent on the stocks held by the Credito Italiano (which was about to become a publicly controlled company). The problem was how to avoid losing power in Foro Bonaparte.† After long talks Carlo got what he wanted so badly: Edison would remain in private hands.

The man he had to deal with was Beneduce, the new chairman of Iri. The two had known each other for a long time and respected each other. They were, along with Alberto Pirelli, Giacinto Motta, Giovanni Agnelli, and a few others, the leaders of the various sectors upon which Italian capitalism depended.

————

*The Institute for Industrial Reconstruction, a state-run industrial conglomerate.
†Headquarters of the Edison Company.

October 1934. The regime boasted of stability while it passed a
law obliging all Italian citizens to declare any assets held outside
Italy. Carlo's state of mind is not hard to imagine: electrical stocks;
German, Austrian, and American bonds; and holdings in lumber
companies (a good part of the Feltrinelli portfolio) were all abroad.
The game was beginning to get tough, but he decided to honor the
new obligations. According to Giannalisa, his lead was not followed by his brother Antonio, who was against declaring the assets
held in the name of their mother, Maria von Pretz, by then eighty.

The months that followed were particularly difficult. In 1935 the
authorities managed to bribe some employees of the Bankverein in
Zurich. They laid hands on the Feltrinelli family files and on those
of another sixteen people. Checks on Carlo's position seemed to
correspond with the statement of his assets. But they did not for
Antonio and Maria von Pretz.

On 28 October, the national holiday in commemoration of the
March on Rome, the Prefect of Milan sent a coded cablegram to the
Ministry of the Interior, saying that Mussolini had ordered, through
the Finance Ministry, the interrogation of some persons resident in
Milan. They had to answer for assets held in Switzerland. The list
included the name of Maria von Pretz. Three days later, the chief of
police stated he had interviewed the lady "concerning the existence
of 165 kilograms of gold, as well as foreign stocks to the value of two
million, deposited in her name in the Bank of Switzerland."

Maria von Pretz said that she didn't know, she couldn't remember. Carlo and Antonio were also summoned. Neither denied the
existence of the deposits, and they immediately telegraphed for the
contents to be transferred to the foreign exchange department of
the Bank of Italy. But by then the scandal had broken; the head of
a powerful man, who had been a source of embarrassment for an
autarkic regime, was at stake.

In the following days it was rumored that Antonio and his
mother might be arrested. On 6 November, Carlo went to Rome to

seek the eleventh-hour intercession of the governor of the Bank of
Italy. He returned to Milan at night, apparently reassured. But he
did not know that in those very hours Alberto Beneduce had received a government order requiring Feltrinelli's resignation from
all his posts within the Iri group.

The meeting took place on 7 November, at 6 p.m., in the offices
of Bastogi. Carlo went with the managing director of Edison, Giacinto Motta, his influential partner in many a business venture. The
words he heard were said with sympathy, but their meaning was
all too clear. Carlo could not get his breath, his heart rate went
through the roof, and suddenly he collapsed. This, at least, is the
story as reported in a night cablegram sent out in code by the chief
of police.

Suffering from this heart attack or embolism, my grandfather
was taken by Motta to Via Andegari. His secretary, Teresa, saw him
being carried into the bedroom. Giannalisa called the specialist
and told the children not to make a noise: daddy had a bad head-
ache. By the following evening, Carlo Feltrinelli was pronounced
dead; forty-eight hours before that, he had played the piano for the
last time. He was fifty-four.

The propaganda machine immediately talked of suicide. In his
personal file there are copies of the confidential ministerial memos
that were circulated in the days immediately after his death. Un-
failingly preceded by the words "it is rumored that," these sources
maintain that Carlo Feltrinelli committed suicide in a sleeping car,
in prison, in his own home, with a hand gun, with poison, for fear
of incarceration, and in any case always out of shame.

He killed himself, some said, after discovering the extent of his
mother's guilt, a mother "in the grip of a special form of mono-
mania attributable to congenital avarice." "What a dirty business!"
concludes an anonymous informer. Obviously, it was necessary to
root out accomplices: "it was rumored that" Alberto Pirelli too had

"organized a vast contraband currency ring" and that he and Feltrinelli were aided by the Fascist podestà* Visconti di Modrone,
who was suddenly ousted.

Lending credence to the suicide-out-of-shame theory served to
counter any attempt to exploit the affair in order to discredit Fascism. In the Paris headquarters of Giustizia e Libertá† and in some
parts of Italy, however, there were those who ventured a parallel
between Feltrinelli's death and the Matteotti‡ murder.

A broken heart or a poison capsule? Giacinto Motta's correspondence does not tell us everything we need to know. Five days
after witnessing Carlo's death, Motta wrote to his Neapolitan friend
Emma Savi Lopez:

> It was a most harrowing scene [...]. We were talking calmly, even
> though Carlo was troubled in spirit, in the office of a friend, who half
> an hour before had asked me to join them, when poor Carlo
> clutched his forehead with his left hand while clamping his right
> convulsively over his heart, thus arousing in us the gravest appre-
> hension. A few minutes later, while someone had been sent off to
> call his doctor, two successive cries escaped his lips: "What a pain,
> Giacinto, what a pain in my head! I am dying, Giacinto; I commend
> my children to you!" And he spoke no more.

On 12 June 1936, in a letter to Majno, Motta alluded to a "crazy
gesture" from Carlo without explaining further. This clue supports
the suicide theory.

Vinzio, the delivery man with the Cantieri Milanesi firm who
half-carried Carlo all the way to Via Andegari, is convinced it was
a heart attack, and in all the various branches of my family I have
never heard any reference or allusion to hidden truths, to things

*The equivalent of mayor in the Fascist government.
†A group of anti-Fascist exiles based in Paris.
‡An Italian politician, member of parliament, and secretary of the Socialist
Party, Giacomo Matteotti was an active anti-Fascist. He was murdered by a Fascist
action squad in March 1924.

known but never mentioned. Furthermore, the few people still able to provide some form of direct testimony, like Falck's daughter, Giulia Devoto Falck, flatly deny the suicide hypothesis. But the doubt remains.

Possibly Giannalisa was unable to shed a widow's tears. Sorrow soon yielded to vertigo. At only thirty-two she had an enormous fortune at her disposal.

Her father, Mino Gianzana, and Antonio Feltrinelli insisted on taking over the corporate posts left vacant on Carlo's death, but Giannalisa refused; she wanted to do things her way.

Her first move was to dismiss her husband's most faithful colleagues. Motta wrote to his friend Majno:

> I only hope, and I trust that this will hold for you too, that I will be forever spared further dealings with a person who has put her own resentment and insane fear of losing the hoped-for profit before her sacred obligations toward children already bereft of their father. [...] May God protect those poor children, this is my most ardent wish, to which I add my fond hope that for you too there may soon be an end to the vexations and problems that this family has given you.

Giannalisa's second move was to request an audience with His Excellency Il Duce: "In order to explain the difficulties that I now find myself obliged to face on my own," she wrote. Mussolini, in this instance perhaps more sensible of decency than the widow, did not receive her.

No matter, she resolved to make it on her own and showed that she was more than capable of doing so: she obtained statements of assets, replaced a few trustees, and played her part to perfection.

In the afternoons, every now and then, she lent a hand in an institute run by a renowned Milanese biologist who was doing cancer research. She volunteered to take her mind off things. Her job was injecting tumor cells into rabbits.

Giannalisa loved her children but treated them in accordance with the dictates of an ill-considered logic. She would punish and then repent. She would mortify them and then shower them with kisses and hugs.

Giangiacomo and Antonella, in the meantime, were transported here and there like monkeys. In 1936, after a splendid springtime cruise to Rhodes, it was off to New York by ship; but at Gibraltar the sea was rather rough: better to disembark in Lisbon. In Lisbon it seemed like a good idea to make a quick visit to the resort town of Cascais. A car came to pick them up, and clothing and trunks were promptly stowed aboard because now they had to cross France and Switzerland. The new destination was farther east: welcome to Austria! Attacks of car sickness at every bend.

For Giangiacomo and Antonella, school was out of the question, at most a semester, around 1937, at Milan's Giuseppe Parini High School (according to the recollections of the famous Italian wine expert Luigi Veronelli, at that time Giangiacomo's classmate). It was then that Giannalisa enrolled her son in the Gioventù Italiana del Littorio, the Italian Fascist Youth Movement. The excessive shuttling between the new villa in the exclusive suburb of San Siro and the family's Roman residence on the Aventino persuaded Giannalisa to engage a private tutor. The teacher chosen to give literature lessons was Luciano Anceschi,* the future maestro of the New Italian Avant-Garde, whom Giangiacomo, his first pupil, was to encounter again much later. An alumnus of one of the city's finest high schools was chosen to tutor the children in the family's Roman residence. From him, Antonella and her brother learned the fundamentals of art history. His name was Jean Piva. Today, he is a retired doctor, and I have met him.

He says he well remembers the yelling in the Feltrinelli home, so much like a grand hotel, which always smelled of the wax used to polish the brassware, and where a pair of dirty hands was

---

*Anceschi (1911–95) was a publicist, literary critic, and professor of aesthetics.

enough to start an uproar. On the pretext of visiting a museum, Giangiacomo could occasionally go out. He almost always avoided the museum, preferring a field belonging to the family on the Appian Way. Not that it was a special place: a patch of ground with some crops and a few trees. But he felt good there, with a few tools and a little silence. He didn't have any friends.

By way of compensation, one morning at breakfast there appeared Luigi Barzini Jr., a thumb and index finger hooked into the lapels of a gangster-style bathrobe. He was wearing plush slippers and a cigarette hung from his fleshy lips: he was the new fiancé of the richest widow in Italy.

The son of the greatest special correspondent of the early twentieth century, an adventurous spirit who had reported the Peking-to-Paris rally, Luigi Junior was in his turn a journalist. A period spent studying in America had provided him with a lively, modern style that was superior to that of the average Italian journalist. But he was overly influenced by his father's aura, he felt he was the crown prince, and his English clothes hung badly on him. His colleagues, perhaps out of envy, said that he "dressed like a white man," because he always had the look of a black man dressed in European clothes. He was said to be fond of the comfortable life, and not averse to a few luxuries.

In April 1940, two months before Italy entered the war, the young man and Giannalisa pronounced the fateful "I do." It happened in Amalfi, in the chapel of Saint Andrea in the cathedral. The marriage was later annulled by the Rota, but the bride had a clear memory of what she wore that day: "a navy-blue dress with white polka dots and a straw hat in the same color." Like his sister, Giangiacomo was dressed in a page's outfit, and his task was to toss silver coins in the air when the bride and groom emerged on the steps, causing amazement and pandemonium among the local children.

A few days after the wedding, on the point of leaving for his

honeymoon, Gibò, as Barzini was nicknamed, was arrested by the
Fascists. It seems that for some time he had been playing at espionage: during a spell as the London correspondent of the *Corriere
della Sera,* he had passed on useful information to the authorities
in Rome. On his return to Italy, in the course of a dinner with some
British diplomats, prompted by a desire to show off, he let slip
something about the messages in code sent out from their embassy. In short, he gave them to understand that the Italian intelligence service could read the messages with ease. The British
checked this out right away: they sent a message quoting what
Barzini had said. The Italian secret service, which was in fact listening in, was obliged to collar the newly wed groom.

Thanks to his father's connections. Luigi Barzini was sentenced
to confinement there in Amalfi, in the Hotel dei Cappuccini, together with his wife. A decidedly mild punishment for such a serious crime. Giangiacomo and Antonella spent part of the first year
of the war in Amalfi.

The two spouses had to present themselves once a week at the
police station in Salerno to sign the register. But there was no need
to enter the station, all they had to do was knock on the window
overlooking the promenade to receive an "OK, OK" that hardly interrupted their stroll.

My grandmother had been arrested before this by the authorities. In the course of a diplomatic dinner, she had been heard to
speak badly of Mussolini. She got out of this predicament through
the immediate intervention of Enrico Caviglia, a friend she vaca-
tioned with who had been a field marshal in the First World War.
This minor incident came in handy as proof of her "anti-Fascism,"
and she played on it for the rest of her life.

In the meantime, Mussolini's office received Giannalisa's request that an aristocratic title be conferred upon her son. This happened in 1940, and the affair was brought to a satisfactory conclusion

by a substantial check. We do not know if the future Marquis of Gargnano had any opinion on the matter.

Thanks to Barzini Senior, who was on friendly terms with the chief of police, Barzini Junior was allowed to move to Milan. This was in March 1941. His "compulsory residence" was the Hotel Continental on Via Manzoni, because my grandmother did not want any policemen tailing her around the house. But after a few weeks, they were able to savor complete freedom once more and took up permanent residence in Miracielo, their villa in San Siro. Six months later, Barzini's swimming pool was commandeered: they said it had to be converted into an air-raid shelter.

At this point the needle of the compass swung once more toward central Italy. In October 1942, to avoid the worst of the fighting, the Barzini-Feltrinelli family opted for the Argentario, an area on the scenic road to Porto Santo Stefano where work had recently been completed on Giannalisa's dream villa. It stood on top of a promontory surrounded by thick Mediterranean vegetation: myrtle, mastic, and so on.

Looking out from the veranda, you can sense the presence of a sheer cliff face, while to the right the coastline shelves inward and you cannot see the beach, which is hidden by undergrowth. It is a splendid place, but "for us it was sheer murder," explains Aunt Antonella, then fifteen. "We were left entirely to our own devices, but like kidnap victims, without ever going beyond the gate, without ever being able to get to know anybody."

In fact, the human situation was unpromising: when Luigi Barzini was not marching around the estate giving orders (such as ordering sacks to be attached to the backsides of the mules), he was arguing with everybody, Giannalisa included.

It was no idyll, and it was wartime, yet the family multiplied; Giovanna Ludovica was born in September 1942, and Benedetta came along a year after.

The first-born son, for want of an alternative, talked with the only people prepared to listen to him: the gardener, the son of his old nanny Ester (the gardener's wife), the workmen who came to repair the house, his private math teacher (there was no hope for it: really pretty and an anti-Fascist to boot, she lost her job almost immediately). They listened to him; it mattered little if his talk was simple or if he rambled on as adolescents do. "My father even gave him a little money so he could sneak out," muttered the gardener's son in his thick Tuscan dialect.

All this familiarity with the servants and his disregard for the rules stuck in his mother's craw, and, for his part, Giangiacomo hated his stepfather with all his might, a sentiment that was recip-rocated. Giannalisa and her husband did not hesitate to inflict hu-miliating punishments on the boy, such as locking him up in the cellar for days on bread and water. There are witnesses. He suf-fered from claustrophobia from then on.

Later Barzini justified himself as follows:

> I tried to take as much interest as I could in his upbringing, and, at a certain point, to steer him in the right direction with his studies.... Perhaps I am a very poor teacher, perhaps I didn't even have the stuff of a stepfather, perhaps Giangiacomo was a careless scholar, rebellious and hostile, or perhaps there was no way we could un-derstand each other, as he and I were profoundly dissimilar. The fact is that I don't think I ever taught him anything that stuck.

In the meantime, the war proceeded on its inexorable course. After the Anzio landings, the Argentario, thought a safe place at first, became a key base for German supply lines. The bombs rained down almost every day–175 air raids in all–and the Barzini-Feltrinelli household was regularly shaken by the blasts. At night, Luigi would shriek out the latest news culled from the radio trans-mitter. Giannalisa would yell, "Moron, moron!" if Antonella woke up the little ones ("But Mummy, shouldn't we run to the air-raid shelter?"). The estate filled up with poor people because the Croce neighborhood had been wiped out, and even the church in town had a hole in its cupola.

At that point, Giangiacomo "got the hell out." Armed with a pistol and accompanied by the future village butcher, he went into hiding in the maquis at the top of the hill. The only person with any chance of locating him was his friend the gardener, and in fact he found him: "I'll come back only if you'll put me up for a while in your place," Giangiacomo told him. It was a deal.

One fiery night in May 1944, Giannalisa hid her jewels in a mule's excrement sack. Barzini's latest invention. They had to move fast and abandon the villa, while the chauffeur and servants grabbed what they could. At the top of the cliff, they jettisoned seven demijohns of grain, which were too heavy. After a night of bombing, the evacuees were left with a few shards of glass.

It is not clear if Giannalisa knew where her son was when she left with family and staff. He was right there, close at hand, in the servants' quarters just below the citrus orchard.

The flight of the seventeen-year-old Feltrinelli lasted only a few days. Giannalisa, who reached Rome after many adventures, sent the cook (she called him "the malign hunchback") to bring the boy home. Giangiacomo appeared beneath the pergola over the gardener's doorway; he came along without protest.

His mother never forgave him for that first escape. Many years later, recalling the episode, she attempted to justify herself for having abandoned her son during the bombing: "My duty was not to take any risks with the lives of the two little girls"—there were three, but she had quarreled with Antonella, who was removed from the list.

Back in the family fold, Giangiacomo was sent off to school in the monastery of Saint John Lateran in Rome, where he spent the middle part of 1944. He struck a deal with his mother: once he got his school certificate, he would be free to enlist in the struggle against the Germans. "She never expected me to succeed in this," he confided in an interview years later, "but I did."

He had a friend in Piva, his young tutor, and found another in Luigi Aurigemma, who was a few years older than he. Aurigemma's father, an archaeologist, was curator of the Museo delle Terme, where he lived with his family. Apart from the funereal little parties in the Feltrinelli home, Aurigemma remembers his strolls with Giangiacomo in the courtyard designed by Michelangelo.

Fifty years on, Aurigemma is over seventy and lives in Paris. A psychoanalyst, he has translated the complete works of Jung into Italian. In the evenings, he says, when the museum was free of visitors, Giangiacomo and he would stroll together "talking of heaven and earth," and if there was a word that resounded under the arches more often than the others, "that word was justice...." He may well have yielded to nostalgia, but the image is crystal clear.

In November 1944, Feltrinelli joined the Legnano combat unit, a volunteer corps in the Fifth Army. After brief training in the Naples area, he made his way back north. He stopped for a while near Lake Bracciano, where a married couple from Gargnano put him up. By chance they too were called Feltrinelli, but they were not relatives and so Giangiacomo took an immediate liking to them. One morning, corpses were found lined up along the village streets. The couple went to turn them over, one by one. No, the young man they had treated for dysentery the day before was not among them. Perhaps he had already left for Tuscany.

In the area around Siena, where the presence of his division is documented in early March 1945, the young soldier underwent more military training and joined the Italian Communist Party (PCI). From one of his autobiographical notes: "I was introduced [to the party] by Comrade Monti, another member of my unit (an old comrade who had done a year in Civitavecchia [prison] for political reasons), and Comrade Ciafrè Vincenzo of the Siena federation."

They all trooped off to the front, near Bologna, for the days of the Liberation. Once a mortar shell missed him by a whisker. Using his index and middle fingers to mimic the act of digging, he described to me how he poked around in the earth for the shell case.

The few months spent as a soldier in wartime turned him into a man who made his own decisions. Demobilized in August 1945, he went back to Rome and enrolled in the Polytechnic.

Like a well-disciplined militant, he frequented the local party branch in the evenings, but the officials of the PCI preferred to use him for another kind of task. They wanted to exploit his capacity to gather information, especially in monarchist circles.

But on 28 April 1945 the party newspaper *L'Unità* blew his cover by publishing an article in which the Allied intelligence service also took an interest. At that time, the referendum* campaign was in full swing, and the article contained information that someone in the Feltrinelli household had overheard. Here is a salient passage:

> On the basis of information received from an excellent source we are able to provide news of an important meeting held in the home of a family of big industrial sharks, the Feltrinellis. The meeting was attended by Duke Acquarone, as the direct representative of the House of Savoy, the president of the outgoing senate, the Marquis of Torretta, Senator Bergamini, the Hon. Porzio, and the well-known slanderer of office workers Epicarmo Corbino, the treasury minister. At this meeting, the discussion centered on the suitability of a *coup de théâtre* on the eve of the Constituent Assembly, in order to restore the virginity of a compromised monarchy: the abdication of Victor Emmanuel the elder and the subsequent renunciation on the part of Umberto in favor of Victor Emmanuel the younger. Minister Corbino proposed an even bolder move: the withdrawal of the entire House of Savoy along the lines of the withdrawal of Alfonso XIII in Spain...

During the meeting, there was also talk of a more precise coordination of the conservative press, with a major role reserved for

*The referendum held to decide whether Italy was to remain a monarchy or become a republic (1946).

Barzini. By that time, Giannalisa was financing his activities: he
ran the Sì press agency and two newspapers, *Il Globo* and *Libera
Stampa*. My grandmother enjoyed this kind of commitment; she
did not lack fighting spirit: on the eve of the referendum, she personally distributed pro-monarchy pamphlets through the streets of
Rome. From her Rolls.

Given the climate (and also the foul-up caused by *L'Unità*),
Giangiacomo had to make himself scarce. He went to Milan,
where, again in the late spring of 1946, something important happened to him: he met a young militant from the Socialist Party of
Proletarian Unity (PSUP), Bianca Dalle Nogare.

The piles of snow remained on the streets until April. Milan was
still a great wounded city that no longer stank of burning debris,
but was still full of blackened patches where the fires had been put
out, and of strange abysses inside apartment blocks awaiting reconstruction. But life in the city had started up again, the various
social classes and categories were in search of a new equilibrium,
the newspapers were coming out, the theaters had reopened, and
the schools were once more crowded, with a new generation of
children. Their overcoats were made from American blankets sold
in the markets.

Giangiacomo and Bianca took to each other. At first, theirs was
a platonic relationship. She was a beautiful girl, from a family that
had been fairly wealthy before the war.

But in the aftermath of the insult suffered by her monarchist
friends, Giannalisa was horrified by the turn her son's career had
taken; she was scandalized both by his spells on the run and by the
company he kept. Having a Communist for a son was tantamount
to having a son with the plague. She formed a plan. Probably acting on Barzini's orders, four bogus soldiers in uniform were to confiscate the firearms her son had brought back from the front.
Following a sham search of the premises on Via Andegari and a

convincing threat of arrest, they were to persuade him to run, perhaps to Spain or Portugal, where Antonella was already living.
Then there would be the referendum, and if the monarchy lost, or
so my grandmother's reasoning went, the entire family would take
its leave: crossing the Atlantic from Portugal was a bagatelle.

The plan worked perfectly: frightened by the prospect of a sentence for the illegal possession of arms, Giangiacomo went to Lisbon via Madrid, leaving Bianca without a word.

The account of the immediate aftermath of the referendum of 2
June, again taken from my grandmother's recollections, is a minor
masterpiece that explains many of her future moves.

At eleven a.m. of the 4th, His Majesty was expecting me at the Quirinal. Unfortunately I could not go, because a short distance from the
palace my little car was struck and wrecked by a Polish truck on the
road that runs alongside the gardens owned by Prince Aldobrandini.
Passers-by extracted me from the wreckage and laid me on the pave-
ment, offering me handkerchiefs to stem the blood that was flowing
from my head, but I did not accept them for fear of infection. I caught
a glimpse of a carabiniere and summoned him with my right hand,
begging him to go to the porter's lodge of the Quirinal to leave word
that I could not go to His Majesty because I had been struck by a foreign truck. Finally someone knelt at my side and said, "I am a doctor,
you cannot stay here, allow me to accompany you to the Villa Bianca
Clinic. I shall stop a car." We went to the clinic. They took me straight
to the X-ray department and after every plate taken, they came to me
announcing in amazement that nothing was broken except for a frac-
ture in the wrist at the side of my right hand, and that it was natural
that I was in pain all over on account of the knock I had taken. [...] I
was extremely annoyed about being in the hospital without a telephone in the room, and on the fourth day I begged the doctors to
send me home in an ambulance. I was champing at the bit, so I managed to gain my bed. Alberto Bergamini visited me many times every
day. On the evening of 12 June at 7 o'clock General Graziani called
me to say that His Majesty wished to dine with me without other persons present, and I replied that only Bergamini was with me. "That's
perfectly all right, let him stay." At nine in the evening, Bergamini
was at the door of my house to greet His Majesty. He brought the king
to my room. The windows gave on to the garden where gently sway-

ing cypress trees screened the Baths of Caracalla. It was a splendid
night. His Majesty kissed my hand. The table was at the foot of my
bed, and at my side there was an armchair for him to sit in after dinner. My absolutely wonderful cook performed miracles, and my but-
ler served them up in his tailcoat. The nurse helped me eat because
of the plaster on my wrist. But in everybody's heart a nightmare
loomed over this serenity. Gi [Barzini] went to the *Libera Stampa*
newspaper offices before eleven, and I implored him to phone with
any news. After dinner the table was cleared and the four of us
sat there waiting for something no one wanted to talk about, something far worse than anything we could imagine. Shortly before one
o'clock, the telephone at my side rang. De Gasperi* had called an
emergency cabinet meeting to proclaim immediately, without waiting for 18 June as agreed, the results of the referendum. The monarchy had been defeated. Whiter than the nightdress I was wearing, I
turned to the king, saying, "Your Majesty, I always told you that De
Gasperi was not to be trusted." Fraud had certainly been committed. [...] The king talked of Queen Maria Pia of Portugal and said that
he would follow Carlo Alberto into exile in Oporto. He was wearing a
gray suit. Bergamini's look held all the horror of what we were going
through minute by minute. A millennium of the House of Savoy,
which had begun with Umberto Biancamano, was coming to a close
with Umberto II because of the damned corrupt and treacherous politics of the Christian Democrats. With arrogance and injustice, they
had demolished a monarchy that had endured for centuries. This
sorrowful historic act was unfolding amid dimmed lights and the
dark outlines of the cypresses that seemed projected into my room.
The words followed one another in a disconnected stream. Every
now and then the king would take a glass of champagne from an an-
tique silver salver and put it to his lips. I tried not to cry, but when he
bent over to embrace me, my tears fell on his hand. It was four thirty
in the morning of 13 June. What anguish. Alberto Bergamini accompanied His Majesty to his automobile. On his return to the room, he
paced up and down like a wounded lion, unable to talk under the
weight of the destiny that was about to come to pass. "I told you De
Gasperi was a traitor," I exploded from time to time.

*Founder of the Partito Popolare (1919), a Catholic-inspired party that was to be-
come the Christian Democratic Party in 1943, Alcide De Gasperi (1881–1954) was a
committed European and anti-Fascist who served as prime minister on several
occasions.

From then on, Giannalisa could visit the king only in Cascais. God knows if there is any truth in the story that she brought him rounds of Gorgonzola cheese to alleviate his homesickness.

In the meantime, her son was holed up in Lisbon following the charade of the threatened arrest. According to Antonella's recollections, he was in the worst possible spirits and never uttered a word. "He didn't write to me for two months," recalls Bianca.

> Then I received a packet containing all the letters he had never sent me. They were letters full of profound despondency. I replied, telling him to come back, on foot if necessary, but to come back. He arrived by train traveling third class. He was exhausted, he had bronchitis and needed looking after. I couldn't put him up in our house because my mother, my sister, and I were all staying with friends. So I asked a socialist comrade to put him up for a few days.

In those same weeks of July 1946, Giannalisa left Italy for Cascais, along with her two little daughters. She was entirely unaware of her son's intentions. She telephoned the hotel where she thought he was waiting for her. They told her he was not there, that he had gone back home. Infuriated, she decided to enlist the aid of the Italian minister in Lisbon with a view to having Giangiacomo arrested at the border. Nothing doing. Leaving daughters and nannies at Cascais, she boarded a plane for Italy and, after shuttling between Rome and Milan seventeen times, she finally found him. Face to face. There were no reproofs. She merely told him that she intended to leave Italy in the very near future. That was all. It was one of those moments when people just stand there looking at each other.

A few months later, Giannalisa took herself and the family silver off to Rio de Janeiro. It must have struck her as a place that was as far from any kind of Communism as possible. The only concession to the enemy was the broker she hired in New York: his name was Charlie Marx. As Lacan says, the signifier never lets you go.

2

Milan, late summer 1946, the end of the long break and the return to his city. Giangiacomo still mumbled like many who are shy, but he seemed more relaxed when he met convivial people his own age who might be considered friends. From somewhere or other the first girlfriend appeared. (I know who she is; she now lives a quiet life in the provinces.)

A tall, thin, bespectacled twenty-year-old who walked with his head held high and his toes turned slightly outward, he became a familiar sight in the Milan branch offices of the party. Some turned up their noses at his pedigree, but others took a liking to him right away. Most people had other things to worry about.

Giangiacomo also got to know Bianca better. She had joined the PCI, and he felt he might impress her by showing up in the suburb of Sesto early in the morning to accompany her to the office. But, wearing that strange blue suit made by a refined tailor hired years ago by his mother, the admirer-militant turned up in the evening too: to organize with Bianca and her sister, the wall newspaper for the following day. His suit hung off him; perhaps they found him a bit ridiculous.

At that time they made frequent evening visits to the house of a young Communist Party official, Armando Cossutta.* His mother used to welcome them with platefuls of delicious pasta and beans.

After a sheltered childhood, Giangiacomo now encountered the misfortunes of a more normal life. He suffered belated attacks of measles, German measles, and scarlet fever, but these were minor inconveniences.

In July 1947 he married Bianca Dalle Nogare. Neither Giannalisa, who thought Bianca was a "Muscovite Pasionaria," nor Barzini came to the wedding. But Giannalisa's father, Mino Gianzano, was present. "It was a civil wedding," recalls the bride, "extremely rapid and entirely nonconformist, without invitations and without photographers. We said I do, and then we said good-bye right afterward. I went back home to my mother; Giangiacomo went back to his place. We did not meet again until the next day, when we set off on our honeymoon." The destination was Prague, which was the venue of the world youth festival. They drove a smoky-blue Buick convertible and took along their dog, a German shepherd by the name of Gisa. "Gisa" might have been an abbreviation for "Giannalisa."

Giangiacomo probably did some serious thinking when he got back from his honeymoon. For not only had he married, but he was also over twenty-one; in other words, he was no longer a minor and this brought him rights and obligations whose consequences were hard to foresee. He wanted to study engineering and possibly earn a living through some profession, but he was also the sole male heir to Giacomo, Giovanni, and Carlo, to the Feltrinellis who counted: what they had left behind them in the world was now in need of good management.

Being rich, as the Italian saying goes, is better than grazing goats on someone else's land. But it is also like riding a roller coaster, where you pick up speed, then throw up, go off the rails, or

*Born in Milan in 1926, Cossutta became a leader of the PCI. In 1991 he founded Rifondazione Communista and in 1998 the Italian Communists.

else have to jump off. Many men who wind up rich do not have the faintest idea how to handle money. The Feltrinelli heir, who was forever in conflict with his globe-trotting mother, found himself in that boat.

As soon as his sister came of age, she married and went to seek a new life in France (with André D'Ormesson, the son of the French ambassador to the Vatican). From Paris Antonella brought a suit against Giannalisa, accusing her of having given her daughter an incorrect share of the inheritance. Giangiacomo, who was as much an injured party as his sister, did not feel like taking the family to court. He let the matter drop.

Given this climate, given these conditions, Giangiacomo must have seriously considered getting rid of the damned money and "handing it all over to Togliatti."* He was heard to say this by several people. In a personal profile for the party, he wrote with regard to his "extensive fortune" that the inheritance came to "weigh on me." What's more, "until he was twenty he didn't even know what a bank check looked like," as his wife recalled in an interview. It was thanks to Bianca that he became a more thoughtful man. He threw himself into the study of economics and gradually began to find his feet in business matters.

But while he had no inclination to "play the rich man" and was looking for his own road to follow, even managing to be a good Communist, he was nevertheless a rich man. One in search of an equilibrium not easy to understand, precarious, and possibly unattainable. According to the usual stereotypes, he ought to have been a spendthrift or a zealous philanthropist, or a businessman bent over his accounts. He turned out to be none of these things.

----

*Palmiro Togliatti (1893–1964) was the leader of the Italian Communist Party from 1926 to 1964. Close to Stalin, he wielded considerable influence in the Kremlin during the Comintern period. After the Twentieth Congress (1956) he favored pluralism in the Communist world. He had a genuine interest in culture—which explains, at least in part, his privileged relations with Feltrinelli.

The outcome of the elections of 18 April 1948, which resulted in a clear majority for the Christian Democratic Party and confined the Popular Front* to the opposition, corresponded to the logic of Yalta. The alternative would have involved a serious risk of political instability. Palmiro Togliatti too must have thought this. Thus began Italy's long post-war period, the endless aftermath of Fascism with its reconstruction and stagnation. Those tempted by the idea of a Fascist revival were energetically opposed by a now mature public opinion: the war of liberation, the referendum, and the constitution had all created a new order. But there were moments when the slightest thing could have brought the whole house of cards tumbling down.

"I was eating, I must have come back home about one, when I heard someone calling me from the yard of my house, on Via Paolo Sarpi. I looked down, Feltrinelli was searching for me: 'Get down here, come on, Togliatti's been shot.'" It was 14 July 1948. Silvano Giuntini recalls dashing first to the offices of the Federation and then to the local branch office of the party, where all the party members had to be sent home because they were too steamed up and, above all, armed.

Giuntini, who was to become a commercial specialist with a renowned Milanese publishing house, was in charge of propaganda at the party's Via Cantù office, a big branch with about 1,500 members in the heart of the city. He met Feltrinelli when Feltrinelli invited him to his home in San Babila, where they spent the night listening to Yugoslav folk music. A few years before, Giuntini had received a call from Alberganti, the secretary of the Federation, announcing the arrival in the local branch office of a "particular" comrade.

In the course of musical evenings, snacks prior to visits to the branch office, and a lot of political work, Giuntini and Feltrinelli

*An electoral coalition of the parties making up the Italian left.

became close. In the immediate aftermath of the attempt on Togliatti's life, they probably shared, as did everyone, the same sense of chaos and confusion. The only certainty was that the CGIL labor union had called a general strike.

The national political scene was in a feverish state: the party line was "Take it easy," but in Genoa, Turin, Venice, and Livorno militants occupied whole districts. Seven thousand people were either arrested or questioned.

In Milan, where things were not much calmer, four or five young men from the "Duomo" party office, Feltrinelli among them, went out one night to stick up placards. This was fairly minor militancy. "About four in the morning, on Via Meravigli, the police caught us with placards in hand. They took us downtown and then to San Vittore [prison] the following morning, for five or six days." Comrade Sergio Monti, now in retirement after a long career in the cooperative movement, has a clear memory: "It wasn't so bad. Our misfortune put us in a good humor, and what's more, I lived well in prison because I had a share of the food Bianca brought in every day. We were always hungry in those days."

Revolution, the armed variety, was not on. The conditions were not right. In the days following the wounding of Togliatti, who was soon declared out of danger, this fact became more evident. The tension began to abate.

While the PCI was a powerful advocate of a different, alternative world, it had accepted electoral methods and moderation three years before, when its increased share of the vote was considered "the principal instrument with which to shift the balance of power in parliament and consequently in the country."

Monti became a good friend of my father's. They went on selling *L'Unità* and sticking up placards together. Feltrinelli did not feel himself above these tasks in any way, often using the smoky-blue Buick. "People were scandalized when they saw us coming to do those things in a car like that, but Feltrinelli didn't give a damn. It was a good car, but windshield defrosters hadn't been invented yet and I recall coming back from a meeting near Lodi (it was a cold, foggy night) when we had to take turns hopping on to the hood and taking a leak on the windshield to defrost it."

In 1948, Monti attended a summer camp organized by Feltrinelli and a group of young party members. They went to the villa at Gargnano on Lake Garda, the residence and emblem of the Feltrinelli family: "a kind of Bavarian mausoleum," according to the description of a writer friend. Half the time indoors, half in the park, the group of fifteen lived it up for two weeks. There was also the painter Giovanni Fumagalli, known to everyone as Fuma, who was the secretary of the Duomo branch office and an advocate of socialist realism in the polemic about contemporary art that had just begun. His convictions were probably highly debatable, but it wasn't the campers' aesthetic preferences that upset the parish priest. It was the idea of all those Communists using the villa as their meeting place that rankled. The priest wasn't going to stand for it, the master of the house had to be discredited: hence the stream of official complaints, denunciations from the pulpit, and posters on the walls. The posters spoke of Feltrinelli's marriage: he had gone through a civil ceremony, not a church wedding!

But if my hunch is right, organizing the summer camp was more than just a provocation. It meant several things, even on an unconscious level. In October 1943, villa Feltrinelli had been commandeered to serve as Benito Mussolini's personal residence. After he was dramatically rescued by German paratroops from the Gran Sasso for the short-lived Republic of Salò, Mussolini, who detested lakes ("a hybrid of rivers and the sea"), had to live isolated in our home under the protection of the crack troops of his ally and master. When he left this blind alley, it really was the end.

While Fascism had been defeated, six hundred thousand amnestied supporters of the Republic of Salò didn't just disappear.

Some sang party anthems in the slums and hoped to return one day for the "reckoning." But many had already returned, some as shirtsleeved bureaucrats full of scorn for "goddamn democracy," others masquerading as right-thinking folk who wore starched collars out of class arrogance. In the courts there were judges who took great pains to do what damage they could to ex-partisans, turning trials on their heads the way a cheese maker turns a churn: on the other hand was the Volante Rossa.*

This explains the extravagant gesture, the campsite set on the grounds of the villa that had once been Mussolini's. It was a deliberate move and a clear warning to the Fascists: Come back, and you'll get yours.

This summer camp was to become a talking point the following year, 1949, when people in Milan were getting alarmed about the Ciappina gang, also known as the "everywhere gang." Ugo Ciappina, who was little more than a boy but dangerous, and the Armenian Colust Megherian, both members of the Carrobbio cell, had developed a reputation for the improper use of arms that had been kept hidden even after 25 April. But this was not politics, merely armed robbery. They recruited half a dozen shady characters, and two of them, when they were arrested, stated they had decided on a life of crime in the summer camp by Lake Garda. Perhaps the parish priest hadn't been so far wrong.

Feltrinelli was arrested once more, again in Milan. It was the work of the political office of the city police: "Have you heard? We've taken in your buddy the millionaire!" said one cop to a reporter from the *Milano Sera*. But Feltrinelli had nothing to do with the affair: at that time he was a party regular, disciplined in his work and offering total adherence to the party line.

The misunderstanding cost him a day in jail, and worried comments began to appear in the conservative press. For the first time,

*A Resistance group that did not lay down its arms on the cessation of hostilities.

they began to talk of "Giangi the millionaire." The political office
sent the following note to the Ministry of the Interior: "Feltrinelli
(a major financer of the party) was arrested and then freed. He
was suspected of having financed the well-known 'everywhere
gang.' [...] Feltrinelli is an activist and his wife Bianca Dalle Nogare
is a madwoman in the service of the PCI terrorist organization."

After his second arrest, Feltrinelli had to give up his normal activities at the branch office. (He had recently replaced Giuntini as
the press and propaganda officer.) It was proposed that he become
a member of a working group at the Milan offices of the Federation. The party decided to protect him: they appointed a former
partisan to serve as his chauffeur, factotum, and bodyguard. A kind
of guardian angel for the most expensive party card* in Italy.

But what did it mean to be a militant in those days, whether
Communist, socialist, grass-roots Catholic, or even Christian Democratic? Comrade Monti said it was necessary above all to "get
things done," maybe a kindergarten, a school, Female Comrades'
Week, Communion, or a gesture of working-class solidarity. It was
a militancy some today might object to, but there's no denying that
it was socially useful.

Obsessive hypercommunism, fanatical anti-Communism, extreme clericalism, there was something for everybody, but after the
war a little passion was needed to keep the flag flying, red or white.
The truly democratic impulse could not find a suitable channel between the colossi of the two "churches" of Catholicism and Communism. The state? It was chronically weak, needless to say.

"We lived through some damn tough times, but they were con-
structive times, you understand?" Giuntini and Monti, members of
the Duomo branch in those days, greeted me with these words.

---

*Party members paid their dues on a discretionary basis. On receipt of the
yearly payment, which was a hefty sum in Feltrinelli's case, a stamp was stuck in
the party card.

They told me that Feltrinelli wanted to make a summer camp out
of the former Fascist village near Canzo, that he wanted to make a
film about the rice weeders in Lomellina, or, possibly, to establish
a local library.

Apropos of "getting things done," in March 1992 *L'Unità* published a fine article by the journalist Anna Del Bo Boffino. I barely
got to know Anna before her death, but I knew about her because
she had been married to the man I used to call Uncle Sergio and
other people knew as Professor Del Bo.

> In '49 we were two newlywed couples: Giangiacomo with his first
> wife, the girl from Sesto San Giovanni, as beautiful as a Tanagra fig-
> urine, I with Del Bo, who was six years older than us and always
> acted as our big brother. We all had been involved with the Resis-
> tance and were members of the PCI. Together, we were looking for
> a space between the dogmatism of the party and the hypocrisy of
> bourgeois culture. At twenty, one has many dreams, and the desire
> to be "new" is a powerful one. We were no different. But those were
> the days of commitment, when the model of the "organic intellec-
> tual" was the only model one could adopt with honesty. They were
> also hard times: during demonstrations, we were the ones who had
> to run from the batons of the riot cops. Communists had no access
> to the world of newspapers or publishing. And all-out strikes were
> weakening the proletariat, bringing it to near starvation. We knew
> about an extremely prolonged strike on the part of farm workers in
> the lower Po Valley, and we really needed to show our solidarity. We
> did this with words, but Giangiacomo could do more. In Gargnano,
> where his family came from, he owned half the town: he had a part
> of the old folks' home cleared (there were only a very few old folks
> there at the time), and it became possible to take in about thirty
> children, who arrived from one day to the next. We, the two women,
> were detailed to look after them, and for a few weeks we fed,
> clothed, and took them out and about. A little blond boy, all skin and
> bones, with a dazzling smile, had head lice, and all the other kids
> caught them from him. We cleaned them up, and I would have fed
> them ten times a day just to see them put a little meat on their bones.
> So that's how it was: we had dreams, and we kept them locked away.
> Giangiacomo could make them come true, and it seemed miracu-
> lous to have him on our side.

It is not easy to deal with someone one thinks "miraculous." Difficulties can arise in relationships. I discussed this issue with Anna in the summer of '95: "Coexisting with Giangiacomo, who had huge possibilities, was not easy. He could just turn around and decide to do anything he wanted. All dealings with him had this dual aspect."

Also, his marriage with Bianca was soon on the rocks.

Uncle Sergio, Anna's husband, was Giuseppe Del Bo. Milanese, born in 1919, he had studied theology at the Gregorian University in Rome. He was a priest. During the war he enlisted as an army chaplain and was imprisoned in Tunisia. He managed to get back home at the time of the liberation of Naples, after which he made his way back up the peninsula with the Allies, calling himself Sergio. It was his nom de guerre. At the end of the war, in Milan once more, he resumed his studies. He enrolled in the Università Statale, where he met Antonio Banfi, who was teaching and advocating a new and universal culture. Banfi waived two years' worth of exams for Uncle Sergio and introduced him to Anna.

At the end of 1946, Sergio went through his toughest existential crisis. In love with a woman, attracted by Marxism: it was his moment of truth. The bishop of Como had him recalled to the seminary, but it was to be the last time. By 1948 the story was over, all dilemmas resolved, and Sergio decided to marry Anna.

The man who was said to be able to maintain relations with the Vatican and Palmiro Togliatti at the same time found his first job in the Cantoni Bookstore in Corso Vittorio Emanuele. But he soon went to work for the ex-partisan Vando Androvandi, in the Einaudi Bookstore on Via Filodrammatici. The journalist Alberto Cavallari recalls meeting him there "while he was transporting packets of books on his bicycle."

Giangiacomo met him in the back of that bookstore. There was nothing strange about this: cultural life, the first House of Culture, the meetings of the magazine *Politecnico*,* the encounters among the bookshelves with writers like Vittorini, Pavese, and Fortini: this was the place where it was all happening. Nearby, the dairy run by the Pirolini sisters and an eating house called Il soldato d'Italia on Via Fiori Chiari offered the luxury of a good cheap meal. The publisher Giulio Einaudi[†] recalled that "Feltrinelli came to the meetings out of curiosity, to listen. I remember that he would sit on the floor, good as gold, listening." Feltrinelli financed Einaudi's activities, lending him money. The PCI had asked him to do this.

Togliatti dined at the Brasera Meneghina on his fleeting visits to Milan. It reminded him of when he was the editor of *L'Unità* in the mid-twenties. They always brought him his favorite dish, ossobuco con risotto. According to Cossutta's reconstruction, it was there that Togliatti and Feltrinelli met one evening. The party leader liked Feltrinelli's idea to undertake the construction of a library devoted to the history of the workers of the world. Apparently the idea came from a priest (Giuseppe Del Bo).

But before describing what Feltrinelli and Del Bo engineered together, we must first take a look at an important document. In order to take part in the courses held by the party's regional school, Giangiacomo, who was twenty-four at the time, had to write an autobiographical profile. It reappeared many years later in the basement of the former offices of the Federation.

The date was early 1950:

To the Cell Office of the Milan Federation of the P.C.I.

Re: PROFILE

Giangiacomo Feltrinelli, son of the late Carlo and Giannalisa Gianzana, born on 6/19/1926 in Milan, residing at Piazza S. Babila 4/b.

---

*Founded by the writer Elio Vittorini in Milan in 1945, it was a lively forum for political and cultural debate.

[†](1912–99). Head on one of Italy's most important publishing houses.

My father was one of the most outstanding figures in the world of finance between 1927 and 1935. The Chairman of the Credito Italiano and of Edison, as well as of other companies in which he was the majority shareholder, he was a classic example of how finance capital can be merged with industrial capital. He died in 1935.

My mother, a banker's daughter, is still alive; in 1940 she remarried with Luigi Barzini junior, from whom she is now separated. She lives in Rome.

I was brought up in a manner that was as orthodox as can be from a bourgeois point of view, with nannies, comforts, travel, etc., and I was always kept apart from children of my own age. Until 1942 I never attended school and was privately tutored. I thus grew up practically without friends.

Given this situation, how did it happen that I came first to join the PCI and then to serve as an activist within its ranks? What were the elements that influenced me decisively and led me to understand the necessity and the importance of joining the PCI to aid the organized vanguard of the working class in the struggle against capitalism, in the cause of socialism?

A first important element was, I believe, the following: in '36 my mother acquired a large garden, which, over a period of years, was constructed by workers, laborers, and farmhands. I very soon made friends with these workers and laborers, and for the first time I came to know another world, which was not the glittering one I knew; I came to understand the lives that the workers led, the efforts they had to make to keep their families, the inadequacy of their wages, and the constant threat of unemployment that loomed over every one of them. I thus realized that there were two different and quite distinct social classes. Later, in 1938–39, amid the bitter debate on international events, war became a grave threat that impinged upon the already hard lives of the workers. I realized that it was not the gentlemen who were calling vociferously for war who would have gone off to fight. On the contrary, I saw that the wealthy could hope to gain from a war while the sacrifices would have to be made by the workers.

In 1940 I made the acquaintance of a worker from Erba, Augusto Sala. It was from his accounts, and from discussions I had with him that I first came to know the details of the people's struggle against the Fascists in 1921. For the first time I learned of the existence of other parties and in particular of the socialists and the Communists. The account of the heroic episodes in the people's struggle against the Fascists and their action squads, financed and backed by industrialists, filled me with enthusiasm. Obviously my parents were worried by the direction I was taking. They posed as anti-Fascists, especially after my stepfather was confined to Amalfi as a consequence of his excessive fondness for double-dealing between the English and the Fascists.

I was still a mass of contradictions: I was a member of the GIL, the Fascist youth organization, and I was glad when the war was going well and the Fascist armies were advancing; at the same time I was listening to Radio London, I was against the Germans, and could see no good coming of the war. I hoped that the monarchy would grasp the first opportunity to get rid of the Fascists.

In the meantime the war continued, and by the end of 1942 the situation was becoming tragic: the first bombing raids on the cities, the arrival of the first Germans in Italy. In this situation I realized that the overthrow of Fascism and the cessation of the conflict were two tasks requiring urgent action that could not be brought to completion without an effort, without a struggle in which everyone had to give something. It was at that time that I met Renzo Negri, resident at Via Melzi d'Eril 22, who was in contact with the Resistance. It was the end of 1942. I only had occasional contact with him because I had to move to Tuscany with my family. Nevertheless, it was through him that I had news of the heroic strike of March 1943. It was then that I contributed one hundred lire to a clandestine newspaper. This and other episodes, even though insignificant, contributed to the development of a closer bond between me and all those who, even if I did not know them personally, were fighting against Fascism, that is to say the working class.

During that period I read *The History of Italian Literature* by Concetto Marchesi, which helped me make a qualitative leap and to put in perspective for the first time those events, those feelings, those ideas of justice that had developed in me and that had led me to be against the Fascists.

In fact I was particularly struck by the essay on the struggle of the Gracchi in Ancient Rome. Marchesi took his cue from that event to demonstrate the existence of two social classes fighting each other: patricians and plebeians, the exploiters and the exploited. This scheme of things, which holds to this day, matched my experience, and political events, Fascism, and the war took on a new meaning.

I subsequently studied what little historical material was at my disposal. In particular, I recall reading Croce's *History of the Risorgimento,* which told me, albeit in a harshly critical tone, something about the international socialist movement. I also read a book by Bissolati on the history of the Italian labor movement. From these books I learned about the men, the parties and the events of Italian political history; I learned about the labor unions, the strikes, etc. The opportunism and the compromise that oozes from every line of Bissolati had only a slight momentary influence on me. The very situation, current at that time, of bitter struggle, provided evidence of the bankruptcy of all reformist ideas.

After the liberation of Rome, where I found myself on 4 June 1944, I had the good fortune to read immediately two works of particular importance and topicality: the *Communist Manifesto* and Lenin's *State and Revolution.* In the *Manifesto,* as had previously been the case with Marchesi's book, I was impressed by the analysis of society and its division into classes locked in continuous struggle, while historical materialism helped me understand the development of society by giving me a new method for understanding history.

In November of 1944 I enlisted as a volunteer in the Legnano combat unit that was attached to the American Fifth Army, not without having first listened to the views of a comrade, Trombadori, I think, who was introduced to me by a young comrade of my acquaintance.

Armed with this admittedly limited theoretical background, I joined the party in early March 1945, while we were in training with the division in the province of Siena. I was introduced to Comrade Masotti, who was also in my company (he was an old comrade who had spent a year in Civitavecchia prison for political reasons), and to comrade Vincenzo Ciafré of the Siena Federation. Shortly afterward the division was sent to the Bologna front, and in August of 1945 I was demobilized.

I returned to Rome, where I resumed my studies (I attended the Rome Polytechnic). Until April of 1946 I carried out no political activities inasmuch as comrade Fulvio Iacchia of the Rome Federation preferred to use me to gather information in milieus hostile to the party. My cover was blown in April 1946 when, as a result of an error, *L'Unità* printed a detailed report of a monarchist meeting that had been held in my home and that I had in part attended. Subsequently I moved to Milan, where shortly afterward my parents, aided and abetted by the British intelligence service, and knowing that I still had the weapons I had possessed at the time of my discharge from the army, orchestrated a phoney arrest in hopes of frightening me and persuading me to leave Italy. In fact, this fitted in with their plans because they, fearing the advent of the Republic, were organizing a general exodus of the family.

I went to Spain and to Portugal, from where, still in July of 1946, I eluded the surveillance of my parents and returned to Italy, taking up residence in Milan.

I then began to work for the party on a regular basis, first in the press and propaganda department of the Bietolini branch office, and then in the Duomo branch, in the youth sector and then in press and propaganda. This was in April 1947.

In July of 1947 I married Bianca Dalle Nogare, who had come from the PSIUP and who had been a member of the PCI for a year. I attended the Youth Festival in Prague in the summer of 1947.

In the meantime, I had come of age and so the administration of the inheritance left me by my father came to weigh on my shoulders.

In the summer of 1948, following the attempted assassination of comrade Togliatti, I was arrested together with some other youths for having posted unauthorized placards.

It was subsequent to this arrest that the Duomo branch office put me in charge of press and propaganda activities.

I was also a member of the branch office committee. In November, I attended a six-month series of evening classes run by the local Communist Party Federation. These classes were very important for my theoretical training as a Communist activist. The histories of Italy and the political economy I studied there gave me a whole new perspective on the bourgeois notions I had learned in normal scholastic courses, while the study of the history of the Russian Communist Party prepared me particularly well to deal with the practical problems I had to face in my day-to-day work for the party.

At the same time I was called in to head the Financial Committee of the Milan Federation.

How did these posts within the party influence my political position? How did I perform these tasks?

My work with the rank and file in the Duomo branch of our party was certainly very useful. As a liaison officer between the various cells, I got to know the comrades, their shortcomings and their strengths. I learned to recognize the responsibilities connected with the party's various aspirations and requirements. I learned to control, at least in part, my impulsiveness and my impetuosity; I learned method in debate, in the work of persuasion and clarification that I had to carry out among the comrades. I learned to spot concealed opportunism, both behind compromises and generic extremist statements. Of my work as head of press and propaganda, I have to say that too often I erred in taking too much upon myself, and only toward the end did I make concrete efforts to obtain some co-workers and to guide and direct them in their work, which is a more difficult task. I therefore fell into the trap of empiricism, thus losing the overall view of the work I had to do in order to concentrate solely on one sector or another. The fact that today I can make this criticism of my grass-roots work for the party is, I believe, the best demonstration that this work was not negative and served to further my ideological training.

The job with the Financial Committee of the Federation was from various points of view rather less fruitful. I brought to the task a certain lack of experience in the field of business. Above all, I lacked the qualities required of a doer (in the business field), while in this case there was less demand for managerial qualities (based essentially on common sense) than for the technical skills possessed by a doer (I also became aware of this shortcoming of mine in my own work, but recently I seem to be on the road to improvement). At the end of 1949 the Financial Committee was rightly incorporated into the Administrative Committee and I became an activist on this committee. In the autumn of 1949 I was once more arrested by the political section of the Milan police. A group of young bank robbers arrested shortly before, some of whom had been members of the PCI (and expelled when their provocative activities had come to light), had stated under questioning at the police station that I had financed their gang, which had strange connections with the world of espionage. I was released the day after my arrest, but this did not deter the tabloids from unleashing a violent smear campaign. I had in fact met these young men at the time they were members of the PCI, and some of them had also taken part in a summer camp that, in my capacity as the youth officer for the Duomo branch office of the party, I had organized in the summer of 1948.

I have had no contact with them whatsoever since their expulsion from the party, far less have I financed their enterprise or lent them money, even on a personal basis.

After my arrest, I was transferred to the Federation cell and my political activity was limited exclusively to work with the Administrative Committee.

By attending the party's regional school, my aim is to attain two basic goals:

1. to further my theoretical knowledge by applying myself to the study of the themes and the writings of those who have led popular movements, who have led the party to power in some countries, and who in other countries are still leading it in the struggle against domestic and foreign imperialists;

2. to learn from three months of collective life to live in a community, therefore modifying my character, and to learn what it means to work alongside other comrades. I feel that this second objective is especially important because of the particular conditions in which I live, and because by so doing I may improve myself and thus work better for the party.

Feltrinelli's "autobiography" caused a sensation in the offices of the Milan Federation. Lidia Lefebre, who worked there as a secretary in 1950, recalls the great impression it made on everyone: a mixture of admiration for a comrade who had exposed himself so openly, and of pride in the party's powers of attraction.

I have met some of the comrades who had dealings with my father in the early fifties.

Giovanni Pesce, who was awarded the Gold Medal of the Resistance, met Giangiacomo in the offices of the Milan Federation of the PCI, or perhaps late one evening in the corridors of *L'Unità* as they waited for the first edition to appear. He says: "The first time it was I who approached him. I said hello, and he greeted me without smiling. That missing smile made me feel a little uncomfortable, and I sensed he was not an easy person. This aroused my curiosity, because I have never liked easy people, the hail-fellow-well-met types." The battles waged by Pesce's combat unit against the Germans were legendary.

Feltrinelli also met Vittorio Vidali at this time. Vidali's curriculum was an impressive one: prison, wounds, mutilations, a life on the run between Algeria, the USSR, France, Germany, and Austria. A spell in the America of mobsters, Sacco and Vanzetti, and Rudolph Valentino. The Spanish Civil War and the command of the Fifth Regiment of the International Brigade. Mexico and the "Giuseppe Garibaldi" anti-Fascist alliance. The marvelous Tina Modotti. After twenty-five years, his return to his native Trieste was dogged by the rumor, vague but never really denied, that he had been among the killers of Leon Trotsky.

The twenty-year-old Giangiacomo must have got a kick out of talking with characters like Vidali. But what interested him in the underground movement wasn't heroic deeds and guns: he was struck by the spirit of "getting things done." Historic events generated expectations that required initiative and strength of spirit, just as in the days of the Resistance. What people accomplished then was only the beginning of a grandiose project.

Giovanni Pesce: "When we met, what Feltrinelli wanted most was for me to explain why the Resistance, despite its victory, was half canceled by the political and economic interests that handed power to the same ruling classes that had given birth to Fascism and the monarchy."

I never met Pietro Secchia,* the number 2 man in the party at the time. He has been described as the strong man of the Resistance, the shadowy figure who lived above Togliatti in a condominium in Montesacro, from where he manipulated both the leader and the entire party network. "One branch office for every bell tower" was his motto. They say that he was often in disagreement with the official party line and acted closely with the "supreme" party on the other side of the Iron Curtain. He was a

---

*(1903–72). A leading figure of the PCI, Secchia was a hard-line Communist, member of parliament, and senator.

difficult man, with a subtler intelligence than current historiography would lead us to believe.

While Secchia had a friendly relationship with Feltrinelli, he told his factotum, Giulio Seniga, that he thought Giangiacomo might be an able manager of his own business affairs but was less open-handed with the party.

Between September of 1950 and the following summer, Feltrinelli made various trips to East Germany, Czechoslovakia, and Hungary. The pretense was to tend to certain commercial matters: Meissen porcelain from Germany; vacuum flasks, refrigerators, and gas stoves from Czechoslovakia; things like that. But the party was his partner in these ventures, at least fifty-fifty. Secchia introduced him to the Czechs as a comrade who "enjoys our full confidence." Though these dealings were of little account, they boosted his status as a businessman who worked with Eastern Europe. A fat wad of confidential reports was added to his file in the political archives kept by the Ministry of the Interior and by the military intelligence service.

The house in Piazza San Babila where Bianca and Giangiacomo went to live was furnished in a sober, functional style. Bianca tried to create a pleasing ambience. A couple of dogs had the run of the house, and on one wall, among the old masters, hung a portrait of Stalin.

Political activity took up almost all their free time. This meant very little social life and few friends. During the day, Feltrinelli the businessman struggled to elude the traps laid for him by his rapacious mother. He had learned in a hurry, on the job, and therefore he took care not to expose himself too much. He had good sense, and a sixth sense, too, especially in his choice of colleagues. He promoted as his assistant a young accountant and devout Christian, Gaetano Lazzati, whom he encouraged and trusted.

His holdings were concentrated in construction (with the Edilizia Centro Milano and the Compagnia Imprese e Costruzioni, both owning important real estate in Milan and Rome) and in lumber and lumber by-products. Within the parent company, Feltrinelli Industria e Commercio Legnami, there was a difficult coexistence with the Accademia dei Lincei, Antonio Feltrinelli's child. There were other holdings in the construction sector (Ferrobeton) and in building materials (Loro & Parisini). Then there was a majority holding in the Banca Unione (before 1918, the Banca Feltrinelli). The owners of this small but distinguished private bank, which stood near the Milan Stock Exchange, were anything but united. Giangiacomo's fellow shareholders were his mother and his sister, the Bastogi Corporation, and the Vatican Bank. So a young businessman, ostentatiously Communist and in a period of high Stalinism at that, was the principal stockholder in a merchant bank, side by side with a representative of the Vatican's IOR,* the minority partner.

Giannalisa prepared for a tough fight; at least, this is the way Lazzati remembers it. She wanted to oust her son from the board. She succeeded, but even that wasn't enough for her.

During a street demonstration, perhaps in the days of the *legge truffa*,† the police arrested Giangiacomo right next to the Banca Unione. He was carrying a copy of *L'Unità*. The telephone lines of the bank management were red hot: "It's a scandal!" The scandal was the newspaper he held. Giangiacomo's mother again moved to force her son to sell his shares. And that's what he did, in 1953. Twenty years later, the Vatican found itself in partnership with the notorious Michele Sindona,‡ this time as the majority shareholder.

Politics came into everything, contaminating life and business.

---

*L'Istituto per Opere Religiose, or IOR, is the Vatican Bank.

†According to this law, decried as a fraud by the Left, the coalition that won 50 percent of the votes would obtain 65 percent of the seats in parliament.

‡A shady financier, Sindona met his death in mysterious circumstances while awaiting trial in prison.

Feltrinelli made deals with politicians, and he was appreciated by those in politics. A straight question: How much importance was attached to party card 0735668 in the name of Giangiacomo Feltrinelli? "A lot, a lot," comes the reply in chorus, with closed eyes and much nodding of heads, from three men who were party leaders or officials at the time: Armando Cossutta, Gianni Cervetti, and Elio Quercioli.

There are anecdotes: "He would make up the losses on the Federation's balance sheet"; "A million a month for the Milan office of the newspaper"; or the story about local party secretary Alberganti, who, when he couldn't meet the payroll, would say, "I'll see to it" and go off to phone you know who.

These things were well known at the Ministry of the Interior. Since 1948, Feltrinelli, a "major financer" of the PCI, had been under the systematic surveillance of the Milan police. They kept a record of his business activities, his arrests, his travels, the people he invited to dinner, and the money given to Togliatti for the administrative elections—everything. In August 1951, the Office of Confidential Affairs received a report from the Milan police in which it was alleged that Feltrinelli had salvaged the publishing house "run by the Communist son of the president of the Republic" (namely Einaudi).

The three men I interviewed—Cossutta, Cervetti, and Quercioli—offered similar descriptions of the relationship between Alberganti and Feltrinelli. Although there was an age difference of twenty-five years between the two men, they were linked by strong ties: "Alberganti always protected and defended him!"

Giuseppe Alberganti, whose roots lay in a blend of anarchism and labor unionism, had been a partisan in Emilia and possessed the physical courage of a man of action. He was one of those who stayed at the barricades. After the strike called following the Togliatti assassination attempt, he did not return to his post at the Federation: he couldn't stand the idea of facing all those workers who

were tearing up their party cards because they were not allowed to
go into action.

I am sure that my father was fond of Alberganti, who treated
him with a quasi-paternal regard. But shortly before he died, the
nonagenarian Fuma, the painter and former secretary of the
Duomo branch office, told me, "On the day of the revolution, Alberganti wouldn't have struck your father off the list of those to be
taken out."

Perhaps Giangiacomo himself was aware of it. He may have
been young and enthusiastic, but he was intelligent and learning to
deal with people, to take their measure, and—why not?—to be suspicious. He did not see the Communist cause as a bandwagon to be
abandoned whenever it was convenient. Communism was his
ideal.

The man who really counted was Secchia. How far the trust extended between Feltrinelli and Secchia is proven by a brief note in
Secchia's hand, written on the day that marked the end of his political career. It was 26 July 1954 when he learned that Giulio
Seniga, his right-hand man, had flown the coop a few hours earlier
with the party's secret cash fund: $421,000 and some confidential
documents (the exact sum was revealed to me by Seniga in 1996).
Secchia wrote:

> At eight in the morning I came across the first theft. [Seniga] had
> taken everything from Bundazia [the nom de guerre of Oddino De
> Laurentis] and then from all the others. I took Valli everywhere I
> went in order to have a witness if any sums were found or if every-
> thing had disappeared. [Seniga] did not manage to go to Giangia-
> como's apartment or to Turchi's, and in these two places I found all
> the sums deposited.

In other words, a part of the PCI's reserves was hidden in a
Roman house put at the party's disposal by Feltrinelli. According to
Seniga, there was another Feltrinelli "safe" in Milan, but he did not
want or was unable to visit it.

In the early fifties, Togliatti would occasionally go to dinner at the San Babila apartment. When he came to Milan, his every move was top secret for security reasons, and the party preferred him to eat in the houses of comrades in order not to attract attention. Passing from the hall to the living room of Giangiacomo's and Bianca's apartment, he had to steer a zigzag course through the piles of books lying on the floor.

The idea is simple. It is not possible to study the labor movement without collecting sources, material, documentation. It is necessary to piece together the threads of a tradition that Nazism, Fascism, and the war severed. To take stock of a world that resembles an open wound and find the right instruments to repair the body. This is what Feltrinelli and Del Bo had in mind, and the result of the challenge they faced can be seen today. All you need do is take a tram to Piazza della Scala in Milan.

Here you get off, and after you pass a few banks and diners with marble-topped counters where the clerks take their lunch, a low doorway leads to the reading room. A domed ceiling pierced by thick bull's-eye windows provides light for reading. In the room you must be quiet; people have come a long way to study here. A cultivated librarian can take you to the private chapel for religious services dating from Grandfather Carlo's time. Today, below the crimson banner of the Paris Commune, there are two hundred periodicals from the time of the Communards and the First International. Returning to the reading room, you can see a first edition of the *Encyclopédie,* together with a collection of original editions of the most important works of the Enlightenment. Out back, among the ranks of metal shelves, it takes a while to get your bearings among sections on the old economists, Russian populism, English industrialism, the Spanish Civil War, the French, German, and English utopians... There are more than 300,000 books and 30,000 periodicals. But a discerning eye will spot a rare

edition of Thomas More's *Utopia* alongside first editions of Rous-
seau's *Social Contract,* Bayle's *Various Thoughts on the Occasion
of a Comet,* Mary Wollstonecraft's *A Vindication of the Rights of
Woman,* and Saint-Simon's *Political Discourses.* Verri's *Il Caffé*
close to the satirical journals of the Risorgimento, *Civiltà Cat-
tolica,* Viesseux's *Anthology...* Or Cattaneo's reflections on the
1848 uprising in Milan, Herzen's *Thoughts,* the essays of the phys-
iocrats, and pamphlets on the effects of the industrial revolution... If your interests run to history more, you have to go down
to the basement, where cartoons and caricatures from the siege of
Paris, May 1871, stand next to Marx's working notes, Engels's
notes, Victor Hugo's letters to Garibaldi, the letters of the young
Bakunin, Proudhon's correspondence from exile in Belgium, and
the canvas-backed notebooks in which Angelo Tasca* kept an account of his years in Paris, as well as his correspondence with
Salvemini,† Rosselli,‡ Togliatti, and Nenni.

Reaching the exit, before you get your breath back, you might
spend a few minutes looking at the only extant copy of the *Patriotic
Journal of Corsica* (1790), or the collection of *Die Neue Zeit* (1883).

Every library embodies the fascination of its construction, of its
intrinsic rationality, of its unpredictable nature. That's why its development is a journey that meanders through a maze of tempting
possibilities—perhaps a new collection here, maybe a new section
there—in search of an unattainable completeness. A library resembles any ink blot: in some places the form is denser, in others

---

*(1892–1960). A political exile in Paris. A founder of the PCI, he was expelled in
1929 for his criticism of Stalin.

†Gaetano Salvemini (1873–1957). A historian and opponent of Fascism from the
start. He taught at Harvard in the thirties.

‡The Rosselli brothers, anti-Fascist intellectuals, were assassinated by Mussolini's thugs in Paris: Carlo (1899–1937) was an economist, Nello (1900–37) a historian of the Risorgimento.

more tenuous. But undeniably there is a form, a balance, a center of strength.

In April 1951, a confidential report informed the chief of police:

Within the sphere of the various activities of the PCI, we ought to include the work of the well-known Communist businessman Giangiacomo Feltrinelli, resident in Piazza San Babila 4, which is made up of an enterprise, already well under way, aimed at attracting young people of all classes desirous of culture to a library that bears the name of the aforementioned Feltrinelli and is located in a building owned by the same Feltrinelli—or at least so we have been assured—on Via Domenico Scarlatti 26.

According to this information, this "little university of Marxism" was in reality a meeting place for "young Communist fanatics" who were being given a training in culture as well as in the work of "action squads."

Feltrinelli sometimes scolded his youngsters when he found them in the bar across the way, absorbed in a hard-fought game of pool. This was apparently as close to action as this particular squad ever got.

In the first offices of the library, not far from Milan Central Station, a group of young intellectuals got down to work. While Giuseppe Del Bo, beginning in 1948, was the main source of inspiration, between 1950 and 1952 Feltrinelli created the library's real structure. From Rome, following a request sent to the PCI, came the high-school teacher Franco Della Peruta* (recommended by Gastone Manacorda), the philosophy student Gastone Bollino (the secretary of the Rome University cell), and Franco Ferri, a graduate of Normale di Pisa University, who had been chosen by a group of colleagues very close to Togliatti. These were joined by the socialist

---

*(1924–). Professor of the history of the Risorgimento at the University of Milan.

Gianni Bosio, the founder of the magazine *Movimento operaio,* and
the first bursars or collaborators, like Stefano Merli and Luigi
Cortesi. Almost none of these people belonged to the generation
that had fought in the Resistance, a further indication that a historical epoch had come to an end. As scholars, they recognized that
the inherited canon had been delegitimized. Retaking possession of
the history of the workers' movement, which was their declared
aim, meant the systematic and unified collection of all the material
that had survived the war, the book burnings, and the censors. This
was to be done by updating both documentary structure and bibli-
ographic research methods, without neglecting an analysis of the
social problems that were already developing.

Feltrinelli's investment called for specialists, who were recruited
almost exclusively from the ranks of the activists in Sesto San Giovanni, the Milan suburb known as the Italian Stalingrad: two employees to look after administration, two for secretarial duties, one
delivery man, and three filing clerks. It was necessary to forge
ahead in the creation of an inventory of archival sources: books,
pamphlets, periodicals, manifestos, flyers, and photographs. The
material began to flow in.

The researchers combed the stores specializing in old books, region by region, and delved into address lists, family by family. The
result of their efforts was an increased store of documents on the
Risorgimento and Italian socialism. Franco Della Peruta spent
most of his time working on the Italian section, while Del Bo supervised the acquisition of collections of old foreign publications,
especially French material. Feltrinelli wanted to give the research
an international slant from the outset; he had already made several trips to European countries. Many years later, he spoke to a
German journalist about his first hunts for material:

> It was 1948. Germany was still in ashes and ruins. Only the cultural
> and literary spheres showed signs of life. On one of my frequent trips
> to Hamburg, I learned in a bookshop that someone in Osnabrück

was selling a first edition of *The Communist Manifesto.* Together
with Professor Del Bo, I immediately left for Osnabrück. We almost
wanted to draw out the pleasure of anticipation, but we were afraid
someone might get there before us. So, having arrived early at our
destination, we waited in the car, eyes peeled. But we were the ones
to be spotted: a stranger came up to the car and asked if, by any
chance, we were the friends interested in the collector's item. Then
he took us to a dusty attic, where we found a couple of enormous
bookshelves. The first of these contained the most comprehensive library of socialist literature I had ever seen: articles by Trotsky,
court-case documents, party circulars, manifestos, and resolutions. I
bought the lot for forty thousand marks. I did not let that treasure
out of my sight until I had transported the thirty boxes to my apartment in Milan. But I passed up a tremendous bargain: the second
shelf contained the most valuable collection of erotic literature I had
ever seen.

Feltrinelli and Del Bo were like brothers. Both men had not followed a linear course in life; both were linked by the ideal of a just
secular society. Sometimes Feltrinelli would listen to his friend's
advice, other times he would play his cards close to his chest.
There was also a playful aspect to their relationship, and no lack of
amusing episodes. They were like kids.

In a legal deposition made when they were no longer kids, Del
Bo was to say this of his friend:

> Given my fraternal contacts with Feltrinelli, I wish to describe what
> I feel was his character. He was undoubtedly a man of considerable
> intelligence, impulsive, with a tendency to take the lead. He seemed
> wary, but in reality he was prepared to embrace other people's opin-
> ions with enthusiasm and to espouse their cause if he thought fit.
> But he was just as prepared to abandon a cause, without standing on
> ceremony, if he felt it was outdated or did not serve his way of think-
> ing. His enthusiasm was easily aroused. He believed in what he did.

Feltrinelli loved Citroën cars and drove his with the skill that
comes with great familiarity, not worrying about getting dents. If
he was a terrifying driver, he was also a tireless one. His forays
with Del Bo as they combed Europe in search of books and papers

were to become family legends: "That time when Sergio nearly had his first heart attack because of the way Giangiacomo was driving the car, with a broken window, at three hundred kilometers an hour..." Thanks to these missions the two travelers in the black Citroën soon had acquired a network of experts, consultants, and dealers, all of top quality.

In Holland, they went to Herbert Andreas, a very special character. Born in Hamburg in 1914, as a young man he had developed a passion for history, mainly of the origins of the workers' movement and Marxism. In the early thirties he changed his name to Bert, as a tribute to Brecht, joined the German Communist Party, contributed articles to his local newspaper, and published an antimilitarist novel, *Mata Hari*. About midway through the decade, after a couple of arrests, he opted for exile in Holland and continued his subversive activities with International Red Help. After the war, Andreas settled in Amsterdam, where he established himself as a collector and bibliophile. His first contacts with Feltrinelli date from 1951, and he was to work closely with him for ten years. Thanks to Andreas, and despite the fact that in Germany at that time there was scant interest in the history of the socialist movement, the library's sections on Marx and Engels, German social democracy, and the Hegelian left began to take shape. Bert Andreas was also perhaps Feltrinelli's first contact with the Marxist–Leninist Institute of Moscow (IMEL).

Another source of German literature was an enthusiastic researcher who lived in Zurich: the anarchist Theo Pinkus. In England, Eric J. Hobsbawm went through lists of old books, though only occasionally. For Russian material, there was a scholar of the caliber of Franco Venturi to oversee populism and Decembrism. For the United States there was Luigi Aurigemma, Giangiacomo's childhood friend from the Museo delle Terme in Rome. The official reason Aurigemma gave for his journeys to America was that he was in search of material on the Utopian colonies of the nineteenth century. But if he chanced to come across some documents

on McCarthyism, in full flow at the time, so much the better. He
often came to Paris, and when Feltrinelli went there to see Del Bo,
they would dine on snails.

Those trips and the frequent visits to Paris were good for Giangiacomo; the change of air and the water gurgling in the gutters
gave him the sense of a great city, beautiful and free. In Paris he
took a shine to a lady dining at the next table in the Deux Magots.
I suspect this was the beginning of an intense affair.

The heroic Archives of the Revolution period was the first half
of the twentieth century: thefts, confiscations, bombs, rescues, secret handovers. The revolutionary movements tried to halt the dis-
persion of socialist manuscripts, letters, books, newspapers, notes,
reports, and minutes, particularly those of Marx and Engels and
their contemporaries. On 2 February 1921, Lenin wrote to David
Borisovich Ryanazov, the director and cofounder of the Marx–
Engels Institute in Moscow: "Can we not buy [...] the letters of
Marx and Engels? Or copies of them? Is it possible to take the collection of extant writings and bring them together in Moscow? Is
there a catalog of what we already have?" The situation was not
promising. After the First World War, the rich inheritance of books
left to Germany had been scattered. In the Soviet Union, most of
the works in circulation were photocopies of material that was either inaccessible or impossible to find. Even the publication of the
works of Marx and Engels was a sketchy affair, and editions were
often incomplete.

Most progress was made in Amsterdam, thanks to the efforts of
Nicolaas Wilhelmus Posthumus and Nehemia de Lieme. The former was a pioneer of economic history in Holland, an enthusiastic
captain of industry; the latter was the founder of an insurance company whose profits went partly to finance the cultural development
of the working classes. Posthumus came from the social democratic
tradition, De Lieme from the liberal socialist school of thought. In
1934, the two men joined forces to found the International Institute

of Social History. In the space of a few months, with the help of invaluable associates, Posthumus acquired the SPD archive; the libraries of Max Netlau and Karl Kautsky; the archives of Leon Trotsky, Mikhail Bakunin, Wilhelm Liebknecht, and Valerian Smirnov.

But these gains made in the twenties and thirties were threatened by the advance of Nazism. Much material was lost, and research became more and more difficult. It was 1946 before the Institute in Amsterdam managed to recover some of the documents confiscated by the Germans during the occupation after 1940.

After the Second World War, the plan to create a temple for revolutionary papers became an obsession for Moscow. The Institute of Marxism–Leninism sent 127 correspondents out into the world. The forms of Marxism were multiplying, and the Cold War was on its way.

The Soviets noticed the Italians in 1952. The first expression of interest in Feltrinelli's library came from their embassy in Rome, while in Moscow a special top secret document was drawn up on 4 April 1953. It gave information about the library and was addressed to Comrade Pospelov, one of the secretaries to the Central Committee, a former director of the Institute of Marxism–Leninism and soon to be elected to the secretariat of the first Central Committee of the post-Stalin era.

Six days later, a second document, its contents similar to those of the document of 4 April, landed on the desk of Nikita Khrushchev, the prime candidate to succeed Stalin. The note suggested that it might be worth approaching Pietro Secchia about using Feltrinelli as an intermediary with the institute in Amsterdam (Moscow could not hold negotiations directly: the institute was headed by persons "hostile to the USSR"). Secchia, the deputy chairman of the PCI, was said to be the middleman through whom Feltrinelli passed on "important material support" to the party. Moreover, the note advised the intervention of the Soviet embassy in Holland with a view to obtaining accurate information on the materials kept in Amsterdam and on the heads of the International Institute of Social History. It was also urged that Feltrinelli be invited to come to Moscow; his visit could perhaps be camouflaged among the many foreign delegations due to arrive on the occasion of 1 May.

Feltrinelli let it be known that he would prefer a personal invitation. However, in the Kremlin they had other fish to fry: Stalin had not been dead a month, and the struggle of Khrushchev and Zhukov against Beria was already under way.

Talks began again in July 1953, when Secchia went to Moscow for a briefing on the new line regarding Beria. It is probable that Feltrinelli was mentioned. The personal invitation materialized after the summer, and the trip was made toward the end of 1953. Giangiacomo arrived in the Soviet Union via Vienna and Prague, accompanied by his wife, Bianca.

Moscow was celebrating Old Year's Night. On his arrival at Pushkinskaya 15, my father must have walked the red carpet together with the heads of IMEL, reviewing all the busts and icons on display. Then he must have visited the cellarage, where the doors are in cast iron and archivists wearing aprons show you picaresque little drawings by Lenin aged twelve. Then they must have taken him to the upper floors, where any conversation was always preceded by a glass of steaming hot tea.

The focus of conversation was the collaboration between IMEL and the Biblioteca Feltrinelli in Milan. The first lists of things to be exchanged were drawn up. Moscow was interested in copies or microfilms of Marx's correspondence, as well as that of the members of his family, Engels, and the writings by Lenin kept in the archive of Camille Huysmans,* including the lists of material on the First International. The Soviets agreed to provide microfilms, books, and registers of contents.

*(1871–1968). A Belgian socialist who was secretary to the Steering Committee of the Socialist International in the forties.

Feltrinelli found himself in a strange position, as the third party of a triangle that was Milan, Moscow, and Amsterdam. With the Dutch, "cooperation was restricted to persons with the same view of things," recalls Rein Van Der Leeuw, then a young functionary with the Institute of Social History. As the only person who could contact and work with the Soviets, Feltrinelli promised them he would do all he could to find out what was kept in the institute in Amsterdam. He also had to find out about the Marx–Engels archive that Columbia University was interested in acquiring. He would try to get the Dutch go give him an inventory of the archive, or buy a part of it, or at least get hold of a copy. He declared his willingness to search for valuable documents in the West, in mutual agreement with the Institute of Marxism–Leninism. He made the same promise to the Dutch, with whom he was on excellent terms. His role was to build bridges between two worlds that did not communicate with each other, as well as to look after the interests of his own library. Up-to-date research on the sources of Marxism could not be made without the help of the Soviets, but relations with the Dutch were just as vital.

The idea of temporarily moving a part of the Milan archives, mentioned in the Pospelov report, did not seem to get off the ground in the course of the talks with the Soviets. But the fact that Feltrinelli had considered this should not surprise anyone: at that time, a part of the archives of the PCI was still in Prague, and there was talk of sending it to Moscow for safekeeping. In Italy, after the electoral clash that had brought down the *legge truffa*, the troops had closed ranks and the international climate encouraged and fed the growth of a cold-war paranoia from which no one was immune.

The meetings held in Moscow in early 1954 only partly met the expectations of those involved. Perhaps the party showed its more monolithic side. Perhaps the Soviets found it difficult to understand this strange Italian.

3

In the late afternoon of Saturday, 18 June 1955, four young men and a young woman met in a bar on Via Manzoni, a stone's throw from La Scala opera house. One of the four was the fledgling publisher Giangiacomo Feltrinelli, whose twenty-ninth birthday was that very evening. The other three men were his editors, and the woman was his secretary, interpreter, cashier, and receptionist, who always carried under her arm a stenotype machine fresh from America, as expensive as it was superfluous. The little group toasted the new publishing house and its first books.

The two books just off the presses were *The Scourge of the Swastika* by Lord Russell of Liverpool (translated by one of the editors, Luciano Bianciardi) and the *Autobiography* of Jawaharlal Nehru.

They had left the advance copies in the office, because they wanted to forget those few typos that elude the watchful eyes of copy editors and proofreaders and then, when the book is nicely printed and bound and jacketed, stand out with brazen insolence.

In a television interview given ten years later, the publisher recalled that these two books were no casual choice.

They corresponded to three of the principal threads that made up
the leitmotiv that the house had developed with particular care: the
first was a consistent and coherent anti-Fascism; the second involved the quest for a form of coexistence between countries with
differing economic and political structures, a coexistence that–and
this was the third thread–did not accept the crystallization of the
politico-economic geography of the day, but worked on the assump-
tion that it was possible for the new forces of the Third World, the
countries that were emerging from colonial domination, to find their
own equilibrium and to take their place forcefully in the global political system.

Back in 1955, in the bar on Via Manzoni, those present were well
aware that it was only a beginning, that the real difficulties were
still to come, and that anyone could print two books, but you
needed ideas and means if you were to last, and luck too.

In the immediate postwar period, in 1949 to be precise, the editorial department of an evening paper, *Milano Sera,* housed in the
former headquarters of the Fascist *Popolo d'Italia,* had launched a
series of low-cost, low-priced (100-lire) paperbacks: the Universale
Economica del Canguro. Corrado De Vita, the editor of the newspaper, backed the launch with a high-profile promotional campaign.

The idea was to revive a glorious Italian tradition of the late
nineteenth century, when a few publishers, Perrino, Barbera, and
Edgardo Sonzogno (to mention only the most important names),
with an eye to the educational-humanistic aims of the nascent socialist movement, had gone after the mass market, printing the
classics of world literature and offering the books at an absurdly
low price, around twenty-five cents.

Against this background, during a period of reconstruction that
also included culture, the colorful dust jackets of the new Canguro
series began to emerge at the rate of one a week. "A book a week
against obscurantism" was the slogan that announced the first
four: *The Confessions of an Italian* by Ippolito Nievo, *The Indiscreet
Jewels* by Denis Diderot, the *Life of Jesus* by Ernest Renan, and the
scholarly essays of the English scientist J. B. S. Haldane. In the

provinces, the occasional priest would caution retailers against these books: Better not have them on display.

One month before (in May 1949), Rizzoli had launched Bur, another renowned "universal" library destined to enjoy enduring and well-deserved fame. Both ventures, albeit for different reasons, were linked by the idea of exploring the new possibilities of the popular paperback book. But "popular" then did not mean a low-quality product—quite the opposite.

Canguro got off to a remarkable start: the readers liked what they saw, and print runs reached a peak of 35,000. The rate at which new titles appeared made it necessary to create a regular working structure right away, complete with a business name: Cooperativa del libro popolare. It was shortened to Colip. More editors were hired, and they set to work under Luigi Diemoz, a man of great refinement who was painstaking to a fault. He looked like a Hapsburg aristocrat, down to the monocle he wore in his left eye.

It ought to be added that the decisive impetus for creating the cooperative came from the PCI, on the advice of the party leader. "I remember one thing very clearly," recalls the art historian Mario De Micheli. "It was Togliatti who pressed for and later made the decision. Both De Vita and Feltrinelli assured me of this." In the early days at least, the editorial office in Milan was under the strict control of the central cultural committee in Rome. Ambrogio Donini, the historian of religion in charge of the party's publishing activities and a member of the Colip board, was the middleman between Milan and Rome.

Among those who worked with the new publishing house was Feltrinelli, still very young and already passionate about the publishing business. His presence within the cooperative, at first as a simple financial partner, was soon transformed into a far broader commitment, especially when things began to take a less favorable turn.

After the initial enthusiasm, it became apparent that something was wrong. Booksellers did not earn much out of Canguro's publications: the price was too low. As a consequence, sales plummeted. Things seemed to have gone into a dangerous spin until, at the last moment, the call went out for someone to help the company avoid the worst: so my father found himself directly involved in the way things were managed. This was toward the end of 1950.

The publication of a new book every week was resumed, print runs were more prudent, prices slightly increased, and the distributor changed. "The new management, thanks to the impetus provided by Feltrinelli, has succeeded in reestablishing a little order, and a good part of the accumulated debt has been paid off." Thus Ambrogio Donini, in a letter to Giancarlo Pajetta dated February 1951.

It wasn't just a matter of accounting: the need to broaden the range of publications had become pressing. As the months went by, the Universale Economica label became less and less suited to the robust body that had outgrown it and promised to grow even more in the future.

At a meeting of the readers' committee held in September 1951, Feltrinelli spoke on new publishing ventures to be undertaken by Colip in support of the Universale Economica series:

> In other publishing houses [...] popular editions are part of a far broader output, which makes up for the small income derived from the low-priced series. Colip has to go the other way, backing up the Universale Economica series with more profitable publishing ventures that make for greater profit margins, for Colip and retailers alike. That way, booksellers will treat our low-priced production with more respect.

The house launched two bigger series, one devoted to literature and the other to history. This led to the publication of *The Social History of the French Revolution* by Jean Jaurés and *Italia qual è*

*(1908–88). Professor of the history of political doctrine.

(Italy As It Is) by Francesco Saverio Merlino. Giorgio Candeloro* was commissioned to write a history of Italy.

But realizing this project required financial resources, which were not always available to cooperatives of this kind. Once more, Feltrinelli stepped into the breach with systematic injections of fresh capital. In the most difficult period, his contribution amounted to more than five million lire a month, which fell to a million around mid-1952 before falling again to seven to eight thousand lire in March 1953.

His was the support of a committed militant, which made it possible to consolidate the enterprise. And with hindsight, it proved a good investment too. For the Colip project needed to be not merely supported or broadened, but completely reinvented. And the day came when Feltrinelli was obliged to wind up the accounts of the cooperative and shoulder the deficit. The venture ended, the idea remained.

In the meantime, the Italian political landscape was changing, because huge changes were under way in world politics. In the cultural field, there was a greater willingness to accept other points of view. The PCI began to take less interest in Colip's activities because the need for an "anti-obscurantist" offensive was no longer a priority. Other urgent matters and new issues were beginning to emerge.

Having laboriously attained the goal of two hundred titles, in early 1954 Canguro took the plunge: publication was suspended to make way for the establishment of the newborn Giangiacomo Feltrinelli Editore.

Nineteen fifty-five must have been a tough year.

Three days after the launch of Feltrinelli Editore, Italy was rocked by the usual government crisis: Mario Scelba's first government was ousted to make way for a new administration led by Antonio Segni. Within the Christian Democratic Party, a struggle began over the inheritance left by De Gasperi. As far as the Communists were concerned, Scelba was the inventor of the motorized riot police who broke up "seditious" demonstrations with a liberal use of batons and rifle butts. In this case, "seditious" meant everything from the protest against the use of chemical weapons in Korea to the tilling of uncultivated land on the part of unemployed farm workers, or any form of protest by laid-off workers.

In Rome, there was a new ambassador with an energetic approach to the prevention of Communism, Claire Boothe Luce, while America was still going through the aftermath of the anti-Communist campaign unleashed by Joseph McCarthy and his numerous acolytes on the Senate subcommittee on investigations: the electric chair for Julius and Ethel Rosenberg had recently underlined the effects of their crusading zeal.

Claire Luce immediately won over the Italian national press. The support of Scelba and the Vatican was a foregone conclusion. In the spring of 1955, the Italian premier had made a trip to the United States, complete with a visit to the Empire State building and a triumphal motorcade through a Brooklyn decked out with Italian flags, some with the arms of the House of Savoy, others with the symbols of Fascism.

America's new ambassador soon enjoyed the unconditional support of Italian industry and high finance, whose leaders had little fear of an imminent Italian Communist revolution but could not tolerate their influence in the labor unions and factories.

Italy's biggest company, Fiat, set about reorganizing their personnel department. Every worker had a dossier and uniformed supervisors and informers were at work inside and outside the factories. Fiat also encouraged the establishment of a "yellow" labor union, a pro-management organization detached from the political left.

Fiat buzzed with rumours of plant restructuring, modernization and automation; in other words, the adoption of modern American methods. All this was in the interests of cost-cutting. To speed things up, labor militants were detailed to special departments, from which it was easier to dismiss them on the flimsiest of grounds: insufficient productivity, prolonged sick leave, or on the basis of other treachery cooked up by the personnel office.

The newspapers commented on the defeat of the farm workers and on the flight from agriculture. And in the south, in the other Italy, people were still dying of starvation in the outlying districts of the cities and on the great landed estates of Puglia, Calabria and Sicily.

The cultural climate of 1955 was fervent, restless, full of promise and menace. The new publishing house sought a form of expression that was different from journalism, but just as aggressive and striking; there was a desire to move beyond a certain academic culture, whether liberal or Catholic or Marxist, then dominant in the biggest publishing houses, and to try out original and heretical forms of thought.

All this fitted in perfectly with a specific plan. In September 1952, Feltrinelli had set up a distribution company called Eda (Editori Distribuiti Associati) to promote Colip and other Italian publishers, but also to import prestigious foreign presses like PUF, Plon, Oxford, Juillard, Pergamon, and Reclam. (Eda was headed by Franco Osenga and Adolfo Occhetto, the father of Franco, later to become a Feltrinelli manager, and of Achille Occhetto, the last leader of the PCI before its dissolution.) A few years later, in 1956, Feltrinelli Libri Spa was established to run small bookstores: Feltrinelli intended to create a single circuit (publisher plus distributor plus bookstores).

In the meantime, the task of consolidating the Feltrinelli library was well under way, and a research team was working on the difficult process of renewing and reorienting the study of the workers' movement. Occasionally, in the new headquarters on Via Scarlatti, the president of the republic, Luigi Einaudi, would drop in to consult the archives.

The only thing that seemed to be missing from this well-articulated plan was a newspaper. With the failure of *Milano Sera,* an evening paper founded in 1945 and promptly labeled "crypto-Communist" by the Ministry of the Interior, the idea of Feltrinelli's possible entry into the world of daily newspapers was strongly advocated by the PCI. The space left vacant by *Milano Sera* could be occupied by a new venture in competition with the other evening papers. Enthusiastic about this idea, Feltrinelli set to working on it day and night, without letting any of his team know about his plans. The administrative staff were kept in the dark to the last. But with the journalists all hired, only a few days before the launch, Feltrinelli put everything on hold. Something did not add up. His people explained to him that the PCI had not kept faith with the initial agreement. Feltrinelli reminded both Amerigo Terenzi and the party leadership of this in a letter dated 28 October 1954. The new paper was to have "inherited nothing from previous ventures" and to have "no connection with the tradition of pro-Communist newspapers." It was to contribute to "a new political orientation in the country, by surrounding itself with all those national forces that, although they could not be considered supporters of the party, nevertheless shared some common views on fundamental foreign and domestic policy issues." The initial agreement also called for a broadly based share package so that one person (Feltrinelli) would not have to take all the risks.

The reason given for the sudden decision to drop the project had no polemical intent but was to foster "a calm analysis of the situation."

According to Cossutta, the project was opposed by President Einaudi himself, whose threat to reveal dossiers on the past activities of the Feltrinelli family was sufficient to prevent the creation of a politically aligned newspaper.

At first, the new publishing house, whose head offices were on Via Fatebenefratelli 3, aroused a certain curiosity, largely because of the founder's name. Italy already boasted plenty of publishers.

The newcomer might last a year or two, in the opinion of some condescending observers. Italo Calvino was the only one to express his good wishes, in the pages of a news sheet from the Einaudi publishing house. But Feltrinelli's position was effectively different from that of his competitors, as he pointed out himself in an interview granted to Sandro Viola in the early sixties:

> I had two advantages. One was my previous experience; since 1945, I spent years working on the reorganization of the companies within the Feltrinelli group, learning about balance sheets, how to assess an executive, how to foresee market trends. The other advantage, perhaps the more important one, was that the great transformation of the country began precisely around 1955, just as we were getting started. This arguably allowed us to grasp the reality of those changes faster than others and to graft them onto the house's commercial and cultural program.

The offices on Via Fatebenefratelli were staffed by a group without much experience in publishing: the first editors, contributors, and consultants did not come from universities or other large institutions. In almost all cases, Colip had been their only training ground. They learned quickly.

The first thing the publisher did was ask his staff to sound out the Italian market. Their reports on every single competitor were complete, detailed, and meticulous. The commitment of the people who wrote them is clear, as is the fact that they were alert and able. But who were they?

The most immaculate description comes from Luciano Bianciardi. He had been offered a job in a city that he never cared for. Plucked from his native Maremma in Tuscany, Bianciardi, today presented in a rather euphemistic light as "sarcastic" or "angry" (I see him as an evil genius with a big heart), described Milan and the Feltrinelli company in a letter to a friend. The letter was published in a recent biography by Pino Corrias.

> At work in the publishing house, I have been lucky enough to find some really smart kids and I have become a close friend of one of

them, Onofri, the manager. Onofri is an older and worse version of
myself. I mean to say that he is a "Vitellone,"* enthusiastic, generous,
rough-and-ready, frivolous, a good sort. Naturally he is also a
bigamist. [...] The others are good kids too. I'll run through them for
you. Giampiero Brega works across the desk from me. Twenty-eight,
a tad on the tubby side, with a degree in philosophy, he tends to play
the moralist and is, in his own way, a very good person. Valerio Riva,
twenty-five, socialist, tall, bespectacled, with a mouth like a sucker
cup. He looks after fiction, is the most practical one among us, and is
potentially the most authoritative. He will go far. Luigi Diemoz, the
chief editor. Age hard to guess and never stated. Forty-five? He is
small, thin and worn out by five years of Milan, restaurants, and a
gastric ulcer. Always bitter, skeptical, he has an enormous mustache.

Libera Venturini, forty, a widow for ten years, completely dipshit
after years at Montecatini. I don't know how she ended up here.
Then there are the two girls, Renata and Giuliana, tall and blonde
the former, petite and brunette the latter.

Then comes Feltrinelli, nicknamed the Jaguar: twenty-eight,
glasses, mustache, tall and robust, ignorant, and filthy rich. He has
interests in lumber, the construction business, refrigerators, and
Coca-Cola. Outwardly he is very cordial and free-and-easy: when
we meet it's all slaps on the back and phony punches in the gut. He
likes me. Upstairs there are the managers, two of them, and the
graphics office, two people there as well. Then, still upstairs, there is
Cinema nuovo, which is Feltrinelli's thing too. Aristarco, Terzi, a girl,
and a young kid work there. Aristarco is a king-size ball breaker.

Our office is very pretty, they say: it looks like a perfumery; all
modern tables, glass, and colored plastic. The decor is the work of
the boss's wife, known as Mrs. Jaguar, an ex down-and-out who has
risen to the heights of wealth and power: she is odious and pretty.

Bianciardi, who was in charge of paperback editions of Italian
fiction, did not last long because his unrepentant determination to
remain out of step got on everyone's nerves. Most nights he was
the last to leave Milan's legendary Bar Giamaica, known in Italian
literature as the Bar delle Antille or the Portorico. Even spinsters
knew that this was the bar frequented by artists whose shaggy

*A young provincial unemployed person, from Fellini's film *I Vitelloni.*

manes heralded the longhaired hippie look. Bianciardi was eventually invited to continue working as an out-of-house editor, author, and translator. I know that Giangiacomo cared for him.

Valerio Riva had to do the work of two or even three people: "There was no book we didn't go after; no translation we didn't redo, sometimes from start to finish; no text we didn't rewrite; and no book was ever published without fresh ideas (often surprisingly good ones) for every launch. It seemed as though we could never do enough." Riva also wrote: "No one wanted to come to Feltrinelli; if anything, people tended to leave. And those who stayed were hated outside the business." So where was the fun? "We were all young, we were all equals. And sure, the level was high. And nonconformist. In short, it was an independent publishing house."

The third editor, whose interests lay more in nonfiction, was Giampiero Brega. He was to have a long association with Feltrinelli. When this trio was joined by Mario Spagnol, Enrico Filippini,* Giampaolo Dossena, Vittorio Di Giuro, Alba Morino, and Attilio Veraldi, with Gerolamo Marasà at the control panel, you could say that they made up the best publishing staff of the day.

Also worthy of mention was the management department run by Silvio Pozzi, a former dispatch rider with the resistance movement. After the Liberation, Pozzi worked for a brief period with the Coca-Cola Company; then, thanks to a letter of introduction from his boss, he found a position as an accountant with Eda, the distribution company. Here he met Feltrinelli for the first time. Pozzi recalls:

> I met him one day in the head office on Via Cavour. He came into the waiting room, I was tying up a parcel, and he asked me: "Is the accountant around?" "Who are you?" I asked him. "Feltrinelli," he said. Embarrassed, I continued trying to tie the parcel. For a while he watched me, and then he said: "That's not the way. Look, first you

*(1934–88). A journalist and German scholar who introduced some of the most important German-language writers to the Italian public.

have to make a kind of slip knot and they you can pull it tight." I
didn't know, because it wasn't my job after all. So he showed me.
That's how I met Feltrinelli.

Pozzi went on to become a director of the publishing house, and
for people like him the term "feltrinelliano" (Feltrinelli boy) was
coined. According to Pozzi, the editors saw Feltrinelli as a friend, a
peer; they would all go to dinner together, and there was a good
deal of familiarity. At the same time he was the boss, with a rigorous managerial style that scared the younger members of the editorial staff.

But the atmosphere was good. Michele Ranchetti, formerly an
assistant to Adriano Olivetti* and the first manager of the Feltrinelli
Bookstores, recalls an anecdote that reveals the spirit of the group:

> One time Brega told me the story of one of the many rows between
> Feltrinelli and Bianciardi. Regarding a book that was to be trans-
> lated, Bianciardi told Feltrinelli he had already discussed the matter
> in sufficient depth with the deputy asshole. Feltrinelli wanted to
> know who the deputy asshole might be. "Everyone knows it's Brega,"
> shot back Bianciardi. Feltrinelli laughed, guffawed in fact, and re-
> peated the wisecrack to Brega himself, who, a touch resentful but as
> cool as possible, asked: "So who do you think this deputy asshole is?"
> Feltrinelli, gleeful: "*You* are the deputy asshole. You ought to feel
> flattered, because who do you think the asshole is?"

Feltrinelli wanted to establish a modern firm, where books
came out on time, where the accounts department was buzzing
and where punctuality was the rule. Riva again: "Feltrinelli taught
us to talk with Italian authors on an arithmetical basis: print runs;
industrial, general, and advertising costs; list prices; multiplica-
tion, subtraction, and addition. If the figures added up, the book
could be done, otherwise forget it."

The balance sheet? Losses. Often, almost always. But there was
no philanthropic logic behind Feltrinelli's practice of making good

*(1901–60). An entrepreneur, engineer, industrialist, publisher, and member of
parliament.

on losses: there were no funds to lose for the sake of mere prestige. The following anecdote told me by Pozzi refers to a later period, but it throws light on the attitude:

> One time, it must have been in the mid-sixties, Feltrinelli took me to Cuccia,* at Mediobanca, to ask about long-term financing. We made the standard pitch, put forward our request, then Cuccia called in one of his people and made the introductions: "This is the famous Mr. Feltrinelli, his hobby is publishing...." Feltrinelli turned on his heel and walked out without even saying good-bye. I just stared at the ceiling. Cuccia was speechless.

From one meeting to the next, in a rather undisciplined and informal climate, with no respect for academic rigidity, books and series took shape. "Our style corresponds, as is obvious, to a certain aspect of my personality, and people are getting used to it. At Einaudi, for example, they are more systematic in their planning. But we are all ups and downs," the publisher was to say in public.

The first titles to be published soon won shelf space in the bookstores, both because they captured something about the places where culture was to be found (Germany, Russia, Latin America, the United States, Egypt, China) and because Feltrinelli had invested in paperback editions (unfashionable in those years) not only of fiction but also of nonfiction books and manuals. These were no longer low-priced versions of previously published hardbacks, but entirely new products. An important role was played by the competence of various consultants, like Carlo Muscetta, and by the covers designed by a pioneer of graphic design such as Albe Steiner. Moreover, to guarantee a visible presence on the shelves of the bookstores, Feltrinelli offered booksellers across-the-board financing for all the titles in a publisher's catalog, an innovative arrangement that is still in use today.

*Enrico Cuccia, the legendary boss of Mediobanca, for many years Italy's most powerful banking concern.

It was not long before Feltrinelli did away with the traditional
working method by which all human knowledge was divided up
into fields, with one person in charge of each field counting on his
own collaborators, in descending order. This was the same hierar-
chical model as the Communist Party's division of the city into federation, zone, cell, and section. One casualty of the decision to
sacrifice this system was Fabrizio Onofri, ousted by Feltrinelli following a direct clash between the two men that left onlookers
dumbstruck.

Anna Del Bo Boffino, the publicity manager at the time, recalls:

> We realized we were very lucky, living in the eye of the cyclone. On
> the one hand, the office was ruled by a sort of party discipline, and
> we had a comrade who was also the boss. But every time Giangia-
> como went over the intellectual score, so to speak, then everything
> had to discussed, and at that point the fact that he was the boss be-
> came a problem: because our boss was also a comrade.

But what does the boss's secretary, Tina have to say? While still
very young, Tina Ricaldone had given up her job with the Communist Federation (where she had been Alberganti's secretary) in
favor of a position with Feltrinelli in the Via Fatebenefratelli offices. There, she swore an oath of fidelity to her publisher that was
to prove more lasting than any wedding vow.

Tina was and still is a very reserved person; even though she
called my father by his first name, and is to all intents and purposes a member of my family, when we talk of him she never says
"Giangiacomo" or "your father," but invariably only "Feltrinelli."
Feltrinelli, she says,

> created the publishing house to give purpose to his life and to pro-
> vide the political left with a tool. He could not bear the idea that
> some people thought of the publishing house as being on a par with
> a factory for the production of stock cubes. With many of the people
> who came to work with us, maybe on the strength of a recommen-
> dation, relations were broken off as soon as they revealed any sign
> of bureaucratic attitude.

But for the people who stayed, those years were remarkable. "The feeling was that we were leaders across the board, and not just the first to acquire the right books. I'll give you an example: ours was the first house to establish the forty-hour week...." To this day, Tina will not say any more.

Feltrinelli was on the verge of becoming a real publisher, "with his head in the clouds and his feet on the ground," as someone was to say. But he was more than that. He had a liking for newspaper sellers. Tough folks already at work in the city fog long before daybreak. He liked the tradition of the *pontremolesi* or *bancarellai*, the men and women who carried books around in panniers and sold them on the street. He toyed with the idea of setting up a mobile bookstore that might do the rounds of the markets and fairs. Some older booksellers still remember a very young Feltrinelli rummaging through the shelves and the tables with the latest publications, not only to inquire about the sales of his own editions but also because he was interested in the day-to-day problems faced by booksellers: discounts on orders, problems with suppliers, the pressure applied by the big publishers, the increasing impoverishment of their stocks...Problems he was to tackle personally when he took over the first stationery and bookstore on the outskirts of Milan, and other established bookstores in Pisa, Rome, Milan, and Genoa.

Some have talked of him as an off-putting man, divided in two by his dual role as boss and comrade and prone to sudden likes and dislikes. Says Carlo Ripa di Meana,* then the manager of a small Feltrinelli bookstore in Forte dei Marmi: "His real problem, apart from the sad story of his family, was his immense wealth. He was tormented by the suspicion that he was surrounded by people who wanted to exploit him, who were his friends only because his name was Feltrinelli."

*A socialist, former member of the European parliament, and founder of the Italian green party, Lista Verde.

At first sight most people seemed to find Feltrinelli disagreeable. He was a good listener, but his sincere and humble impulses were blended with an aristocratic reserve. He was a difficult man given to a certain type of risk, along with a surprising irreverence that speakers of Yiddish would describe as chutzpah.

Those who threw in their lot with Giangiacomo in those years, and who resisted temptations like idleness, glibness, opportunism, or adulation, were treated as equals. Guided by his own highly sensitive radar, he could be standoffish or charming, brusque or exquisitely polite. With everybody, and without bias. This freedom in interpersonal relations allowed him to call himself rich in the truest sense of the word, unfettered by considerations of class.

In the early years of the publishing house, apart from questions of friendship or compatibility, all knew they were part of a great undertaking: to make up for lost time and to link Italy to world culture.

"New ideas were emerging, albeit in a vague form. Old conceptions were called into question, and it was a period of study and research. We tried to exercise our influence on all aspects of a rather fluid society and politico-cultural system. It wasn't a question of lack of commitment, our commitment was decidedly wide in scope." This was how Feltrinelli recalled his early days in publishing in an interview with *Publishers Weekly* in the mid-sixties.

At its inception, the new publishing house was the interpreter of requirements that were still confused, uncertain, and often contradictory. But it was explicitly a part of Italian anti-Fascist culture, and its editorial approach was organized along Marxist lines.

In the publisher's introduction to the first historic catalog, published in 1965, to mark the house's tenth anniversary, Feltrinelli wrote:

> To our way of thinking, anti-Fascism was not and still is not merely a criticism of the outward aspects of the Nazi-Fascist phenomenon, of its errors and horrors, but the search for the images and causes,

in the recent and distant past, of the crisis affecting a system that
was not resolved with the fall of Fascism. This is why we took our
analysis of the past well beyond the limits set by conventional historiography, and also tried to stimulate and develop an understanding
of the present, of politico-economic structures, and of the ideas that
were developing in this new context, as we sought a solution to
those problems that the fall of Fascism had left unresolved.

Much has been said about the "cultural hegemony" of the left
during the postwar period in Italy. The fifties, for example, was a
time when people were searching for a synthesis intended to solve
all problems. But what counted were precisely those cultural fer-
ments that, in their desire to be complementary to a political line,
ended up diverging from it: against the deference of the left,
against the intemperance of the right.

Feltrinelli immediately acquired dissonant books, in other
words the liveliest work then coming out of Eastern Europe: the
acts of the Eighth Polish Plenum, Lukàcs's *Discourse to the Petöfi
Circle,* and *Political Writings* of Imre Nagy, an anthology on labor
problems in the USSR, the Programme of the Yugoslav League.

Within the left, Feltrinelli proceeded at a syncopated pace toward the goal of an open society. His decisions were also dictated
by his instincts. "If in 1955 I had not been a Communist, I still
would have proposed exactly the same range of material I had proposed at the time, because I am sure that it was exactly what contemporary Italian culture was interested in." He said this much
later, in an interview.

Forty years after the uprising in Hungary, the Italian press ded-
icated a lot of space to the final months of that "terrible" 1956.
There were recollections, historical analyses, and anecdotes, like
Pietro Ingrao's* account of how Togliatti made a sardonic toast
during the first hours of the Soviet intervention. But to summarize

---

*A major personality within the left wing of the PCI, he was the editor of *L'Unità*
from 1947 to 1957, and president of the National Assembly from 1976 to 1979.

that *annus horribilis* for Italian Communism: the PCI's defense of "socialist gains" (in opposition to the arguments of the Hungarian workers, the intelligentsia, and the students) was to put the party's "democratic evolution" on ice.

The steady trickle of news—the unheard-of things said by Khrushchev in his report to the 20th Party Congress (February 1956), the fifty-four workers killed by the militia during the strikes in Poznań (June), the feeling that a tragedy was looming in the interim between the Red Army's first and second interventions in Budapest (23 October to 3 November)—triggered a malaise that involved both questions of policy and intellectual issues. A qualitative leap forward was required in the critical capacities of the entire left.

It was clear that certain concepts expounded by the Third International and by Marxist theory in general—particularly the naive expectation that capitalism would be stricken by a general crisis—were belied by reality, making it necessary to bring certain theories up to date. The sheer capacity for development of the forces of production and the technical advances in industrial organization had been underestimated. This was the subject of debate in the Istituto Gramsci throughout 1956. These were the first and most important signs of dissent.

In the sectors close to the Feltrinelli Library, the debate hinged on the orientation of historical research following the closing of the magazine *Movimento operaio* and the polemics that marked the International Congress of Historical Studies held in Rome in 1955. The Soviets, making their first ever appearance at an international congress, cut a pitifully poor figure.

A variety of papers, letters, and documents enable us to check Giangiacomo Feltrinelli's career as a militant. His contacts with the Communist leadership, at least until 1955, were cordial.

His relations with Togliatti also remained good. In December

1955, Feltrinelli had addressed the party leader in elaborately deferential terms. "Dear Professor," he wrote, "I am very glad that, after talks with Professor Carlo Muscetta, you have agreed to grace our series of monographs on Italian and European periodicals with a volume including selected material from *Stato Operaio*,* a task to be undertaken in collaboration with a reliable person of your choice." The fee agreed upon was, for those days, astronomically large: four hundred thousand lire.

Early in the summer of 1956, Feltrinelli and Del Bo, who had recently been promoted, met with Togliatti as a seaside resort. Important changes had taken place in the top echelons of the library. On 24 May, Feltrinelli had called a meeting with all the employees and a good number of freelance collaborators. The day before, Franco Ferri had resigned after a series of close encounters of a decidedly nonconvivial kind with Feltrinelli. In the course of the meeting, the running of the library was officially handed over to Del Bo, and a radical change of course was announced. All present were asked to endorse this move: those who could not relate to the new program were more or less invited to resign.

What was to be the future of the "institute" (as Feltrinelli then called it for the first time)? To become a "duplicate of a cultural committee or of a body like the Gramsci Foundation" in order to satisfy needs of an immediately popular nature? Or to be a scientific body with its own instruments, and with policies and programs that were truly extensive in scope? Was it necessary to deal with modern and contemporary history in general, including all the issues dear to Gramsci? Or was it preferable to adopt a standpoint clearly oriented toward the history of socialism and the study of its origins, toward the social, economic, and political sciences? Was some form of geographic limitation necessary, or would it be better to put Italian historiographical interests within a broader context?

*The PCI's monthly magazine. It was published in France from 1927 to 1939, then in New York from 1940 to 1943.

In Feltrinelli's view, the working hypothesis was very clear and he backed it with vigor: the institute had to have a purely scientific character, it had to make a name for itself in the history of the labor movement without a doctrinaire approach to thematics and methodology, and it had to have an international outlook. "Without a doctrinaire approach" meant, for example, not overlooking certain areas such as the Hegelian left or certain philosophers like Labriola (who were marginalized by mainstream Italian Marxism), and "international" meant attacking the Italian cultural structure at those points where it was weakest: its provincialism. This was one of Feltrinelli's typical changes of direction: back to the founding principles of the early days and then off out of the swamp in which his fellow travelers had become mired.

Togliatti, Feltrinelli, and Del Bo discussed all this during their meeting in the early summer of 1956. The party leader shrewdly encouraged them to press on. It was an important conversation, the last really fruitful one between them. The events that followed would throw this fellowship into disarray.

On 23 October 1956, the people of Budapest rose in rebellion, and Soviet tanks moved in to restore order. The brief insurrection was suppressed at the cost of many lives. But it was hard to establish the extent of the repression; some talked of dozens dead, others of hundreds, and some of several thousand. The lead editorial in *L'Unità* of 25 October was headlined "From One Side of the Barricades, in Defense of Socialism." But the party was on the ropes, and shaking like a leaf.

In Rome, the students immediately took a stand: "The executive of Communist students, having met on 25 October, has resolutely affirmed its support of the process of democratization." That same evening, news came in that prominent labor unions had also reacted critically. Three days later, again in Rome, it was the intellectuals' turn to take the field: they produced a document that was to go down in history as the Manifesto of the 101. Signatures were collected at the Rome offices of Einaudi and of the magazine *Società*. The text, censored by the Communist newspapers, was leaked and picked up by a "bourgeois" press agency. The signatories who did not dissociate themselves were attacked bitterly by *L'Unità* and by the party.

On the other hand, there were no public consequences for the eight Communist personalities, from Milan this time, who a few days later signed a similar protest addressed to the Central Committee. No newspaper talked about it. Yet one dramatic evening, the document was delivered to *L'Unità*. Outside the editorial offices, a group of Fascists was demonstrating against the PCI and the Red Army, while inside, the editor, Davide Lajolo,* known as Ulysses, was thundering that he could not publish the document in question. While the verbal exchange was raging, Feltrinelli, who was present, must have thought of sending the whole crew to the devil: PCI, *L'Unità,* and its editor alike. The shouts of the Fascists down in the street must have reinforced his sense of belonging. He managed to keep calm and to put forward his point of view without raising his voice too much.

Here the text of the letter to the Central Committee (dated 29 October) that the Milan-based group would have liked to publish:

> The undersigned Communist intellectuals deplore the fact that the communiqué sent out by the Party Central Office on 25 October defined the tragic events in Hungary as "an armed counterrevolutionary struggle, openly aimed at the overthrow of the people's democratic government, at interrupting the march toward socialism, and at restoring a reactionary capitalist regime" and that, until this moment, a clear position has not been taken that recognizes in the origins and fundamental nature of the Hungarian movement a strong plea for socialist democracy.
>
> They also deplore the fact that the arrival of Soviet troops at the behest of government officials and politicians has not been deemed the latest and most serious error of a policy line that the 20th Congress of the CPSU has condemned and abandoned.

*(1912–82). Journalist, writer, and editor of *L'Unità*. Elected to parliament in 1963, he was a member of the Central Committee of the PCI until 1975.

They insist that their position—confirmed by the development of events—is the only one in line with the party's socialist and internationalist ideals and with the rational implementation of its political line for an Italian road to socialism.

They therefore pledge their support for this same position in the congressional debate, with a view to arriving at a correct approach to the theoretical and political problems that these events have reintroduced in such a compelling fashion to their conscience as militant Communists.

Luigi Cortesi, of the Biblioteca Feltrinelli

Giuseppe Del Bo, of the Istituto Feltrinelli

Giangiacomo Feltrinelli

Enzo Modica, of the Milan editorial office of "Contemporaneo"

Giuliano Procacci, of the Istituto Feltrinelli

Rossana Rossanda, of the House of Culture

Vando Aldrovandi, of the Libreria Internazionale Einaudi

Marcello Venturi, of the editorial office of *L'Unità* in Milan

The signatories, almost all of them within Feltrinelli's orbit, were summoned in the space of a few hours and shut up in a room inside the Federation offices for a brusque rebuke and a reminder of the need for discipline. Armando Cossutta and the party official Italo Busetto were both called in to restore order. Cossutta, on the point of liquidating even hardliners like Alberganti in the name of the "Italian road to socialism," proposed mediation and promised transparency during the imminent pre-congress debate: Everything is postponed, for the time being be good!

Feltrinelli threw himself into the congress of his new party section, on Via Milazzo. Hours and hours of discussion and thousand of cigarettes smoked, hundreds of preambles, a single conclusion. Locked up for five days in a meeting held to discuss everything, "from manhole covers to Peking." The words were heavy as living beings, and the winners were those who showed the most tenacity.

The concluding motion deplored the fact that the national dignity of the Hungarian people had been impaired and, at the same

time, criticized the "generic nature of the criticisms" made by
the leadership of the PCI on the subject of de-Stalinization. The
provincial congress, held shortly after, and the national one, held
in Rome that December, were not so satisfactory.

The historian Giuliano Procacci provides us with an illuminating episode from that period (a couple of weeks after the second
intervention in Hungary):

> One morning I went to the Feltrinelli library, with which I had been
> collaborating for a while. When I got there (before opening time), I
> found the door open. In the reading room was Giangiacomo Fel-
> trinelli, absorbed in the pages of *Das Kapital.* You could see from his
> face that he had been up all night, "Nothing makes sense here," he
> said to me, "we're in the shit right up to our necks."

In January 1957, Feltrinelli had a row with Lajolo, because he
had published a polemical reply in *Pravda* in response to an article
in the Polish periodical *Nowa Kultura*–neglecting to give the Polish
point of view.

As a publisher, Feltrinelli had excellent contacts with intellectuals in Yugoslavia, Hungary, and Poland. In Poland, the house had
profited from the good offices of Eugenio Reale, a former Italian
ambassador to Poland, a personal friend of Gomulka's, and a supporter of a "third way" between a capitalist and a Stalinist regime.
In fact, Reale had recently been expelled from the PCI for this very
reason.

The library was the epicenter of a different way of thinking, even
with regard to the politics of the day. Del Bo, Cortesi, and Della Peruta were joined by Procacci, and the historian Enzo Collotti (for
the German section) and Luciano Cafagna. Cafagna, an expert on
economic history, joined the team in January 1957. The six men
were thinking in terms of a new classification for the existing collections of material, and promised new research programs.

The closing of *Movimento operaio* was interpreted by orthodox
Communist historians as a gesture of intolerance. Basically, the

problem was that of going beyond the classic boundaries established by the history of the working and agrarian classes. This was why, as Gianni Bosio's magazine was closing, the library, later to become the institute, launched the *Annali*, its most important publication. The idea behind the *Annali* was to set up a dialogue with the *International Review of Social Science*, published in Amsterdam.

Until that time, Italian historiographical research had been limited to studies of the labor movement in Italy and of the pre-Fascist period. The history of the Third International and the history of the PCI itself were taboo, terrain into which it was hazardous to venture. But this was precisely the ground that the *Annali* series was interested in exploring.

The series Il Pensiero socialista (Socialist Thought), produced by Feltrinelli in collaboration with the library, was on the same wavelength. Among the first publications, Hilferding's *Finance Capital* and Kautsky's *The Agrarian Question*, with an introduction by Procacci, were of particular note.

Between 1956 and 1957, in the Feltrinelli Library the debate was about how Italian big business was changing, about technological development and industrial relations. This training ground had a name: Center for Study and Research into the Italian Economic Structure. The round table was made up mostly of men who were not Communists.

The party protested, suspected, and hurled anathemas, especially because of the unforeseen presence of certain party members like Bruno Trentin (Research Center of the CGIL Labor Union).

Dear Comrade, it has come to our attention that you took part in a meeting called by the Feltrinelli Library in Milan to launch a study center devoted to the Italian economic structure. [...] We were surprised by the fact that you did not deem it correct to discuss with us the line to be followed, and in any event by the fact that you did not feel it your duty to inform us about the meeting itself and of any results that may have emerged from it.

The letter was signed on behalf of the party leadership by Luigi Longo.* It was dated 12 March 1957.

Feltrinelli's reply, dated 4 April, was brusque:

> I should be grateful to you if you would clear up this matter, because it strikes me as inconceivable that obstacles be put in the way of a program of scientific research into such an important sector.... Moreover, to this day comrades have never been required to obtain official authorization prior to attending the meetings and encounters organized by the library. The library is a political organization whose work and development do not fall within the general ambit of our cultural and political struggle.

"It is clear," declared Luigi Longo in a letter to Feltrinelli dated 8 April, "that you have been ill informed regarding the tone of the letter." No rebuke was intended, but the failure to notify the party regarding the participation of Communist experts in the meeting gave the impression that there was a wish to maintain an atmosphere "if not of secrecy, at least of a confidential nature." There was a risk of providing grounds for rumors spread by "the adversary" regarding the political purposes of those meetings. "On the other hand," continued Longo, "it would have been natural for the Communists invited to take part to exchange their ideas in advance..., all the more so since, perhaps owing to an oversight, not all the comrades well versed in economic issues were invited to the conference by the directors of the library."

According to Trentin, when asked about this forty years later, the presence of those Communists in the group was a sign of just how open the conflict now was, especially between the party and the labor unions.

Feltrinelli kept up his party membership in 1957, abstaining

*(1900–80). One of the founders of the PCI, Longo was with the International Brigade in Spain. He was secretary general of the PCI from Togliatti's death (1964) until 1972.

from public declarations and letting off steam in private conversations. Disquiet, disagreements, and breaches troubled all parts of the Communist world: directors of the foundation (Fortichiari), representatives of the days of secrecy (Reale), exponents of the generation of the 1940s (Giolitti, Onofri) and of the partisan movement (Raimondi, Seniga). And now intellectuals like Muscetta and Calvino were giving up their party cards, and more. Their defection, in the summer of 1957, provoked an exchange of letters between Feltrinelli and Giorgio Amendola, the leader of the pragmatic right wing of the party. The correspondence between the two is a perfect reflection of that troubled period.

A good number of people had pinned their hopes on Amendola following his speech during the National Congress of the PCI in April 1956. In commenting on the 20th Congress of the CPSU, he had maintained that Italian Communists ought to feel free of external "mortgages." But after the events in Hungary, as happens within the logic of power, he had become more Catholic than the Pope, leading the antirevisionist offensive.

Feltrinelli's letter responded to a statement made by Amendola to the daily paper *Il Giorno*: "The loss of small fringe groups of intellectuals is not an important phenomenon"; the PCI's recent bad patch had affected only a few, and "only that fringe least in touch with the masses."

On 7 August 1957, Feltrinelli wrote:

> I must tell you that it is not my intention to indulge in self-defense, for I neither feel myself to be [a member of any] "fringe," nor am I lost to the working class and the party, nor again do I feel I am part of the "dead wood," as D'Onofrio has defined some comrade intellectuals. But I must express my opinion with regard to your statements.
>
> First of all, it seems to me that the comrade intellectuals who have abandoned—not without a long and painful crisis—the party or who have, at least temporarily, ceased being active party militants or who have left the politico-cultural front cannot be defined as a

"fringe" (of what, indeed? the party? the socialist movement?), and thus be erased and disposed of dismissively.

Moreover, we are not dealing with a few isolated cases but with a group of scholars of national stature: philosophers, historians, men of letters, jurists, and artists. These comrades have not only brought luster to the party, the working class, and the socialist movement but have also enabled us, since the fall of Fascism, to undertake a wealth of politico-cultural projects [...and] enabled the party to integrate more fully with Italian society, thereby paving the way for a range of initiatives that have contributed to the winning of more than one battle in favor of democracy and socialism. [...]

That this situation [of defections] holds within the party is a serious matter, because it involves both comrade intellectuals and the ordinary comrades in the street cells and in the workshops. And the problem is worsening, despite the 8th Congress, which did much important preparatory work for the renewal and reinforcement of the party, with a view to linking political action more closely to the reality and the exigencies of the Italian situation, by concretely articulating a program of political activity that would lend substance to the watchwords of the party's most important assembly.

The congress itself—in proclaiming that the part was more and more oriented toward the Italian road to socialism and in hailing the results of the 20th Congress of the CPSU—assumed, implicitly and explicitly, the necessity [...] for an original ideological formulation of the problems of socialism.

This result—all things considered a positive one—could turn the party into a lively center of debate that would draft programs for political action, not only for our comrades but for the Italian democratic movement as a whole. Can we honestly say we have succeeded here? I do not think so.

Amendola's reply, lengthy, preoccupied, and touchy, was not long in coming. Here are parts of it:

That over the last year a certain number of comrade intellectuals have left the party is certainly not an unimportant phenomenon. [...] It also pains us on a human level, as it signifies a breach in the old bonds of a friendship born during the struggle against the Fascists. What responsibility must we bear for having been unable to prevent this breach? What must we do? [...]

[We must] help the best ones return to the party fold (and some
have already returned) and help those comrades who have still to
make up their minds by discussing matters frankly with them and
by not driving them away. Nevertheless, let me tell you that since I
joined the party in 1929 I have seen many leave! [...] They all left declaring they wanted to engage in a better fight for socialism. Where
did they end up? What did they achieve? But we carried on, because
while these people were leaving, on the basis of the party's political
activity others came to us and offered their support. Today, too, the
essential thing is to pursue just policies that, faced with the threat
to Italian democracy represented by the DC, may express the needs
of those Italians who wish to continue along the road to democratic
renewal and socialism. If we manage to develop a broadly based
plan of political action, as in other crucial moments, in the heat of
the struggle other groups will join us and strengthen our party.

I am proud to have been a Communist since 1929. And more than
ever I feel I have chosen the right road. And this is why it pains me
to see comrades falling by the wayside and leaving us. My hope,
therefore, is that you, after having emphasized the seriousness of
the situation, will make your contribution to containing it.

Giangiacomo must have read and reread this letter, nervously
nibbling at his mustache with his teeth, struck by the generosity of
Amendola's reply, flattered perhaps, but by no means relieved.

Between the first putt-putt of the Fiat 500 and the first beep-beep
of *Sputnik,* the political world was rife with intrigue and discord.
But perhaps politics was not the only theater of existence, perhaps
one could live without the party.

Matteo Secchia, Pietro's brother, was certainly an apparatchik
when he went to confer with the undersecretary of the Soviet embassy in Rome. It was 12 August 1957. The diplomat was to note
down in a diary, five days later, an account of the visit: "Feltrinelli
has yet to state that he wishes to leave the party, but he has stopped
contributing funds."

The return to political life after that summer was marked by
Mauro Scoccimarro's report to the party's Central Commission.

His speech immediately revealed a departure from the previous official line. The non-Communist press noticed the breach, but it was talked about more than it was understood. However, insiders who knew the party machinery could not ignore the terms of the question. The 8th Congress had created new elective controlling bodies, and the traditional wheeling and dealing of the party bureaucrats was still going on? And what price the new statute that made party membership independent of ideological adherence, when Marxist-Leninist doctrine was considered decisive in the choice of a leader? Was the party to be a party of the masses, or a party of Marxist cells?

No answers to these questions were forthcoming, and the pill became very bitter for Feltrinelli when Scoccimaro defined "the right of individuals or groups to autonomy and freedom of initiative in cultural and ideological activities" as a deviation and not a democratic requirement. Feltrinelli noted in his journal: "The old concept forms a homogeneous and tight-fitting block; the new concept has been unable to express itself except as a series of disconnected ideas."

More than ten months had passed since the congress. He had seen people leave, he had been prudent, he had deluded himself, he had attempted to say his piece: nothing doing, no response. He had entered that gray area reserved for those whose loyalties were suspect. Perhaps it would be better to quietly move out of the way.

In the meantime, the first great best-seller in the history of contemporary publishing was about to be born.

4

The words shared by Boris Leonodovich Pasternak and Gian-giacomo Feltrinelli have aged in an old office safe on Via An-degari. My father also hid the photos of a trip to Denmark and some Garibaldi memorabilia there. The key disappeared, so we needed a blacksmith and an oxyacetylene torch to open the safe. Inside was the Feltrinelli-Pasternak correspondence. After forty years, if a secret changes hands, it can slip away like quicksilver.

I start with an article by Feltrinelli published in the *Sunday Times* of 31 May 1970. At that time he had disappeared (gone underground), and no one knew what identity he had adopted. The article, commissioned by the editor Sir Denis Hamilton, ended with the phrase "I am where no one can find me."

In 1955, immediately after the establishment of my company, Gian-giacomo Feltrinelli Editore, I was contacted by Sergio D'Angelo, who at that time was running the PCI bookstore in Rome and was about to leave for Moscow as a member of the editorial staff working on an Italo-Soviet radio program. He suggested that he act as the USSR literary talent scout for my Milan-based publishing house. A few months later D'Angelo told me that an amazing novel written by a Russian poet, Boris Pasternak, was about to be published in the Soviet Union. I asked D'Angelo to get in touch with the author and to request a copy of the manuscript so that a translation might be made immediately. After first publication in the Soviet Union, Russian authors enjoy no copyright protection. By starting the translation right away, I would have the chance to publish at the same time as the Soviet publisher and thus to secure the copyright on the work in the West. By agreement with the author, the manuscript was delivered to me in Berlin in the summer of 1956.

Establishing the rights of works coming out of the Soviet Union was crucial. If a publisher from Europe or America managed to publish *Doctor Zhivago* in the thirty days subsequent to its appearance in the USSR, he would have secured exclusive rights for the Western market. According to the Berne Convention, his would be the first edition. The Soviets had not signed the Berne Convention. But one day over the statutory thirty, and the work would become public domain and anyone could print his own edition, without exclusive rights or any obligation to pay royalties. Antonio Tesone, the Feltrinelli company's legal adviser, made a careful study of the case.

Apart from the question of rights, the reconstruction in the *Sunday Times* corresponds to the version of the facts provided by D'Angelo on various occasions. It might be useful to recapitulate the events that occurred before the summer of 1956. Most of these are already known.

One year after Stalin's death, in spring 1954, Boris Pasternak's name was thrown into prominence following the publication of some poems in the magazine *Znamya*. They were written as an appendix to a novel he was working on, *Doctor Zhivago*. The novel was finished in 1955. Pasternak sent copies to the Goslitizdat publishing house and to a few literary reviews. Then he waited for their decision.

In the winter of 1955, D'Angelo agreed to become a scout for Feltrinelli in the Soviet capital. He had worked with the house occasionally in the past.

D'Angelo left Italy in March 1956. He was working with Radio Moscow. A few weeks after his arrival, during a cultural events program, he came across news of the probable publication of *Doctor Zhivago* by Pasternak: "A novel written in the form of a diary covering three-quarters of a century and ending with the Second World War."

D'Angelo was quick. He sent the information to Milan, and Luigi Diemoz asked him to get in touch with the author right away.

In early May, on a beautiful sunny day, D'Angelo arrived in the Writers' Village at Peredelkino, the wooded area just outside Moscow where Pasternak often spent time with his second wife, Zinaida, his younger son, Leonid, and sometimes with Evgeny, the son born of his first marriage, with Evgenya Lure. Fifteen hundred meters away, on the other side of a small hill, stood the holiday residence of Olga Ivinskaya, the woman with whom Pasternak had been in love for almost ten years and who helped him in his work as a translator.

Pasternak received D'Angelo and listened to him with apparent surprise, lost in thought. He was not at all convinced that his book would be published in the Soviet Union: he had spent a year waiting for a reply that never came. In the end he decided to go along with his guest's request. He had already sent the book to be read by a group of Polish writers who visited him some time ago, and he was also in touch with the Prague publisher Svet Sovetov about a Czech edition.

When D'Angelo rose to leave, the poet made a bitter joke. "You, sir," he said to D'Angelo, "are hereby invited to my execution."

On 13 May, Feltrinelli drafted a first letter to the author. Understanding that this would be a thorny affair, he decided to handle it personally and, when D'Angelo went to Berlin to have a visa renewed, he went to meet him. It was the end of May or the beginning of June. The two men dined in a restaurant where they met two blondes who worked for the Siemens Company, and they danced with them. They never took their eyes off the big package left on the table wrapped in a raincoat. It contained a typescript in Cyrillic.

As soon as he returned to Milan, Feltrinelli sent a telegram to the Slavic linguist Pietro Zveteremich to ask him for an opinion, which he received within a few days. Zveteremich wound up his reader's report with these words: "Not to publish a novel like this would constitute a crime against culture."

On 13 June, Feltrinelli sent off his first letter to his future author, in French. "If ever you receive a letter in any language other than French, you absolutely must not do what is requested of you–the only valid letters shall be those written in French." How Pasternak's message arrived, written on a cigarette paper, I don't know.

The correspondence between publisher and author was made difficult by the length of time it took for letters to arrive. Every exchange required a suitable intermediary to whom the envelope might be entrusted for mailing or personal delivery.

Feltrinelli later introduced the banknote method: the messenger was "safe" if he could show Pasternak the missing half of the banknote in Pasternak's possession.

Milan, 13 June 1956

Dear Sir,

We are very grateful to you for letting us have your novel, entitled *Doctor Zhivago*.

Even a cursory reading confirms the enormous literary importance of your work, which presents us with a vivid portrait of Soviet reality.

Once more, we should like to express our gratitude for your allowing our publishing house to publish *Doctor Zhivago* in Europe for the first time, and also for entrusting us with organizing its publication in other countries, through the assignment of rights to other publishers.

We therefore submit to you our proposals for settling the question of authorial rights, both for the Italian edition and editions in other languages.

With regard to the Italian edition, we feel we can offer you the highest royalty rate customary in Italy, namely 15 percent. Given the high sales price, the rather high publishing costs in our country, and finally the translation costs, which will have a considerable effect on the cost of production, we would not be able to increase this percentage. As for the foreign rights, we propose, as is customary, to pay you 50 percent of the rights income received by us. The money due to you shall be paid into an account to be opened here, which will be available to you for travel or other expenses in Europe, or alternatively into an account with the State Bank of the USSR.

These are the most important points of the contract, two copies of which are enclosed with this letter; please be so kind as to send us one signed copy should you be in agreement.

Yours sincerely,

Giangiacomo Feltrinelli

A cordial letter, standard and efficient. Everything ought to have gone smoothly. On 30 June, Pasternak replied, also in French. Before he sent the letter off, he showed it to his sons, Leonid and Evgeny.

Today, Evgeny has a face like a wood carving, exactly like his father. I owe most of this reconstruction to him. He was thirty-three at the time: "We fully agreed with that letter even though we knew it might lead to dangerous consequences. Our father was prepared to make any sacrifice as long as *Doctor Zhivago* was published. He thanked us and said that he had been hoping for our support."

Evgeny recalls that his father copied his reply, something he usually never did:

Moscow, 30 June 1956

Dear Sir,

Your proposals are admirable, and I shall sign the contract with pleasure. Although I am not entirely uninterested in money, here we live in conditions that are completely different from those in your country. It is no merit of mine if questions of money are nonexistent or entirely secondary for me. In any event, keep all that is due to me under your protection, I entrust it to you unreservedly, and don't let's talk any more of this until I come to you or bring up the matter myself. I am particularly glad that the novel will come out and be read in your country. If its publication here, promised by several of our magazines, were to be delayed and your version were to come before it, I would find myself in a tragically embarrassing situation. But this is not your concern. In the name of God, feel free to go on with the translation and the printing of the book, and good luck! Ideas are not born to be hidden or smothered at birth, but to be communicated to others.

Make sure the work is well translated. In this regard, Professor Lo Gatto has much praised and recommended the poet and translator Ripellino, in Rome.

Yours sincerely,

B. Pasternak

P. S. Please be so kind as to send me a telegram acknowledging receipt of this letter.

A fine letter, showing a sincere lack of interest in economic issues. Says Evgeny, "My father got by with the bare essentials. His study was modest in size, he dressed very simply, and he avoided futile amusements, travel, holidays, and all that derives from the pleasure of spending money."

The alarming thing about Pasternak's first reply to the Italian publisher is that the Soviets knew about it from the start. Recently, in Moscow, an important document came to light. It is stamped top secret, the date is 24 August 1956. The sender was General Ivan Serov, chairman of the National Defense Committee of the Soviet of Ministers of the USSR (the KGB). The recipient was the Central Committee.*

The [committee] is in possession of a series of facts from which it emerges that in May of this year the writer B. Pasternak, through Sergio D'Angelo, a speaker with the radio of the Ministry of Culture of the USSR, an Italian citizen and a member of the Italian Communist Party, delivered to the Italian publisher Feltrinelli a manuscript of his unpublished novel, *Doctor Zhivago,* for publication in Italy.

In the letter of 3 July of this year addressed to Feltrinelli, Pasternak officially agrees to the publication of the novel and asks that the honorarium due to him be left in Italy. On handing over the novel,

*KGB Archives

Pasternak set the following conditions: that the publisher, subsequent to publication of the work in Italy, assign the rights to the novel to French and English publishers.

Pasternak asks Feltrinelli to make sure that the novel does not come out in Italy before it is published in the USSR. Feltrinelli replies that the novel will be published around April 1957.

It is known that in April of this year Pasternak delivered *Doctor Zhivago* to the editors of the magazine *Novy Mir.* The work was reviewed, but permission for publication has not yet been given. On 9 August of this year, Pasternak sent a letter to a certain Danil Georgevich Reznikov, resident in Paris, in which he expresses his doubts regarding the possibility of *Doctor Zhivago*'s being published in the USSR: "I realize perfectly well that [the novel] cannot be published now, and that this is how it is going to be for some time, perhaps forever: so grand and so unusual is the freedom of spirit with which existence is represented in the work, existence in its totality, existence in the world; so free and new is its conception of the world."

Referring to the delivery of the book to a foreign publisher, Pasternak wrote to Reznikov: "Now they will tear me limb from limb: I have this foreboding, and you shall be a distant and sorrowful witness to this event." At the same time Pasternak sent Reznikov a manuscript of "People and Situations" which he had written as an introductory essay to the collection of poems published by Gozlitizdat. He also asked Reznikov to do as he wished with the essay, as if it were his property.

The essay contains a detailed autobiography of Pasternak, accompanied by an assessment of the work of some Soviet poets, in particular Mayakovsky, Tvetaevas and Yashvili. In the essay Pasternak also expresses his opinion on the possible causes of their suicide and of that of the writer Fadeev.

Boris Leonidovich Pasternak, born in 1890, is a Jew, has no party card, and is a member of the Union of Soviet Writers.

During the revolution and in the years that followed, he joined the petit bourgeois literary school known as the Acmeists. A typical feature of his work is estrangement from Soviet life and a celebration of individualism. For a long time Pasternak did not publish any of his works, with the exception of a brief cycle of poems.

Between 1946 and 1948 he wrote the first part of the novel *Doctor Zhivago,* which reflects his idealistic view of the world. The magazine *Novy Mir,* to which he sent the manuscript, refused to publish

the novel because it was ideologically unacceptable. Subsequently
the manuscript of the novel was passed from hand to hand in literary circles.

In those same years Pasternak established contacts with a series
of collaborators in the British embassy in Moscow, through whom
he kept up a correspondence with his sister, who lives in London.

In conversations with some of the representatives of the embassy he made anti-Soviet statements.

It was thanks above all to these contacts that, between 1946 and
1948, Pasternak made a great deal of propaganda in the English and
American press, creating for himself an aura of the "great poet-
martyr" unable to adapt to the reality of Soviet life.

The KGB report both clarifies and complicate matters. In the
correspondence found in the safe along with the Garibaldi memorabilia, there is no trace of the letter of 3 July. There is the letter of
30 June, whose contents are similar to the one that, according to
Serov, was dated three days later.

This leaves two possibilities, or maybe more: one is that, in
some remote archive, the letter of 3 July does exist. But why two
letters in the space of three days with the same content? Unlike
Pasternak's message to Danil Resnikov, nothing in Serov's top-
secret message regarding the alleged letter of 3 July is in quotes.

The reasonable suspicion arises that no correspondence exists
for that day. Perhaps the reference was to the letter of 30 June, and
3 July was the date on which the police intercepted the letter. But
then why should the Soviets have allowed the letter to reach
Milan? In the envelope, probably, there was also a contract: "I sign
without reservations," wrote Pasternak on 30 June. If the contract
was intercepted, why not use it to accuse the poet in public? There
was no shortage of either pretexts or trials.

Another possibility: the Soviet police intercepted nothing at all.
Perhaps someone talked about a letter sent on 30 June or 3 July,
and disclosed some information–the publisher's request to assign
the rights in England and France, for example, or Pasternak's plea

that Feltrinelli make sure that the Italian edition did not come out
before the Soviet one (while the letter of 30 June says the exact
opposite), or the fact that plans had been made to publish the Italian edition in April 1957. Who was present when the novel was
handed over? Who could have known about the correspondence
between Pasternak and his Italian publisher?

The poet's family, perhaps prompted by jealousy, have always
encouraged the suspicion that Olga Ivinskaya supplied information to the secret police. Even the contemporary press in Moscow
today takes it for granted that Olga was an informer. But practically
everybody was an informer in the most rumor-ridden society
imaginable. If Olga passed on information, she might have done so
in a well-meaning compromising way, omitting details and presenting the most reassuring versions in order to make future mediation possible. In a letter to Khrushchev, dated 1 March 1961,
Ivinskaya admitted: "The Central Committee suggested that I keep
Pasternak away from possible contacts with foreigners." And in
another part of the same letter: "It was futile to point out that it was
the Central Committee that had previously put us in touch with
D'Angelo and that through D'Angelo I managed to keep the publication of the novel in Italy on hold for a year and a half."

Ivinskaya had already served a three-year internment (she came
out in 1953). She was not the only person involved in the affair, and
the solution of our mystery might bring us to other suspects. Perhaps some sprightly old domestic was bustling in and out of the
room just as D'Angelo and Pasternak were discussing the deal, or
perhaps D'Angelo himself played the role of "mediator." In any case,
in August 1956 the news was circulating freely within the machinery of the Soviet apparatus. The day after Serov's note was sent, 25
August, the KGB once more informed the leadership of the CPSU of
the effective delivery of the manuscript and, in a separate communication, they also informed our old acquaintance Pyotr Pospelov,
who had by then become the secretary to the Central Committee.

On 31 August, Foreign Minister Dimitri Shepilov called Pasternak's novel "a ferocious libel against the USSR" and gave notice
that "the Department for Relations with Foreign Communist Parties, through some friends, is taking steps to prevent the publication abroad of this anti-Soviet book." This means that the matter
was probably discussed around some samovar with the Italian
Communists, in Russia on vacation or on other business (we are
between the publication of the Khrushchev report and the Hungarian uprising).

The tone adopted by the Soviets was both concerned and agitated,
even though, I suppose, at the time they still thought that with the
help of their Italian comrades everything could be sorted out.

Giangiacomo's article for the *Sunday Times* adds this:

> While the Italian translation was proceeding, publication in Moscow
> was postponed, and the rumor began to circulate that I had received
> a copy of *Doctor Zhivago*. The PCI (of which I was a member at the
> time) received a request to check out that rumor. I confirmed the
> matter with Togliatti, the secretary general of the party. At that time
> I received no request to suspend publication of the book in Italy. I
> was only asked to ensure that publication in the West was concomi-
> tant with publication in Moscow.

The autumn was highly eventful. While the Soviets were making up their minds, Feltrinelli was invited to return the original of
Doctor Zhivago temporarily. The request was made by Pietro Secchia and Paolo Robotti, on their return from a trip to Moscow. The
Soviets had asked the two Italian leaders to take all steps necessary
to clear up the affair. Secchia had talked of his good relations with
the publisher, reassuring them: they would give it a try.

On 24 October the Department for Relations with Foreign Communist Parties received, via the embassy, a euphoric message from
Robotti: the problem was solved! Within a short time the manuscript would be back in Moscow. The communication was endorsed by Leonid Brezhnev.

But the truth was quite different: Feltrinelli, alarmed about the pressure on him, decided to keep the manuscript (until then in the possession of Zveteremich in Rome) in his own home.

January 1957 brought a series of events.

The umpteenth delegation from the PCI, this time led by the deputy leader Luigi Longo, made a visit to Moscow. Despite a fairly heavy agenda, the Soviets brought up the Zhivago affair, showing the Italians letters from local writers expressing their indignation with Pasternak for his ideologically incorrect attitude.

The Soviets were disappointed. After months of secret talks, reassurances, and interparty negotiations, they found themselves empty-handed. Yet again, they asked for the help of the leaders of the PCI, who looked at one another and spread out their arms in that eloquent Italian gesture that says, "We're sorry, but what can we do about it?" Irritated, the men in Moscow decided to change their tactics and take the bull by the horns, breaking their menacing silence over Pasternak.

But, as in a chess game, this sudden change of tactics led to a wrong move, one that began an inexorable march toward checkmate. Pasternak was summoned by Alexey Surkov, the secretary of the Union of Soviet Writers, who offered him a formal contract drawn up by Goslitizdat. But Pasternak was given to understand that it would be necessary to make cuts or maybe even completely revise the book. Then he was told he had to send a telegram to his Italian publisher. The aim was to play for time.

> per request from goslitizdat publishing house novaya basmannaya 18 moscow please hold Italian publication of novel *Doctor Zhivago* for half year until first september 1957 and the coming out of soviet edition of novel send reply telegram to goslitizdat
>
> pasternak

The telegram reached Milan 14 February 1957. It was in Italian, more or less. But as soon as Pasternak left Surkov's office, before sending the telegram, he wrote to my father, in French this time. The date was 6 February.

Dear Sir,

Our state publishers are putting pressure on me to send you a telegram requiring you to suspend the Italian publication of my novel until they bring out their modified version of it. I would propose that you postpone publication for, say, six months at the outside. Grant this deferment, if it does not clash with your plans, and send your reply by telegram not to me but to the address of the State Publishers: Goslitizdat, Novaya Basmannaya 18, Moscow.

But the sorrow that, naturally, is caused me by the imminent alteration of my text would be far greater if I thought that you intended to base the Italian translation on it, despite my enduring desire that your edition be strictly faithful to the authentic manuscript.

Another question: I was the one who saddled you with the burden of the matters covered by art. 4 of the contract while inviting you to deal with the business of the other foreign translations. I have recently made some great new friends in France, who are prepared to work with me and who are connected to the best publishers, Gallimard and Fasquelle, for example. I am prepared to offer you any supplementary concessions you may desire with regard to article 2, if you would hand over the matter of the French edition to the group of French translators about whom you will receive a letter from Mme Jacqueline de Proyart, my representative in Paris for literary matters and the leading member of the group. Otherwise, if you do not wish to give up the management of the novel in France, at least give consideration to Mme de Proyart, Mlle Hélène Peltier, and Monsieurs Michel Aucoutourier and Martinez as translators, of whose services you must avail yourself in accordance with the meaning and purview of art. 4. Please do come to an agreement with them, really, I pray you, it is my burning wish. And forgive me for imposing on you so much. Yours

B. Pasternak

Jacqueline de Proyart, a student living in Paris, from a noble family and a fervent Catholic, arrived in Moscow in early 1957. She knew little or nothing about Pasternak, not even if he was alive or dead. She met him by chance, found him most fascinating, and offered to help with the translation of his works into French. She was on friendly terms with Gallimard.

On receiving Pasternak's letter, Feltrinelli immediately wrote to Zveteremich:

It will be necessary to finish Past. in 3 months. The Russian version will be published in September, and in order for our contract to be valid, and by that I mean that we are to be able to sell the rights, the book has to be on sale by 2 September. I am prepared to make some sacrifices, to compromise, provided I can go to press by that date. Assure me of this, and any suggestions from you would be welcome. I talked to Moravia about a review, but he didn't seem enthusiastic. I'll bring the matter up with Bassani.* In the meantime, make haste.

Then he waited until a reliable courier was available before sending a letter to Moscow on 22 March:

Dear Sir,
Some weeks ago I received the news that your novel *The Story of Doctor Zhivago* will be published in Moscow next September. May I say how pleased I am about this? The Italian translation is proceeding, and after the news of the forthcoming publication in Moscow I have insisted that my translator finish the translation as fast as possible. Yours sincerely

Giangiacomo Feltrinelli

Despite all the assurances, the days passed too slowly for Pasternak; his health and morale were suffering, while the time gained by the Soviet authorities was minimal. Moreover, there was enormous tension in the top echelons of the CPSU, as became evident during the summer with the expulsion of the so-called anti-party group (Molotov and company) and the clampdowns ordered by Khrushchev.

In this atmosphere, in a letter dated 10 June, a good three months after Pasternak's telegram, Feltrinelli informed the state publishers of his intentions.

Dear Comrades,
I hereby confirm that we shall not proceed with the publication of Pasternak's novel *The Story of Doctor Zhivago* until it comes out in the USSR in the month of September. Now that we are finally free to express an opinion on the manuscript, we confirm that this is a

---

*Giorgio Bassani (1916–2000), journalist, novelist, lyric poet, publishing manager, vice president of RAI TV.

novel of great literary value, whose author is comparable with the great Russian writers of the nineteenth century. We believe that Pasternak's prose recalls that of Pushkin. His is a perfect portrayal of the nature, soul, and history of Russia: characters, objects, and events are rendered clearly and concretely in the finest spirit of realism, a realism that ceases to be merely fashion and becomes art.

The reflections of the protagonist and of the various characters in the novel on their personal destiny and on that of their country are on a level so high as to transcend the boundaries of current political contingencies, whether the reader agrees with their political implications or not—an aspect of the work that might give rise to some controversy. However, it seems to me that the importance attached to these reflections is irrelevant and moreover, after the 20th Congress, the revealing of certain facts no longer surprises or perturbs.

Besides, Western readers will for the first time hear the voice of a great artist, a great poet who has made, in an artistic form, a detailed analysis of the course of the October Revolution, the harbinger of a new epoch in which socialism became the only natural form of social life. For the Western public, the fact that this is a voice of a man alien to all political activity is a guarantee of the sincerity of his discourse, thus making him worthy of trust. Our readers cannot fail to appreciate this magnificent panorama of events from the history of the Russian people, which transcends all ideological dogmatism, nor will they overlook its importance or the positive outlook deriving from it. The conviction will thus grow that the path taken by your people has been for them a progressive one, that the history of capitalism is coming to an end, and that a new era has begun.

We have expressed in complete sincerity our opinion of Pasternak's work, and we hold that its debatable aspects are more than compensated for by the arguments in favor of its publication. We have reached this conclusion not only in consideration of our interests as publishers, but also in line with our political convictions, of which you are well aware. Moreover, you are also well aware that, as far as we are concerned, political opinions and the business of publishing are inseparable.

It is important for us to be able to express our point of view, given that there have been some misunderstandings in the past regarding Pasternak's book, and above all given that you have suspected that we wished to lend this publication a sensational character, which is absolutely not our intention.

Yours sincerely,

Giangicomo Feltrinelli

Eight days later, Zveteremich sent a telegram to Milan ("Dear Feltrinelli, I have completed the translation of *Doctor Zhivago*..."), and on the twentieth of the same month Pasternak sent a new message:

Dear Sir,
I have been ill now for three months, first at home, then in a hospital, and now in a sanatorium near Moscow. I thank you again for having granted the postponement requested by the state publishing house (Goslitizdat). But that is all I have to ask of you. The rest is superfluous. I would be deeply pained, grievously disappointed, if the Italian version of the work, in a form faithful to the Russian manuscript, were not published by your house on 1 September. Any delay in [the publication of] the Italian edition would hold up the other foreign translations, whose publication I have entrusted to you (in France, in England, in Czechoslovakia, and elsewhere). Here in Russia, the novel will never appear. The troubles and misfortunes that will perhaps befall me in the event of foreign publication, that is to say without an analogous publication in the Soviet Union, are matters that must not concern us, either me or you. The important thing is that the work sees the light of day. Do not withhold your help from me. Yours very sincerely,

B. Pasternak

In July 1957, Molotov and his faction having been ousted from the Politburo, Khrushchev was firmly in the saddle. Lazar Fleishman, the best biographer of Pasternak, writes:

That same summer they published a selection of [Khrushchev's] speeches to assemblies of the intelligentsia. These speeches were to serve as party guidelines. Since Zhdanov's day, no Soviet leader had expressed his opinions on literary and artistic matters. It was the first time that Khrushchev had spoken on the subject, and the publication of those speeches left no doubt about the fact that it was the conservative front rather than the liberal one that enjoyed his full support in the field of cultural policy.

Fleishman notes that, in the summer, two episodes occurred that infuriated the Soviet authorities. The first was the publication of

some excerpts from *Doctor Zhivago* in the pages of a Polish quar-
terly. How could this have happened? Evidently there were many
copies of *Doctor Zhivago* in circulation, and this preview—the Poles
thought—might be a pretext for the subsequent appearance of the
novel in the West. Especially since a magazine run by Russian émi-
grés in Munich—and this was seen as a second humiliation by the
Soviets—had printed some poems attributable to Pasternak without
citing him as the author. It was necessary to intervene.

Evgeny Pasternak explains: "In early August, the Central Committee drew up various statements in an attempt to deal with the
problem of the planned publication of the novel in Poland and Italy.
At Goslitizdat they wanted to have the text modified, hoping that
Feltrinelli would wait until September for the author's corrections."

The leadership of the Italian Communist Party was once more
informed so that suitable countermeasures might be taken. A substantial delegation from the PCI, including Longo, Alicata, and
Spano, arrived in Moscow for the World Youth Festival. The young
expert in Slavic studies, Vittorio Strada, was also making a visit, his
first, and he managed to meet and get to know Pasternak. Strada
still remembers his surprise when, as he was leaving, Pasternak
took him aside and whispered: "Vittorio, tell Feltrinelli that I want
my book to come out at all costs."

Let's go back to Feltrinelli's *Sunday Times* article of May 1970:

> In the summer of 1957 I heard rumors of the cancellation of plans to
> publish *Doctor Zhivago*. Shortly afterward, the author requested me
> to proceed with publication in Italy and the West, independently of
> publication in Moscow, and to ignore other instructions that he
> might in future he obliged to transmit to me. The agreement be-
> tween Pasternak and me was that I would shoulder all the responsi-
> bility for publication, in order to provide the author with some
> protection from the Soviet authorities.

August witnessed the beginning of the strategy orchestrated by
Dimitri Polikarpov, head of the cultural section of the CC, and

Alexey Surkov, secretary of the Writers' Union. Pasternak was summoned peremptorily to meetings in which harsh words gave way to threats. Instead of Pasternak, who was physically debilitated, the two men often dealt with Olga, who was acting as his representative. A new postponement was expected of Pasternak; it was a last attempt to stop publication. Otherwise, without putting too fine a point on it, they would have him arrested.

> I have started rewriting the manuscript of my novel *Doctor Zhivago*, and I am now convinced that the extant version can in no way be considered a finished work. The copy of the manuscript in your possession is a preliminary draft requiring thorough revision.
>
> In my view it is not possible to publish the book in its current form. This would go against my rule, which is that only the definitive draft of my work may be published.
>
> Please be so kind as to return, to my Moscow address, the manuscript of my novel *Doctor Zhivago*, which is indispensable for my work.
>
> Boris Pasternak

The text of this letter was agreed on with Polikarpov and Surkov on 21 August, transcribed in Russian, and sent in the form of a telegram.

D'Angelo was to describe these events in a long article for a Soviet studies magazine. Olga rushed to visit him, he recalls, and with tears in her eyes she asked him to help her in persuading Pasternak to agree to send the telegram. When the pair went to see the poet, he greeted them angrily: no motives of friendship or affection, he said, could justify their mission; they were disrespectful, treating him like a man with no dignity. And furthermore, what would Feltrinelli think, the publisher to whom Pasternak had just written to say that the publication of *Doctor Zhivago* was his principal aim in life? He would take Pasternak for a madman, a coward.

Only after much discussion was Pasternak persuaded that, given what had been arranged, no further message (especially if not written in French) would be taken seriously. In any case, it was

no longer possible to block the publication of the novel. And so, finally, he agreed to send the telegram.

"The fact that he was not arrested," wrote D'Angelo, "was
thanks to Olga Ivinskaya."

On his return to Rome, Velio Spano, in effect the foreign minister of the PCI, laid his report before the party leadership. It was
14 September:

> In the course of the meeting of the Central Committee of the CPSU
> the question of Pasternak and his book was again raised. The Soviet
> comrades, still concerned over its possible publication by Feltrinelli
> or some other Western publisher, again asked us to take steps. They
> gave me the letter of injunction signed by Pasternak and asked me to
> ensure that one of us show it to Feltrinelli in order to corroborate the
> position adopted by Pasternak himself.

Alicata went to Milan with the copy of the text used for the
telegram. It had been decided to hold the meeting with Feltrinelli
in the rooms of the Milan Federation of the PCI, in Piazza XXV
Aprile. The art historian Mario De Micheli bumped into the publisher, who was waiting on the steps in front of the offices ten minutes before the meeting. "I'm not giving in," said Feltrinelli. De
Micheli also recalls how violent Alicata became as he furiously
brandished the bogus letter of injunction from Pasternak.

Meanwhile Zveteremich, who had been in touch with Pasternak
for some time, was in Moscow, and he spoke of his time there in a
letter to Feltrinelli dated 5 October:

> In Moscow the atmosphere created around the book is very ugly.
> They are turning it into a big scandal. Its publication has been defined
> as "a blow against the revolution." Clearly in bad faith. Especially
> since I have had complete confirmation that the book was to come out
> in the USSR. I have seen the contract between P. and the Soviet pub-
> lishers dated 7/1/57, as well as a letter to P. from a writer who spoke of
> a magazine that intended to publish excerpts from it. I met the copy
> editor. It seems that in the CC of the CPSU, Pospelov and others
> thought it should be published. Everything changed as a result of the

pressure applied by the Writers' Union, which in this case has been
more intransigent than the party and forced its hand. [...] P. asks you
not to pay any heed to this and cannot wait for the book to come out
even though they have threatened to reduce him to starvation and
have already deprived him of work previously commissioned. P. en-
treats you not to let it be known that you have a contract with him on
the basis of which you have assigned him a certain sum. An agreement is fine, but nothing concrete regarding payment. This would ag-
gravate his situation. His safety depends on people believing that he
will receive nothing. [...] D'Angelo is not afraid of any consequences of
the scandal caused by the publication of P., excepting perhaps that he
might be invited to leave the USSR, something that does not bother
him. So he thanks you for worrying and tells me to reassure you.

In the course of a visit, Pasternak gave Zveteremich a brief message for his publisher.

Dear Sir,
I should like to send you my heartfelt thanks for your touching concern. Forgive me for the injustices that have befallen you and for
those perhaps yet to come caused by my wretched fate. May our distant future, the faith that helps me live, protect you.
                                                    Boris Pasternak

Between the end of September and the beginning of October,
Surkov descended on Milan. The false letters, indirect messages, and
the pressure having all failed, he had come to do the job himself, in
a tête-à-tête with Feltrinelli. They were closeted in the publisher's
office for three hours, and their angry shouts could be heard
throughout the floor. Surkov ("a hyena dipped in syrup," according
to Feltrinelli) could not have failed to note the faded photo of Pasternak hanging on the wall at his host's back. Seeing how things were
turning out, Surkov played the card of the extorted telegram. The
reply played the card of the extorted telegram. The reply: "I am well
aware of how documents of the kind are obtained."

Taking his time, for by then it was only a formality, Feltrinelli
replied on 10 October to the telegram Pasternak had sent at the end
of August.

Dear Sir,

I received your letter and your telegram [. . .]. I should like to express my amazement and make the following points:

1) In the text in our possession we see none of the shortcomings you criticize in the manuscript, namely that it is an "unfinished work" and "a preliminary draft requiring thorough revision."

2) We have an agreement with you according to which you granted us the right to publish your book. This agreement was made after you signed a contract with Goslitizdat for publication in the Russian language. This contract does not contain any clause that makes publication of the book abroad dependent on publication in the Soviet Union.

3) As for the telegram that you sent at the beginning of this year in which you asked us to wait a little, until such time as the book was published in the Soviet Union, we willingly agreed to postpone foreign publication. But today, seeing that the Soviet publisher has no intention of publishing your work, we no longer see any reason for postponement.

4) In order to avoid any further tension in Western literary circles, created as a result of your wholly regrettable telegram, and following the various talks held in Moscow between foreign delegates and some representatives of Soviet political and literary circles, we advise you to make no further attempts to hold up the publication of the book, something that, far from preventing it, would lend the entire affair a tone of political scandal that we have never sought nor wish to create. In any event, in consequence of your initiatives and those of the Writers' Union (in Italy and in England), we shall decline all responsibility for the repercussions that the appearance of the work will certainly have as a result of the lack of tact shown by some of your functionaries.

Yours sincerely,

Giangiacomo Feltrinelli

We don't know when Pasternak received this letter, but it is certain that it reached him late. The absence of a prompt reply was a positive sign: *les jeux sont faits,* and time to drink a toast. But the atmosphere was ruined by the need for Pasternak to continue making pseudo statements designed to intimidate the Italian publisher and his French and English colleagues. This is what Pasternak was forced to write to Feltrinelli on 23 October:

> Mr. Feltrinelli,
> I am stunned by the fact that I have yet to receive your reply to my telegram. I asked for the manuscript to be returned to me as soon as possible because I had come to the conclusion that the work [...] was unfinished. I feel that any publisher with a respect for literature and his own reputation cannot refuse the request of an author who considers his manuscript a draft and for this reason asks for it to be returned.
> Your failure to reply leads me to think that, in spurning the direct instructions of the author and in spite of his clear and express wishes, you have nonetheless decided to publish the novel. I do not know if the laws of your country give you such a right. And in this case we are not dealing with a formal right either, because both my telegram of 13 February 1957 and the subsequent letter expressed beyond any doubt my wish not to publish the novel in a version that is still a draft.
> Decency demands that the author's wishes be respected.
> Neither I nor any other writer from my country could allow his manuscript to be published against his will. This would be a clear-cut and crass infringement of the rights an artist has over his work, a violation of his will and of the freedom of that which flows from his pen.
> The request that the manuscript of the novel be returned also holds for those French and English publishers to whom you have given a copy.
>   Boris Pasternak

But the letter sent to Feltrinelli a few days later, on 2 November, was of a quite different tenor. It has never before been published.

> Dear Sir,
> I can find no words with which to express my gratitude. The future will reward us, you and me, for the vile humiliations we have suffered. Oh, how happy I am that neither you, nor Gallimard, nor Collins have been fooled by those idiotic and brutal appeals accompanied by my signature (!), a signature all but false and counterfeit, insofar as it was extorted from me by a blend of fraud and violence. The unheard-of arrogance to wax indignant over the "violence" employed by you against my "literary freedom," when exactly the

same violence was being used against me, covertly. And that this vandalism should be disguised as concern for me, for the sacred rights of the artist! But we shall soon have an Italian Zhivago, French, English, and German Zhivagos—and one day perhaps a geographically distant but Russian Zhivago! And this is a great deal, a very great deal, so let's do our best, and what will be will be!

Do not worry about the money owed to me. Let us put off the financial issue (for me, there is none) until we have a more sensible and humane system, when, in the twentieth century, one can once more keep up a correspondence and travel. I have unlimited faith in you, and I am sure that you will watch over what you have put aside for me. Only in the unhappy event of their canceling my benefits and cutting off my food supplies (which would be extraordinary and there is no sign of it happening), well, I would try to find a way to let you know in order to take advantage of the offers you have made me through Sergio, who, as his name suggests, is a real angel and lavishes all his time and his soul on this regrettable affair.

Yours very sincerely,

B. Pasternak

It is the kind of letter that every publisher would like to receive at least once in his lifetime.

The message also contains an important reference to the rights payments for *Doctor Zhivago*. Judging by the receipts kept in the safe on Via Andegari, periodic payments in rubles began in December 1957. The receipts, written and signed by Pasternak or Olga Ivinskaya, refer to 12,800 rubles delivered on 21 December 1957, 4,000 on 7 June 1958 and another 1,000 that same month, 10,000 in October, 5,000 on 17 February 1959, 3,000 on 28 March, and 5,000 on 1 August.

At first, the middleman who made the deliveries was D'Angelo; then, as we shall see, other channels were used.

To return to the fall of 1957, on 25 November Pasternak again wrote to Feltrinelli:

Dear Sir,
Yesterday I finally received your esteemed reply, dated 10 October, which had therefore been wandering about goodness knows where for a month and a half. As I am unable to go into the details, I hasten

to thank you with all my heart for the fact that all has ended well, thanks to your shrewd foresight, which has informed all the ramifications of this extraordinary affair. I am enormously obliged to you.

I am not wont to indulge in the immodest folly of equating myself with the voice of truth; but I am bold enough to hope to share the striving and aspirations of all who love their native land, life, truth, and beauty with a diligent and grateful love. Now, just as you have done a very, very good thing for me, over and above all measure, so you have striven a great deal for the beautiful, just cause.

I was greatly pained that I made a certain name for myself thanks to trifling things like a few verses, disparate like contemporary poetry in general, fragmentary, incomplete, and limited to vague expressions, in such great times, which demand that one live in a resolute and responsible way, stating one's thoughts without reserve. Thanks to a lengthy prose work, the result of long and arduous toil, it has been possible for me to put an end to this state of shame and suffering and begin a new chapter of my vocation, a new period of my life; it has come infinitely late, but it has come. You be the judge, therefore, of how grateful I am to you for having helped it into the world!

I have an important question for you. None of this could have come about without the assistance of S. D'A., who has been our indefatigable guardian angel. While such sincere help cannot be measured in money, do me a big favor: when he returns to you, repay him for all the countless occasions in which he has lavished his time and energies [on my behalf], in the following manner. Take a considerable amount from the sum that you are holding for me for the future and give it to S. D'A. You and he must agree on a suitable sum, and then double it. May we meet again in a distant future, dear friend and artificer of my new kind fate (in spite of its fearful consequences)! Yours,

                                                        B. Pasternak

D'Angelo, to whom Pasternak read and handed over this letter, put a large "no" in the margin, drawing a pencil line through the text concerning him. After Pasternak's death, he was to say that he never refused that most generous compensation (which was never formally requisitioned): all he did was "reserve [the right] to accept." Years afterward, he was to claim a good half of the author's royalties.

Giangiacomo
with his mother,
Giannalisa, and his
sister, Antonella,
in 1929.
*© copyright Archivio
Feltrinelli*

Giangiacomo with
his father, Carlo
Feltrinelli, at the
Lido in 1932.
*© copyright Archivio
Feltrinelli*

Giangiacomo
Feltrinelli,
Rome,
December 1940.
© copyright
Archivio Feltrinelli

Carlo Feltrinelli with Giangiacomo in Switzerland in the 1930s.
© copyright Archivio Feltrinelli

(above) Cover of the first edition of *Doctor Zhivago*, published by Feltrinelli Editore in 1957.

(right) Giangiacomo Feltrinelli at the Frankfurt Book Fair in 1958.
© copyright *Archivio Feltrinelli*

Villadeati in Piedmont, Italy; Giangiacomo and his wife, Nanni De Stefani, bought the villa in 1957. © copyright *Archivio Feltrinelli*

Boris Pasternak with Olga Iwinskaja and her daughter, Irina, in 1959. *© copyright Heinz Schewe*

Giangiacomo Feltrinelli with Alfred Hitchcock in Milan in 1960, presenting Hitchcock's *Supernatural Tales of Terror and Suspense.* *© copyright Archivio Feltrinelli*

(above) Fidel Castro and Giangiacomo
Feltrinelli in Havanna in 1964.
© copyright Inge Schoenthal Feltrinelli

(above) Henry Miller signing the Italian editions of *Tropic of Cancer* and *Tropic of Capricorn* at the Feltrinelli bookshop in Milan, in 1962. © copyright *Archivio Feltrinelli*

(below) Giangiacomo Feltrinelli with James Baldwin, launching the Italian edition of *Another Country* in 1964. © copyright *Archivio Feltrinelli*

The Feltrinelli family:
Inge, Giangiacomo,
and Carlo in 1966.
© *copyright Ugo*
Mulas/Archivio Feltrinelli

(below) Carlo and
Giangiacomo at
Lake Garda in 1965.
© *copyright Inge*
Schoenthal Feltrinelli

Villa Feltrinelli
in Gargnano
at Lake Garda.
© *copyright*
Archivio
Feltrinelli

Giangiacomo Feltrinelli at a May Day demonstration in Berlin in 1968.
© *copyright Archivio Feltrinelli*

(above) Giangiacomo Feltrinelli's last (false) identity card, issued in 1970.
© *copyright Archivio Feltrinelli*

(below) The funeral service for Giangiacomo Feltrinelli, in March of 1972, at Milan's Monumental Cemetery. © *copyright Archivio Feltrinelli*

It is clear that Pasternak uses the expression "double it" in reference to a remuneration for D'Angelo. But a remuneration redoubled does not equal a half share of all the profits.

In 1965, five years after the death of Pasternak, D'Angelo sued the Italian publisher. The courts threw out the suit.

23 November 1957: *Doctor Zhivago* is the book of the hour.

The first figures from the bookstores in the center of Milan were comforting: the first print run (12,000 copies) was selling like hotcakes. The publisher presented the book with a jacket design by Albe Steiner (much appreciated by the author, simple, elegant: "très bon goût... très noble." The text of the novel was introduced by a publisher's note that Pasternak had suggested to Zveteremich in the course of their meeting. There was no reference to contracts or correspondence between the author and the publisher.

> Regarding the preparation of the Italian edition, there was an exchange of letters between the publisher and the Soviet publishing house concerning the worth of the book and its publication date. At that time, an agreement was reached to the effect that the Italian edition would not be published before the month of September 1957. At the end of the summer, when the publication of *Doctor Zhivago* was imminent and there was nothing to suggest that in the USSR any difficulties had arisen over publication, we received a request from the author that we return the manuscript to him as he was anxious to review it. We were unable to grant the author's wish inasmuch as the book was at an advanced stage of preparation and was also ready for publication in other countries. Also, the modifications that the author apparently intended to make to it did not arrive in time [...].

In the only interview he gave in those weeks, Feltrinelli declared that the publication of the book amounted to an "explicit protest." It was a phase in that "battle for tolerance" that Togliatti–years before, in his excellent preface to Voltaire–had described as "still topical and not an easy one to win."

In the winter of 1957, *Doctor Zhivago* was being translated by important publishing houses: S. Fischer (Germany), Collins (United Kingdom), Pantheon (United States), and Gallimard (France). In Italy, it was reprinted every two weeks.

Doctor Zhivago was to be published in the Soviet Union, but, since the USSR was not a signatory to the Berne Convention, Western houses would be free to publish it without contracts and payment. The only way to obtain exclusive world rights, which counts economically and provides protection for the work, was to have the translation ready within the critical thirty days following publication in the USSR.

On the Italian side there was no lack of willingness to wait for the original Soviet edition, at least until Pasternak's personal letters arrived. But, after publication in Italy, it was no longer permitted to talk of contracts and letters, even in the event of highly personal attacks. Such information became classified!

Feltrinelli took complete responsibility for publishing the book, and he did this not as the paladin of anti-Sovietism (not even Pasternak would have wanted that), but simply because he was convinced that the work was of high quality. Within the closed ranks of the Soviet leadership it was thought to the last that the book would not be published in Italy (at least not until after publication in Moscow): Feltrinelli, at bottom, was "one of ours." This made the diplomatic, political, and cultural defeat of the world superpower all the more painful. Of course, Khrushchev could have taken the trouble to read that long novel, something that much later he confessed he had not done. He underestimated the power of a book.

There is an emblematic photo of the Soviet defeat. A paparazzo immortalized Anastasy Mikoyan, the vice president of the Council of Ministers, as he was gloomily looking at the window of a large bookstore in New York. The picture was taken on an official visit in the winter of 1958. *Doctor Zhivago* was the only book on display, many copies piled up in the window.

Had the CIA or an agent acting on its behalf orchestrated the publication of the novel, the impact would have been different: half the world would have cried conspiracy, and complaints would have been made about this most ignominious provocation. But this way, everyone was caught by surprise: it was impossible to prepare a counterpropaganda campaign at the last minute.

It may be that the CIA did have a hand in matters, perhaps in attempts to pirate the book. I read somewhere that Her Majesty's secret service was also involved. They allegedly photographed the typescript at the Malta airport when the plane Feltrinelli was traveling in made a bogus emergency landing. But what James Bond was up to in the window seat of the last row, smoking Turkish cigarettes, is a story still to be told.

The strange thing is that Feltrinelli didn't become the paladin of anti-Sovietism even after the book was published. In the history of Communism, being anti-Soviet always means being anti-Communist; you really can't be a Communist and deny the October Revolution, the echo of which is still so enormous.

Feltrinelli never spoke or wrote a word in the language typical of a former Communist; he was never to be an ex-Communist. His personal stance on *Doctor Zhivago* is explained in an amazing letter to Bert Andreas, dated 23 December 1957. The German scholar, concerned about the sensation over the Pasternak case, had written to Feltrinelli shortly before Andreas was in agreement with the reasons for publication, but feared that the repercussions might affect the activities of the Feltrinelli Institute. This is how my father replied to him:

Pasternak. The question is not purely literary but also significant politically. I cannot, nor do I wish to, avoid this. The political significance was hostile not to the Soviet Union *tout court* but to certain powers that still hold very important positions in it. In this sense the whole affair was advised to me by the Soviet Union itself. If Tito and Gomulka have taken an autonomous stance, then this has political significance as far as the Soviet Union is concerned, but it will not lead to these gentlemen returning to the fold of the capitalists.

Several people understand this, even in the USSR. No harm whatsoever will come to the institute out of this. The ladies in M. are not so stupid. When they were here, it was clear that they understood the situation. Orders from on high can hinder good relations, but even if this happens, they can be restored in the future. It cannot be otherwise. On the other hand, all this cannot but improve relations with other institutes.

The phrase "the whole affair was advised to me by the Soviet Union itself" introduces a new element of mystery: with whom was Feltrinelli in contact? Was one of the "ladies in M." lending her support?

An Italian publisher is in opposition to the plenipotentiaries of a political system with which he identifies but considers devoid of innovation. Once the sclerotic moloch is defeated, he thinks, the USSR will begin to show signs of rejuvenation. Feltrinelli was a plenipotentiary in his own particular republic, the world of his books, his writers, his ideas, and his money. He wanted to deal with the superpower on an even footing. It was his foreign policy.

The "novel behind the novel" was to continue for many episodes, with the publisher continuing to defend his copyright and the motives that underlay his editorial decision. After the initial enthusiasm, however, personal interests, opportunism, and moves like those made by Alicata for the PCI's investigation, were to appear. Was *Doctor Zhivago* not the first great best-seller in contemporary (Italian) publishing?

The book remained in Feltrinelli's bloodstream like a drug. His profession, apparently, could have an influence on world events.

He wrote to Pasternak, in his own hand, at the foot of a letter dated September 1958:

Thank you for *Zhivago*, for all you have done for us. In these times, when human values are forgotten, human beings are reduced to robots, and when most people are trying to flee from themselves and the problems of ego by smothering what remains of human sensitivity, *Zhivago* has provided a lesson that cannot be forgotten. Every time I am at a loss as to which path to take, I know that I can go back to *Zhivago* and learn from him. *Doctor Zhivago* will always help me rediscover the simple and profound values of life, even when they seem lost.

Act 2 of the persecution of Boris Pasternak began in October 1958, after the announcement that he had won the Nobel Prize for literature. The Soviet press unleashed an avalanche of accusations, the Writers' Union demanded his expulsion, and, had he dared accept the prize, they would have deprived him of his citizenship and had him exiled. In a recent book of memoirs, Gerd Ruge, a correspondent with German television in Moscow, gave a good description of what was happening.

> The press campaign grew from day to day. *Literaturnaya Gazeta* introduced a special column called "Wrath and Indignation," featuring the hate letters of the readership, letters written by people who had not read the novel and who roundly condemned the author. During a public meeting of young Communists, attended also by Nikita Khrushchev, the leader of the Komsomol, Semitastny, called Pasternak "a pig who fouls his own trough," and called for the writer's expulsion from the motherland.

Groups of young Communists demonstrated in front of the house in Peredelkino, waving banners bearing the word "Judas," and guards were on hand to protect the house from being attacked or set on fire. A doctor was ready to step in should Pasternak attempt to take his own life, like Mayakovsky or Yesenin: another suicide would have shocked millions of readers and exacerbated the scandal. In fact, according to the memoirs of Olga Ivinskaya, on 28 October Pasternak asked her if it would not have been better for them to commit suicide together.

In the end, Pasternak decided to turn down the prize and sent off a telegram to the Swedish Academy on 29 October. He wrote directly to Khrushchev two days after, to explain that the threatened exile to the West would have meant death for him. Perhaps he sensed that the last chapter of his life had begun.

Yet 1958 had opened with his great joy at leafing through the Italian edition of *Doctor Zhivago*.

In a letter to the publisher dated 12 January he wrote:

Dear Sir,
I do not know when I shall have the opportunity to express my immense gratitude for all your amazing accomplishments, of which I am the beneficiary and the witness. I appreciate the circumspection with which you have granted interviews, and also your regard for me, which I can sense from the appearance of the book, given to me by a German journalist, and by the excellent translation, which is highly praised everywhere. The good fortune that has smiled on my book, the editions that sell out rapidly, all is due principally to you, and full of reverence I bow before your kindness, your talent, and your lucky star.

If in my turn I have been of use in some way, I have a request to make of you–grant me this wish.

Since your edition has enjoyed such an extraordinary success, allow me to express the hope that I might see the work published exactly as it was written, in its original language. So, give me leave to place this delicate matter (bound up with consequences that will perhaps prove fatal to me, the way all fancies of a "Zhivagoesque" nature do) in the prudent hands of my good friend from Paris, Mme Jacqueline de Proyart. After clearing up the financial issues with you, the lady, I believe, will choose to have the work published by Mouton of The Hague, the publishers most consonant with it from a political point of view. I cannot see anything in this that might jeopardize or harm your interests, since every book in Russian will carry below the title a statement declaring your reservation of all rights regarding foreign translations, and a most extensive declaration of your copyright. But should this request of mine run contrary to your interests, I beg you to meet me half way, and I shall indemnify you for any losses in the manner provided for by the clauses contained in article 2 of the contract. Give me leave to confer material authority regarding all literary questions concerning my Russian text on Mme de Proyart, and do not hinder her in this activity.

I shall count you among my most wonderful friends, to whom I
shall forever be indebted. Among those [friends] is Mme de Proyart.
I do not want any discord among my friends. Please, sort things
out with her for the best. Do not write to me, do not bring up the
question of money. Behave as you have always behaved with me,
maintain the same silence. I embrace D'Angelo with affection, pas-
sionately. All his acquaintances here send him their fondest greetings. Please pass on my enthusiastic compliments and my infinite
gratitude to dear Zveteremich, whose work reveals him to be a
master of his art, a wizard.
   Yours,

                                                    Boris Pasternak

Over and above the declarations of friendship, this letter is important because it explains some questions that arose later. The
first concerns the position of D'Angelo, who had returned to Italy
and was employed for a time by the publishing house. The second,
more important, concerns the role of Mme de Proyart. She had met
and befriended the poet in January 1957 and, on the strength of this
acquaintance, she now felt she had a role to play in the management of his affairs.

The odd thing is that the letter sent on 12 January 1958 never
reached Feltrinelli. Given by Pasternak to Hélène Peltier, one of the
French translators who was on a visit to Moscow that January, the
letter was in an envelope containing other correspondence for Proyart. But Proyart kept everything and forwarded nothing to Milan.
Perhaps this was because her legal rights as an agent had not been
defined with sufficient precision. Or, who knows, perhaps she
thought she was much more than a mere proxy, or perhaps she
was unaware that, according to international law, *Doctor Zhivago*
was to all intents and purposes an Italian book, and that a Russian
edition was subject to the same contractual obligations as a translated version in English, German, or French.

Proyart only recently gave the letter to Evgeny Pasternak, and
her failure to forward it at the time generated some serious

misunderstandings and even friction between the publisher and
the poet's solicitous lady friend.

It is easier to follow the evolution of this affair through Feltrinelli's own words in the *Sunday Times*:

> While the literary world was acclaiming *Doctor Zhivago* and its au-
> thor, I became aware of the first signs of a battle between me and a
> number of persons and institutions (all connected with the same
> circle of anti-Soviet activities that, in one way or another, were con-
> nected to the CIA). I had commissioned from a Dutch printer a lim-
> ited number of copies of *Doctor Zhivago* in Russian, but, to my
> surprise, a different, pirated Russian edition appeared in Holland. It
> would seem that someone had printed an edition at the request of
> some Russian émigrés in Paris who had certain ties with Ameri-
> cans. At the same time, at the International Expo in Brussels, some
> Russian émigrés were distributing copies of another pirated edition,
> from the Vatican stand! These events put me on my guard.
>
> As a result, I strongly opposed the political use anti-Soviet circles
> might make of the book and feared the consequences this might
> have for the author. I was also seriously worried that my copyright
> might be jeopardized. I therefore took legal action against the pi-
> rated editions circulating in Holland, Greece, and Argentina, and in
> all cases I managed to come to an amicable agreement.
>
> I do not know how close my suspicions were to the truth, but I do
> know what the attorney Tesone, went through. He was then taking
> his first steps in the legal profession, and found himself catapulted
> into the most complex of international intrigues in the field of copy-
> right. It was in everyone's interest to defend the contract and to pre-
> vent the work from falling into the public domain. In order to block
> a pirated edition, Tesone flew all the way to Buenos Aires. "As soon
> as I arrived, I went to the Plaza but could not sleep because of jet
> lag, and I went down to take a stroll along Calle Florida. After a
> hundred meters I was assailed by a news vendor with a copy of
> *Doctor Zhivago*. I unearthed the printer in two days."

Throughout 1958, the correspondence between Feltrinelli and
Pasternak slowed down. Both were employing maximum caution.
On 5 September, almost a year after the publication of the Italian
edition, Feltrinelli sent his author an affectionate statement.

Dear Friend,

First of all, let me clasp your hand in wholehearted friendship and gratitude.

From time to time, I have had indirect news of you, sometimes good, sometimes of a kind that had me worried about your state of health. I hope, and the most recent news confirms this, that you have now recovered from your indisposition of last spring, and I entreat you, also in the name of the innumerable friends you have everywhere, to look after yourself and not risk your health for any reason.

Now let me say a few words about the success of *Doctor Zhivago*. In Italy we have sold about 30,000 copies. An enormous number for the Italian market and hard to beat even for the most famous authors. But this figure has a significance that goes well beyond this. We have had cases of youngsters who, during their lessons at school, read *Doctor Zhivago*, page after page, passing it on from hand to hand. We have testimony from dozens of people who wrote to thank me for having published the work. Wherever I go, people talk to me of *Doctor Zhivago*, the best-loved book in Italy at the moment. Here are a few lines of a message the Italian writer Carlo Cassola sent me:

"Today I finished reading *Doctor Zhivago*. No contemporary book has aroused in me so much enthusiasm, so much emotion, so much intellectual pleasure, or so much comfort and serenity."

Doctor Zhivago has come out in French and is about to come out in England, America, Germany, Holland, Denmark, Sweden, Finland, Norway, Israel, and Mexico. In Sweden it has already aroused enormous interest in the Swedish Academy.

There is more. In Italy, *Doctor Zhivago* won the prize awarded by booksellers, a fact that reflects not only an appreciation of its literary quality but also its success in sales. I am also sending you the most important reviews that appeared in the Italian press as well as a few from abroad.

We are preparing your autobiographical essay for next November, and I should like to ask you, dear friend, to see if one of your friends in Moscow can find the photos mentioned in the list I am enclosing with this letter. We would like to illustrate the book with photos of the people, of the works, and with reproductions from magazines, etc. mentioned here. I am also enclosing a copy of Chekhov's *Cahiers*, which we published last year, to show you how your essay will be presented. Could you have someone find the material we need? Perhaps you already have it in your own records? I hope I am not importuning you with these requests, but time is very short: we must have everything as soon as possible!

I end this letter, dear friend, with the hope that I may finally meet you one day. Thank you for *Doctor Zhivago.*
Yours,

Giangiacomo Feltrinelli

Pasternak ticked off a few items on the list of material requested and crossed out others. At that time he was thinking of sending Feltrinelli a painting by his father, who was an artist, which shows Prince Trubetskoy intent on making a sculpture of his young grandchildren. In his autobiographical text Pasternak talks of the prince, who taught along with his father in the school of painting. Trubetskoy had been assigned a new studio whose skylight gave on to the kitchen of the Pasternak household. That picture was a great present for Feltrinelli, and Pasternak wrote on the back of the canvas: "I send you this drawing as a gift, my dear friend. It was in this very atelier, built adjacent to the window of our kitchen, as is described in my autobiography, that the prince modeled his grandchildren."

It was 19 October 1958. The poet was not to have the time to arrange the complicated delivery of the materials Feltrinelli wanted. Four days later, his life was turned upside down: he had won the Nobel!

"Infinitely grateful, moved, proud, amazed, confused" was his first reply by telegram to the Academy in Stockholm. Even Giannalisa thought it well to congratulate the winner: just for once, was she or was she not the publisher's mother?

5

The Aurelian Way was a strange summertime manger scene with its oleanders, electric lights, wickerwork screens, spaghetti *al burro,* wall posters, magic pine auto air fresheners, little shrines with television sets, and the reflected glitter of the sand all around. On San Lorenzo's night (in August 1957), the usual Citroën was heading for the Argentario. With Giangiacomo there was a Roman woman who was said to be a character if not a beauty. The couple arrived at Giannalisa's house overlooking the sea, where she had left the children to spend the winter after the long sojourn in New York. With them there was only governess number 17. Giangiacomo woke up Benedetta, the eldest: "Come on, there's someone I want you to meet." The introductions were made in the enclosed space between the roofs, lying down on the still warm stones beneath the shooting stars. That is how Benedetta recalls the encounter.

The Roman woman was Nanni De Stefanis, the daughter of a playwright. In those days, Feltrinelli was spending more and more time in Rome: he had had enough of the fog and the late night meetings at the office; in Rome, for a good night on the town, all

you needed was a white shirt and a couple of Gypsies à la Django
Reinhardt. Nanni was on the poetry circuit, and the typical small
restaurants, the trattorias, were still typical.

With Bianca, things had been going badly for some time; the
couple were practically separated. Before Rome, Giangiacomo had
run off too frequently to the Deux Magots and Françoise. In 1955,
Bianca had been seduced by Renato Mieli, an ex-editor of *L'Unità*.
Formerly secretary to Togliatti, Mieli was suspected of being an
English spy and rumored to be on the point of leaving the PCI. I
think that Giangiacomo loved Bianca, despite her rather uncom-
promising character. In Italy, divorce was still in the future, and
there was only one way to get rid of a spouse, apart from murder:
you needed a decree of annulment issued in a foreign country and
this then had to be endorsed by an Italian court. Something only
the rich could afford, obviously, and it was a tortuous process. The
loophole, usually, was that of *impotentia coeundi* on the husband's
part.

Nanni could have made the right companion for Giangiacomo;
she would have brought a touch of Rome to Milan. With her, life
would have taken a more stimulating turn, perhaps a more amusing one. At first, the couple went to live in the family home, on Via
Andegari, refurbished for the occasion.

One day, they took the car and after an ice cream in the square
in Vigevano, after driving through Lomellina, the rice fields of
Mortara, and the mosquitoes of Casale, they discovered the skele-
ton of an ancient castle at the top of a hill near Monferrato. At the
foot of the hill stands a village. In the mid-eighteenth century, a
young disciple of the school of Juvara,* certainly an amateur, had
indulged in a unique enterprise. He designed a two-fronted belve-
dere that was to link up with the village by means of a strange system of steps, underground passages, walkways, and paths. The

---

*Filippo Juvara (1678–1736). Italian architect whose baroque style was tempered
with classicism. He worked in Turin for the royal house of Savoy.

construction he imagined was devoid of depth but spectacular. Around the axis of the central tower, exploiting the sloping terrain, terraces, towers, arches, hallways, exedrae, and balustrades were designed to blend in with exotic plants, gardens, palm trees, and orange and lemon groves. Everything complied with a rigorous symmetry in which even the trees had their own specific place. The spectacle is neoclassical, the syntax strictly Baroque, and the quiet is Arcadian.

But this was not the scene that met Giangiacomo on his first excursion with Nanni. The only archaeological survey from the time provides us with another image. The *Bollettino storico-bibliografico subalpino* of 1942 reported that the construction had been "left at the mercy of the elements and neglect" and was in "a desperate condition. [...] The castle lies lifeless, crumbling, roofless, and at certain points, like the ceilings of the covered stairways in the gardens, there have been some serious cave-ins. In place of the hanging gardens and the flowerbeds, there grew "brushwood, ivy, and nettles."

The village below is called Villadeati. In 1944 it was the scene of a Nazi reprisal, which culminated in the killing of eleven people. A squad of partisans had sought refuge in the ruins of the castle.

It was going to take one, two, maybe three years, and truckloads of gravel; there were bricks to be piled up, seeds to be sown, but in the end the place was restored and, in a certain sense, it resembles him. According to the historian André Corboz, the castle of Villadeati is "an atypical complex, impossible to classify under a single label." It is a folly, "in which formal quality nonetheless prevails over bourgeois vanity. At Villadeati the space already belongs [to the age of] the hot-air balloon, and no longer to that of the horse-drawn carriage." There are photos of Feltrinelli with a wheelbarrow full of mortar working on a cryptoporticus. He was trying to build himself a piece of the future.

The relationship did not work out. Nanni was unstable. She did want to marry him, but she wasn't prepared to give up her Roman connections. She was unhappy in the new city. The wedding took place 19 June 1957, but the marriage didn't last a year. When these things happen, they hurt. Two marriages, two failures. Perhaps the time had come to go away, to get a change of air, to be alone.

In July 1958, Feltrinelli set off with his backpack and his tent and headed north, toward Scandinavia, with a stopover in Hamburg to meet some German publishers. During this trip, he wrote from the lagoon of Grado to his friend the painter Giuseppe Zigaina, who was about to get married. The letter was a long one in which Feltrinelli bared his soul.

> Dear Pino,
> I am still traveling and hope that you will continue to behave sensibly and not get cold feet at the last minute. I really think, dear Pino, that you should have no doubts. Not because I want to see others go through the troubles that have come my way. But for what little, very little alas, I can understand, and above all because I am not emotionally involved in the matter, I think you couldn't have made a better choice. On the other hand, even though I feel scorned and humiliated, I still agree with what Zompitta said about marriage a couple of years ago. Nothing could be better for a man like you, with your wealth of experience, than choosing the right wife and to have from her what only a wife can give, if she loves you, if she is a balanced person, morally, intellectually, and physically. And when the crises come, the doubts and the problems, you will always find in her love the comfort that a man needs. And then there are children. You see, Pino, I envy you. I think you will have all the things I have always desired and do not have. Once, because of inexperience [...] and maybe even out of my malice or imprudence, I spoiled and destroyed something beautiful and sound. The second time around, I got a taste of my own medicine and reaped the hurt I caused another. I envy you, Pino. Because [...] I seem to see Bianca's qualities in Maria. Only with far more sweetness and humanity than Bianca had. As long as you don't do anything silly, you will be very happy. So say hello to Maria from me, and my fondest good wishes to you both. And while we're on the subject, it is sad, Pino, to get to thirty-two years of age, to find the road ahead barred, and to realize [...] that you have played with life and love to the point of throwing it all away. [...] But enough—otherwise I fall into self-pity. Anything but that. I have gained in strength and calm these last few weeks. Being

alone, the contact with nature, and traveling has given me serenity, so I can talk of these things with calm and awareness. At this moment I am going from Naurk to Honnersgung (Nordkapp) on board a small ship. We are going through the Norwegian fjords, among mountains still laden with snow, on a sea that is, I would say, dark periwinkle-blue under a sun that never sets on the horizon. It is a magnificent spectacle, at times almost terrifying. I left the car at Kiruna in Sweden, and when I get back there on Sunday morning, I want to take the road north once more and see these same places from the land. The solitude here is immense. Last week, after a visit of 7–8 days to Stockholm, I took an inland road right across Sweden (1,800 km) and in about ten days I expect to be in Helsinki. This is one of the best trips I have ever taken. [...] Fondest wishes to you and Maria, from your Giangiacomo.

Perhaps it was to ward off bad luck, but there is no mention here of the press photographer Feltrinelli had met in Hamburg in the office of Heinrich Maria Ledig Rowohlt. "I introduced them," Rowohlt later explained. "I invited her to a party in Giangiacomo's honor. I would say that they understood each other immediately and, when they left the party, I don't think they needed anyone else." It may be that after that meeting, under the auspices of the publisher who was a friend of Faulkner and Hemingway, there was a brief encounter on the way back home. Perhaps in Copenhagen, at the court of another publisher, Otto Lindhart, with whom it is a pleasure to talk of books to this day.

The woman, says Rowohlt, had made a name for herself by photographing Pablo Picasso, Ernest Hemingway, Gary Cooper, Gérard Philippe, Greta Garbo, and Anna Magnani, and she learned about photography by interviewing Erwin Blumenfeld in New York. She looked like a blend of Audrey Hepburn and Leslie Caron.

"Have you read *The Leopard?* Did you like *The Leopard?*" So begins a society piece published in the winter of 1958–59:

When the book came out, the question came from friends who frequented literary circles; then it came from colleagues, then from

acquaintances. By now you hear it in the theater or from the row behind you in the cinema. In fact, any cheap yellow cover, lying on a
table, sticking out of a pocket or a handbag, now makes you think of
The Leopard. Anyone buying or receiving the book that has just
come out is advised to hang on to it: it is, in fact, almost a biblio-
graphical rarity.

"Yet," Eugenio Montale was to say, "Lampedusa, who was this person? Until the other day no one could say that Lampedusa was the
name of a writer."

The Leopard arrived in the bookstores in December 1958—as the
result of a blunder. The plan had been to publish the book early in
the new year. The Christmas schedule was already very crowded,
and Osenga, Feltrinelli's sales manager, insisted that "safer" books
should take precedence. But owing to a misunderstanding, a few
advance copies were sent to the critics and Carlo Bo unexpectedly
wrote a review for *La Stampa.* There was no choice but to bring
the book out as fast as possible.

Feltrinelli was to admit, during an interview, the serendipi-
tous nature of Operation Leopard: "*Zhivago* called for a difficult
decision to be made in isolation. Who could have advised me
in that situation? In short it was not, as is almost always the
case with best-sellers, and as it was with *The Leopard,* a stroke
of luck."

In reality, the publishing histories of the two books are to some
extent analogous. As with Pasternak, Feltrinelli was never to meet
the author of his second huge publishing hit. Giuseppe Tomasi di
Lampedusa, duke of Palma, died of lung cancer in July 1957. His
was to be an overwhelming posthumous success. "In the bookstores, delicate ladies of a certain age, angry young men, and petits
bourgeois who usually read only glossy magazines all asked for
The Leopard, almost with the same passion they had asked for
Doctor Zhivago some time before." This was what *Rinascita,* the
theoretical magazine of the PCI, reported on the subject, thereby
inviting the ironic darts of the critic Geno Pampaloni:

In a country divided into a mass of apathetic people and a discor-
dant clique of sophisticates, the fact that a book not only sells tens of
thousands of copies but moreover aspires to being considered
"good" is in itself more than amazing, it is scandalous. And [the
Communists] view the book with the same mistrust that they reserved for *Doctor Zhivago.*

As with *Zhivago,* the publishing history of the new best-seller
contained a sensational rejection. At first there was the oversight at
Mondadori, perhaps the fault of some superficial readers; then
there was the critic Vittorini, who may not even have read the
manuscript. There were explanations, like the ideological anom-
alies in the novel that prompted a refusal from Einaudi. Vittorini
defended himself in a long letter to the author, and he made the
same arguments publicly: even though "serious and honest," this
was a static, conventional novel that denied history. Cassola's *Il
soldato* was better, and so was Testori's *Il ponte della Ghisolfa.*
These works, which had also just been published by Feltrinelli,
had more life and were "steeped in our history."

The events that led to the publication of *The Leopard* form, as
with *Zhivago,* a "novel behind the novel," though not as dramatically. Its protagonists were Elena Croce,* the daughter of the great
Italian philosopher, who remembered the manuscript that lay for a
long time in a drawer before she finally sent it to Giorgio Bassani,
and Bassani himself, the "sparrowhawk" recently recruited by Feltrinelli during his Roman period to direct a series of works by contemporary authors. Croce wrote to Bassani, telling him that the
novel came from an "aristocratic young lady from Palermo." Bassani swooped on the text and managed to recover, after a great deal
of diplomacy and detective work, the text of the denouement with
the famous ball as well as the original manuscript. After publication, it was the critics' turn: was the novel right-wing or not, and
what should be considered left-wing?

*(1915–94). A remarkable essayist and German scholar, she was an indefatigable
defender of literary culture.

Feltrinelli thought that these were pointless polemics: so what if Mario Alicata had labeled one of his books decadent for the second time? Feltrinelli was probably as bored by this as he was by the twittering of the ancient aristocratic crones in their hats (at the zenith of their splendor) that packed the amphitheater where Lampedusa's book was awarded the 1959 Strega Prize.

The Leopard was "the restless ghost of Italian literature after the second World War" (the definition is that of Alfonso Berardinelli), but *Doctor Zhivago,* in its own country, was an even more awkward ghost.

In 1958, after fourteen years as a party member, Feltrinelli was no longer carrying a party card in his pocket. He was rumored to be "on the point of joining the PSI Italian Socialist Party and will run for them as a candidate in the next elections." This was stated in a confidential report to the chief of police on 11 January. The purported leak was subsequently rebutted by two "first-rate" informers, each unaware of the other's work.

When a person has spent years as a militant activist, breaking with the party is often the prelude to strange existential crises whose effects are not always cathartic. There is a real case study to be made of this. Moreover, precisely because the party is an austere body, it is unforgiving. This unforgiving nature engenders the contempt that smothers you, leaving you with no place to turn. To the right, there are the faces you have always detested; to the left, there is that strange family that doesn't want you anymore.

Both Feltrinelli and the PCI played down his breach with the party, and there was no sensation mongering on either side. Feltrinelli said he was "disappointed." And no more.

That the breach was a real one emerges from the ineffable author of a police report (2 April 1959): "It seems that today, especially after the publication of *Doctor Zhivago* and the works of some

American authors, the breach between Feltrinelli and the Communists is complete."

The officials of the American State Department who were examining his request for a visa prior to a visit to the USA came to the same conclusion. The consul general in Milan, Charles Rogers, sent Washington this memorandum of his meeting with the Italian publisher.*

Feltrinelli is a young man, well dressed, wealthy. He gives the impression of a person who takes himself very seriously. His expression is grave. He has a mission, that of achieving a better world for the "downtrodden." His state of mind seems more like that of a nineteenth-century social reformer than that of a twelve-year member of the Italian Communist Party. At the outset of our conversation he seemed ill at ease, but as the conversation led to his political ideas, he relaxed somewhat.

He said he joined the Communist Party in 1947 because at the time it seemed to him the most effective instrument to combat Fascism and to bring about the rapid development of true democracy in Italy. [...] He left the party in 1957 when he became convinced that the Communist Party, due to its relationship with the Soviet Communist Party, both organizationally and philosophically, was no longer a suitable instrument for the achievement of the objectives he wished to support. [...] It is his aim to be a leader of left-wing intellectualism, and, in order to retain his influence in left-wing circles, he wishes to avoid the label of anti-Communism. His present focus of activity is the Giangiacomo Feltrinelli Institute of Milan, a center of socialist studies, of which he speaks with pride. [...]

When I asked him how he would describe himself as a political thinker, he shied away from the term "Marxist" or "revisionist." Under the present circumstance, he said, it is impossible to define a Marxist. As a father of political thought, Marx unquestionably made a great contribution to human development, but in the light of 100 years' experience, many of his assumptions and theses seem mistaken. [...] Feltrinelli expressed his conviction that the powers of the central government under ideal circumstances should be diminished and many functions of the government delegated to the local community. [...]

*FBI archives.

He is especially interested in the problem of the individual's relationship to society in a technological civilization. He believes
there is a parallel between the pressures to which the individual
is subjected as a result of the imposition of doctrine by a tyranni-
cal government under Communism and those self-induced pressures of standardization and social convention under capitalism.
For these reasons, he would like to observe at first hand the effects
of the evolution of modern society in the American democracy. He
has a number of introductions to intellectual circles in the United
States.

Feltrinelli had not been in the USA since the days of Doctor Gottlieb, Giannalisa's dentist. Gottlieb was the best. When he moved
his practice from Vienna to New York, grandmother thought it only
logical to remain faithful to him and not to do without his precious
skills, especially for the children's sake.

Because of his Communist party card, Feltrinelli had been unable to show his face in the USA since 1945. Even as an "ex" he
still did not have that right. But now Washington took only three
weeks to grant the request, probably as a result of the "Pasternak
effect." The publisher had asked to go to the United States in
order to deal personally with various business matters regarding
the management of the rights of his most important author. The
Herald Tribune and the *Washington Post* attached particular importance to the *nulla osta* signed by William Rogers.

Feltrinelli left for America with his new love, Inge Schoenthal. It
was to be a long trip. First stop Mexico City and a quickie marriage
bureau, then the United States and a whole galaxy of publishing
contacts, followed by Cuba in search of Hemingway, and back to
the States. All in four months: from Christmas to April 1959, with a
brief return to Italy in between. This interlude overseas was the
line of demarcation between one life and preparations for a completely new one, sanctioned by a honeymoon spent between Zihu-
atanejo and Baja California.

We began to publish in 1955. With some rare exceptions, our first books were rather poor. Now I have come to America because we are publishing books that are better, much better, and we'd like to publish books that are better still. I felt that personal contact with American publishers could be an important step for the development of our business and one that would give me some firsthand knowledge of literary production.

These were Feltrinelli's opening remarks in his first American radio interview. He spoke excellent English, and the man who was firing the questions at him—Barney Rosset, an editor at Grove Press and the publisher of *Evergreen Review,* the best magazine of the cultural avant-garde—presented him as an intense man who made a strong impression.

New York gave them a special welcome. The Americans noticed a felicitous resemblance between Mr. Feltrinelli and Doctor Zhivago. The aura of *The Leopard* also helped arouse intense curiosity. A curiosity that was reciprocated.

There were important encounters, and new friends were on the horizon. One was Barney Rosset, "a quick-witted, dynamic forty-year-old," noted his Italian guest. They spoke at length about Beckett. Feltrinelli took out an option but, unfortunately, did not clinch a deal. The two got on right from the start. The same thing happened with Jason Epstein (one of the future founders of the *New York Review of Books*), who by twenty-eight had made it to the top at Random House, "a real *enfant prodige,* a sort of Brega." And also with Mike Bessie, then with Harpers, "intelligent and witty, with a profound knowledge of Europe" and even a friend of Luigi Barzini. It was the same story with Bill Jovanovich, the Montenegrin who ran Harcourt Brace, with Roger Straus, to this day in charge of one of America's most admired publishing houses, and above all with Kurt Wolff, Pasternak's American publisher and Feltrinelli's host.

These men were to become his friends in the world of publishing, together with Heinrich Maria Ledig Rowohlt and Gottfried

Bermann Fischer, a close friend of the Mann family who played the cello with Albert Einstein. These are the names of the older generation, the generation that had created the cultural framework of an epoch in which books had not yet become merchandise.

One black day, Rosset was to say of Feltrinelli: "We had the convictions, he had the courage." For his part, Wolff said: "He was the first and only *homo novus* we met." Perhaps they were both thinking of those first frenetic encounters in New York in the winter of 1959.

After the publishers there came the inevitable meetings with authors: in his radio interview, Feltrinelli said he was on the trail of Jack Kerouac. And we know that he approached Nabokov, then an old man, about *Lolita,* an approach that failed basically owing to incompatibility of character. Feltrinelli proposed to Nabokov that he bring out a Russian edition, thereby incurring the (fairly benevolent) strictures of Alberto Mondadori, who had Nabokov under contract. Things went better with Karen Blixen: oysters, champagne, and a deal for *Out of Africa.* Then he dropped in on Arthur Miller at the playwright's home. The famous wife was in the next room, unable to decide on which outfit to wear. Giangiacomo and Inge played for time, talking and talking, but the famous wife did not make an appearance.

My parents moved on to Havana, in search of Hemingway. Inge had interviewed the writer three years before, and now she wanted to introduce him to her husband. In the great casinos the roulette wheels were still spinning, but only out of inertia, and instead of Hemingway, who had left because he was in poor health, the couple found a revolution only a few weeks old. "A magnificent city," Feltrinelli wrote to the faithful Tina, "very chaotic, with Hispanics, blacks, and Chinese, humming with life and color. Every so often, scattered here and there, you come across bearded guerrillas, complete with pistols and submachine guns, lounging on big chairs in front of public buildings, guarding against the enemy."

They took one of the last flights out to Miami and continued their journey by car to Washington, Baltimore, and New York once more. A Ford Mustang lurked in the rearview mirror for a good part of the trip: the FBI?

On his return to Italy, the publisher threw himself back into the Zhivago affair. He had to come to an agreement with the University of Michigan Press in Ann Arbor regarding a new Russian-language edition of the novel. As a precautionary measure, he decided to begin his own version in Cyrillic.

In the meantime, Pasternak's *Autobiography* had been published in Italy in December 1959, along with a collection of poems translated by Sergio D'Angelo. To return to the article Feltrinelli wrote for the *Sunday Times*:

> I received a number of letters from Mme Jacqueline de Proyart of Paris, with instructions for the publication of the autobiography. She said that Pasternak had granted her the widest powers of attorney. I knew nothing of Mme de Proyart's position, and relations between us grew more tense. I was worried because, in such a delicate matter, it might have been dangerous to involve a third person who was not familiar with all the details. Frankly, I also resented the fact that she enjoyed the privilege of being able to travel and have direct contact with the author, something I could not do as I did not have a Soviet visa.

So it was back to the sequence of questions and answers to be enclosed in a sealed envelope and entrusted to the hold of a plane and to hands that sorted the mail in a hangar. On 2 February 1959, Pasternak sent a reply—from Peredelkino, via Paris—to Feltrinelli's letter of 5 September 1958. The publisher had sent Pasternak a first royalty statement for *Doctor Zhivago* one year after publication, with a grateful postscript in English ('Thank you for *Zhivago,* and for all you have taught us').

My very dear friend,
I begin this letter by begging you to convey to your good mother, Giannalisa Feltrinelli, my humblest apologies, and my profound remorse, as well as my warmest thanks for the beautiful and inspiring telegram that she honored me with on the day, so fateful for me, of my joy. Tell the dear, dear Madame Giannalisa that on reading her note, among the others received that day, I could not hold back my tears, and now, as I dash off these impetuous lines, I can barely resist a new bout, at the mere recollection. Tell her too—since such solicitous and penetrating words always express the entire being of those who utter them better than a hundred portraits—tell her that for the rest of her life she will always remain so young, adorable, and passionate, something that will come to pass, moreover, even without my wishes. I bow respectfully before her. I also thank you for all the flattering exaggerations kindly expressed in your letter of 5 September 1958–5 September, just think how long ago it is now! But we must not be surprised that only now have I found the time to reply.

As for my feelings for you, of which you are well aware, words can never suffice, even were I to express my gratitude night and day. I have often assured you, and I repeat this, that it is to you I owe not only the success of the book, but far more: this entire phase of my life, distressing, deadly dangerous, but full of significance and responsibility, dizzyingly enthralling, and worthy of being accepted and lived in glad and grateful obedience to God. I shall confirm everything to whoever may criticize or show interest and curiosity: I mean to say your handling of rights regarding the publication of *Doctor Zhivago,* now translated in all languages, your honesty, your generosity, your fairness in all disputes concerning the translated versions of *Zhivago.* By the way, when the Indian publishers approached me, I forwarded their offers directly to you.

Also, on the request from the Galeria Libertad of Montevideo, who challenged your rights over the Spanish version of the Dr., I told them that you represented me and that any disputes were futile.

But let's change the subject altogether. Recently numerous critics, translators, and publishers have sprung up who are sensitive, devoted, and benevolent toward me, who write about me, translate me, and publish me. And instead of finding in my gratitude and joy, as they would have every reason to expect, given that they have covered me with gifts and gladness, they find in me, as I was saying, ingratitude and a curious sense of bewilderment. They are saddened, the poor souls, and they waste time speculating about what mistake they can have made to deserve my hostility, wondering what it is they can have done to me, apart from pure unadulterated good. They are wrong. They are not the cause of my suffering, I am unhappy and irritated with myself. With my face in some of their photos, they capture the traits of an ugliness that is characteristic, but not something that I would boast about having reproduced. With some passages in my prose works, with some old and unfinished poetry, which I would have preferred to forget and whose imperfections I am reminded of thanks to the perfection of their translations.

If only I knew what to do about all this, how to conduct myself, if only I had some fixed point of view, if only I were able to give clear and precise instructions. Is it possible to suppress everything I did before the Dr., the *Autobiography*, the recent poems, and the translation of *Faust*? Perhaps I am wrong to criticize, to reject everything *en bloc*? Against my will I have devoted fifteen years of my work to the countless bulky translations that take up a whole shelf in my bookcase. My work in the original language is not vast, it is limited in choice. Can I neglect this part entirely? When I am the one who has my writings to hand, I can make a selection. I have put together a selection of my poems from all the editions of the state publishing house. I hoped that, once this book came out, it might serve as a model for the foreign translations. But it was rejected. None of my work will be published here anymore, neither the translations nor my original works. Conducting business, making decisions, and negotiating through a mail service that is so uncertain, slow, and ill-disposed, over such distances, with such tight deadlines–it is a torment, an insoluble problem, a wretched misfortune. Hence, therefore, the need, the reason I find myself obliged, while still having full confidence in you, to create, to recognize in a foreign country another me, an adviser, who meets my requirements in taste, in rigorous selectivity, in critical competence, and who has like ideas regarding what is to be done, to be accepted, avoided, refused, desired, and striven for, amid all the excessive opportunities that present themselves all too frequently and practically everywhere in my favor.

I cannot contemplate either rivalry or conflict between you and Madame de Proyart, my alter ego, who, like me, understands and makes allowances for the ambiguous position that I had to impose upon you out of necessity, forcing you to put up with my statements in silence and without objecting, and even though infrequent and reserved, my words were nevertheless hypocritically slanderous of your honor as they suggested you had acted without my knowledge or against my will, statements made by me with your permission—statements whose falsity the world was able to understand and forgive—statements made solely under conditions of extreme and unspeakable coercion. Well. But there have been imbeciles who, incapable of imagining the deadly weight of this yoke, of this mawkish and gilded cruelty, took my false accusations as the gospel truth, with a view, perhaps, to ruining your reputation. I have cost you dearly, and this pains me, and my second soul, Madame de Proyart, will never forget your merits and your sufferings in all this ambiguous and delicate situation.

To conclude this interminable letter, I shall talk of money and ask you a few questions. I hope that the entire sum (of money) is kept under your protection. For this I am infinitely and I beg you to see that it continues that way. The fact that I am completely lacking in curiosity regarding the various details and how much it all amounts to must not amaze or hurt you, almost as if my attitude were a form of indifference. Truly I have no desire to know all these things, as I do not dare and have no right or chance to think about them effectively. I think that only in a hypothetical case, and that is if they wanted to starve me out, would I decide to avail myself of an official remittance of cash from abroad. The financial authorities would have agreed to this deposit in foreign currency, but for the rest of my life I would have been poisoned by the perpetual accusation of treacherously living off foreign capital.

But I want to begin using this money in another way. With your help and permission I want to make some small pecuniary gifts, by bank order, to some persons. Here is the list (of names and sums); I pray you transfer:

1. Ten thousand dollars to my younger sister Mrs. Lydia Slater, 20 Park Town, Oxford, England.
2. Ten thousand dollars to my older sister Josephine Pasternak

(to the address of my younger sister, in the event of your not being able to find that of Josephine).

3. Ten thousand dollars to Mme Jacqueline de Proyart, 21 rue Fresnel, Paris XVI.

4. Ten thousand dollars to Mlle Hélène Peltier-Zamoyska, Maison St-Jean by St-Clar-de-Rivière, Haute Garonne, France.

5. Five thousand dollars to Mr. Michel Aucoutourier.

6. Five thousand dollars to Mr. Martinez (ask Mme de Proyart for both addresses).

7. Five thousand dollars to the Italian translator Pietro Zveteremich. Mr. Feltrinelli knows his address.

8. Ten thousand dollars to Mr. Sergio D'Angelo, Via Pietro d'Assisi 11, Rome.

9. Two thousand dollars to Mr. Garritano, to be paid in Italy or at his temporary domicile in Moscow.

10. Five thousand dollars to Max Hayward.

11. Five thousand dollars to Mrs. Harari (the two English translators, whose English address can be had from Collins).

12. Five thousand dollars to the Danish translator Ivan Malinovski in Copenhagen, at the address of Gyldendal publishers.

13. Five thousand dollars to Reinhold V. Walter, care of S. Fischer Verlag.

14. Five thousand dollars to Mr. Karl Theens, museum director, Stuttgart-Degerloch, Albstrasse 17, Germany.

15. Five thousand dollars to Mme Renate Schweitzer, Berlin West 30, Marburgerstrasse 16.

16. Five thousand dollars to John Harris, 3 Park Road, Dertington, Totnes, Devon, England.

17. Ten thousand dollars to Gerd Ruge in Germany.

I end this letter in great haste. A thousand thanks to you.

Yours, B. Pasternak

As had happened before, this letter never reached its destination and remained in Mme de Proyart's personal archive. For what reason? Perhaps, yet again, she was not entirely satisfied or not prepared to settle for second best. In the past, Pasternak had hinted at the prospect of her playing a specific role in the management of his literary estate. But, now, her role was described in a rather

confusing and embarrassing way. Her position might be misinterpreted as that of a mere confidante regarding matters of taste or
critical selection.

This time, Mme de Proyart expressed her point of view to
Pasternak. He agreed to let the letter drop, and said he would write
another. Feltrinelli was to learn about Proyart from Proyart herself,
without any prior intimation from Pasternak.

D'Angelo, by then back in Italy, on bad terms with the PCI and
briefly employed at Feltrinelli, was in touch on his own account with
Proyart and with Pasternak himself, through the Moscow correspondent of *L'Unità*, Giuseppe Garritano, who was also a beneficiary on Pasternak's list. One of the reasons the letter of 2 February
never reached Feltrinelli might have been a last-minute intervention
on the part of Olga Ivinskaya, a move requested by Garritano, who
perhaps feared something and wanted nothing to do with the list.

Feltrinelli received a letter from Jacqueline de Proyart. She presented herself formally, complete with power of attorney, claiming
to supervise "all the rights" to Pasternak's works in the West.
Amazed, Feltrinelli could do little else but write once more to his
author. He did this on 16 February 1959, having returned to Italy
from the United States.

At that time, the courier most frequently used to pass correspondence on to Pasternak was Heinz Schewe, the Moscow correspondent of the German daily *Die Welt*. Ruge, who is mentioned in
the following letter, is Gerd Ruge, a correspondent with German
television and a colleague of Schewe's, who was also involved in
this kind of mission.

Dear Pasternak, dear friend,
Last month I tried to reach you but in vain, all efforts failed; now I
have come up with a new way, and I hope this letter may find you.
    Months have gone by since my last letter, months full of anxiety
and excitement, sorrow and admiration, humiliation and joy.
    Following the political free-for-all that has livened up these last

few months, *Doctor Zhivago* is still being read by hundreds of thousands all over the world, and continues to be appreciated for its worth, and for all that it is capable of giving and teaching humanity. Recently, Ruge brought me news of you, he told me that you are in good health, and that made us feel easier. Dear friend, look after yourself. We have just published the *Autobiography*, of which I am sending you a copy. Only after its publication did I come to know of a certain Madame de Proyart, who informed me that you apparently wish to have only the second version published, with a different ending.

Alas, the version you delivered to me was the first one. I never received any instructions regarding your preference for the second, which has been published by Gallimard.

With regard to Madame de Proyart, I must confess that it came as a sore blow to me to learn of your having made her your representative for Europe, without a word to me, when for a long time I was the one who in practice had the honor and responsibility of representing you. For reasons I fail to comprehend, Madame de Proyart has thought to present herself only now, all but reproving me for not knowing what she herself has concealed from me for a long time.

I have borne all sorts of humiliation without batting an eye, but this last blow is the hardest of all to take. I have conducted, I think, all the various publishing operations, with their considerable burden of responsibility, in conformity with your instructions, or, when these were not available, in the spirit of your wishes. Now, to find myself bereft of your trust, of the support of your authority, is an unexpected surprise, and an extremely painful one.

Madame de Proyart is causing me many problems with regard to the *Autobiography*, which you entrusted to me and for which, even though we have been unable to draw up a contract, I felt responsible, handling its publication in several countries, as I did with *Doctor Zhivago*. As a matter of fact, Mme de Proyart is calling into question everything I have done, hindering me and threatening me with legal action regarding ventures undertaken before she declared her position. She is demanding that I hand over all contracts to her. Agreed, I will do so, if this is your wish. I wonder, dear friend, why I must be threatened and treated like a fraud by Madame de Proyart. This too is a humiliation I do not think I deserve.

But, dear friend, I ask you to explain once more the following points, on which your thinking, even in the letters to Mme de Proyart, is not clear:

1. Can the Russian-language editions of *Doctor Zhivago,* one in Europe and one in America, be considered as included in the contract we stipulated for this work?
2. With regard to the profits deriving from the editions of *Doctor Zhivago,* what are your wishes? That I entrust them to Mme de Proyart, that I hold them for you here or in Switzerland, that I have them sent to you by diverse means and in what annual amount, or that they be held and managed in common by me and Madame de Proyart?
3. Our contract for *Doctor Zhivago* does not cover the rights for a film version. What is your wish? Do you want a film to be based on it? (In this case, please, sign the letter herein enclosed and send it back to me. I am of the opinion that a film version could be made in one or two years' time, but this is up to you, I cannot know what your wishes may be. What percentage would you want? The same as for the translations of *Doctor Zhivago*? Do you have sufficient faith in me to leave me sole control over production? (I shall not conceal the fact that any collaboration with Mme de Proyart would lead only to disaster: there is nothing like incompetence for spoiling all ventures.)

Dear Pasternak, I am saddened at having to subject you to commercial questions, and at boring you with my worries and my anxieties, but it is indispensable for me to know your opinion.

Dear friend, let me know all you need and desire.

I am, as ever, your friend.

Giangiacomo Feltrinelli

P.S. In any event, it is necessary for you to sign the letter of attorney herein enclosed (document no. 2), which is indispensable if I am to be able to take more effective action against all arbitrary initiatives.

So sign both documents, if you would be so kind, and send them to me, along with your wishes and your opinions.

Giangiacomo Feltrinelli

P.S. Please send your reply to Olga. Mr. Schewe will come to collect it in a week's time.

The two enclosures for signature were a letter of clarification regarding the rights to *Doctor Zhivago* and a letter of attorney for the film rights. There was talk of two projects for a film version of the novel, but neither Feltrinelli nor Proyart had power of attorney. In this instance, too, Feltrinelli had to call on his lawyers to nip the film plans in the bud. Without clear instructions, the copyright could not be defended for long. But Pasternak did not sign.

For the first time, Feltrinelli had to face the issue of relations with Paris. He must have pondered for a long time the reasons for Pasternak's recent decisions regarding Proyart: what were they up to? Why name a new agent? Feltrinelli thought that Pasternak probably had faith in Proyart, and in her attorney husband. He could communicate with them at no risk, and then she spoke to the poet as an expert in Slavic studies, consulting him on the philological aspects of the various translations, and so, of course, she was good for the "need for taste, for rigorous selection, and critical competence." But was this enough to subvert an excellent relationship between publisher and author?

As the correspondence reveals, it is hard to believe that Pasternak was dissatisfied with the management of his contracts. Not even from a financial point of view. He knew that his earnings were in the West and that it would be difficult to dispose of them at that time. Publishers from all over the world were paying his royalties into a Swiss bank. *Doctor Zhivago* was by right an "Italian" book, but one whose contract could be neither revealed nor officially registered in Italy: it would have been proof to the Soviets that Pasternak had made a deal directly with a foreign publisher. For this reason, Feltrinelli required foreign publishers to pay royalties directly into the Swiss account, while he did the same for the author's share of Italian sales.

In the meantime, Schewe had become the most reliable middleman for cash consignments to Moscow, the receipts for which were initialed by Pasternak or Olga. Their principal source of income derived from the rubles secretly purchased in some north European port.

But to return to Madame de Proyart. While she had a sincere concern for anything that might help Pasternak, her behavior betrayed signs of an overweening ambition. She thought she could do a job about which she knew nothing, and do it better than anyone else. By superimposing herself over Feltrinelli in the management of the rights to the *Autobiography*, she caused bewilderment among Pasternak's publishers. Her activity also concealed some obscure points, such as the role she played in the matter of the pirated Russian-language edition distributed at the Vatican stand at the Brussels Expo. This edition was subsequently adopted by the University of Michigan Press, complete with numerous typos that Pasternak was to complain about to the Italians.

It is worth remembering that Proyart had not forwarded to Feltrinelli the letter Pasternak had sent a year before, the letter containing the reference to the edition published by Mouton. Both parties were unaware of Proyart's failure to deliver the letter. Feltrinelli had to bend over backward to establish, at the last minute, his copyright on an illegal and certainly flawed edition; Pasternak in his turn thought that Feltrinelli had not followed his instructions for the Russian-language edition of the book. On the strength of the author's trust, Proyart had played things her way and, as the Italians strongly suspected, perhaps on behalf of others.

In mid-February of 1959, relations with Proyart suddenly worsened: alarmed publishers called in from all over the world. Five days after his last letter, Feltrinelli again wrote to Pasternak.

Milan, 21 February 1959

Dear Friend,
The more I think of the situation that has been created following Mme de Proyart's activities, the more I am filled with consternation. Today's telephone call from Kurt Wolff in New York—amazed and indignant about what has happened as a consequence of the power of attorney you have conferred upon Mme de Proyart—has persuaded me of the necessity to appeal directly to you requesting you to revoke immediately all powers vested in Mme de Proyart by sign-

ing enclosure no. 1 and adding the title of the *Autobiography* in your own hand. All must be signed in the presence of Ruge or Schewe, who must be asked to countersign the above-mentioned documents (without forgetting the date).

Dear friend, I imagine that, by conferring the mandate upon Mme de Proyart, you meant to do only good, but in all honesty allow me to say that the gesture has had some highly negative effects.

I would advise you not to take similar initiatives in the future. If you wish me to pay Mme de Proyart money, specify the amount, and I shall do so.

You have attained a position of universal esteem, and now much caution is required both in business matters and in making statements to the press.

In my opinion, you can have faith in two people, Ruge and Schewe, and if one day they should no longer be in Moscow, I will always find a way of establishing contact with you. In case of emergency, have someone you trust take a letter addressed to me to the Italian Embassy: it will reach me in a few days.

Dear friend, forgive my frankness. Let me know what you need. Make no statements to the press regarding your next books. If you are writing, write. Then, we shall see.

If only I could come to Moscow, I would embrace you, and chat with you and explain so many things to you. I feel that someday this will be possible.

Giangiacomo Feltrinelli

The correspondence between author and publisher was getting in a tangle, above all because of the unpredictable amount of time required for transmission and delivery. The letters for Pasternak were sent to Schewe's office in Germany and from there, through a diplomatic pouch, to him in Moscow. Finally, Schewe would take them to Olga.

In early April, when Pasternak rewrote the letter of 2 February (the one that had remained in Paris), it seemed as if he had not yet received the letters sent by Feltrinelli on 16 and 21 February.

Dear, great, and noble friend,
The despondency that has accompanied me of late has now been compounded by the great sorrow caused me by the suspicion that

my letter of January, addressed to your good mother, the admirable
and marvelous Giannalisa Feltrinelli, has gone astray and cannot
now be found. [...] I shall merely repeat my warmest thanks, expressed in the vanished letter to your good mother, for the honor
she generously desired to make me with her felicitations of last fall;
also, I shall express my gratitude to you, Sir, for your long and sweet
letter in two languages (half in French, half in English), for your
generosity, for the sentiments you have nurtured for me, and for all
you have suffered on my account [...]. You are well aware that I am
hindered in my affairs to the point of paralysis, that I can neither
take any decision concerning them nor keep up a correspondence,
that my hands are tied in my attending to my affairs from a distance
and even in my taking an interest in them. Under these circumstances, you have acted with supernatural infallibility, like some di-
vinity of fate. I have no reproaches to make you except for the fact
of your having spoiled me and dazzled me with your splendid, inexhaustible successes. If I may be granted the right to dream or
hope of surviving, I would like to imagine a completely different period, two or three years hence, calmer, more joyful and tolerant, in
which I should be able to forget *Doctor Zhivago,* supplanted and put
to flight by three new works, regarding which I should deal first
with you through a completely free and licit exchange of letters, or
better still, by meeting you in the flesh during my trips to Europe.

I have decided to write 1) a theatrical piece in prose about the
serfs on the eve of their liberation; 2) a poem on the theme of love
and freedom, personified by some Serbian female figure (instinc-
tive appetites, a lover of independence, the mountains, the sea, the
world of the Adriatic, with a hint of the style of Mérimée); 3) a novel
on the way the ancient and the contemporary world are inter-
woven, set in the early days of our era somewhere in the Iberian
Peninsula and in some imaginary excavations in the Caucasus.
(You could encourage and give your blessing to the venture by
sending me material, books on points 2 and 3, so that I may know
more about the Yugoslav situation and on the topic of archaeological digs—life, events, documents, interesting and dramatic ideas,
and by passing on to Fischer and Collins the same request for published sources.)

In the meantime, the singularity of the current situation has created, alongside my relations with you, other relations, which are in
no way deleterious to your rights or your interests, or to my esteem
for you, but which are nonetheless just as important and respectable.

Your fine Russian-language edition of the novel abounds with errata, of which a considerable part probably could have been avoided if the text had been edited by Mme de Proyart, who knows the work well, not only because as a Slavic scholar she had a hand in the French translation of the work, but also because she still has in her possession manuscripts revised and corrected personally by me.

It is an entirely natural consequence of our meetings if Madame, who is now familiar with the projects I have discussed with her and the written texts I have entrusted to her, has taken on this burdensome responsibility and has gradually become my ever more exclusive and plenipotentiary agent. In all this there is no trace of offensive preference to the detriment of any other friend of mine, or of discontent or disapproval in anyone's regard. I wish that during this lengthy period in which it has been impossible for me to act, exercise an influence over things, choose, keep up a correspondence, enjoy the fruits of your business activity and my ideas; during this period in which not only am I unable to know the results of all these things but am even unable to want to know about them, I want your two functions, yours and that of Madame, to be clearly and efficaciously separated. I want you to continue to profit from your contract regarding the novel in translation (which is doubly advantageous for me, in both a moral and a material sense), and to profit from all new agreements you intend to make with the consent and approval of Mme de Proyart.

I want you to see Madame as my stand-in, I want her to act in my stead as regards your accounting needs, for decisions regarding the allocation of funds or consultations about new ventures. Because for the time being (which is destined to last for a long time to come) I do not exist, either for her or for you; you must forget that there was a man with this name, you must delete it from your memory.

These were my intentions when I wrote you the letter enclosed herein. I enclose it, recopied word for word in my own hand, along with the letter I am about to write and send to Mme de Proyart. Believe in my devoted gratitude. I owe you so much! All might have gone differently, were I not deprived of the most elementary liberties.

B. Pasternak

P.S. (very important) In the letter addressed to you that went astray there was a list of sums and of persons to whom I wanted to send said sums as a gift (including ten thousand dollars to Sergio D'Angelo,

ten thousand that I now correct to fifteen thousand, to Gerd Ruge,
etc., etc.). Fortunately a copy of this list reached Madame de Proyart
and is now in her hands. Do not hinder and do not delay these dis-
positions, dear sir. I wish the donations to the various persons mentioned to be made as soon as possible. Mr. S. D'Angelo has offered
me material assistance in the extreme event of my finding myself at
my wits' end. Perhaps I shall be obliged to take advantage of his
offer, but he shall have to consult Mme de Proyart about this, in accordance with the certification herein enclosed, without troubling
you with this problem.

B. P.

Enclosed with the letter was the following statement, dated 4
April 1959:

I have the honor of confirming, dear sir, that I have assigned to Mme
Jacqueline de Proyart de Baillescourt full control over the management of all my royalties and likewise control over the cash transfers
I shall request of you. In my absence, please be so good as to account
to Mme de Proyart for all my royalties, including those of the novel.
I confer upon Mme de Proyart—or upon whosoever she may wish to
designate in the event of her decease—freedom of disposition.

B. Pasternak

Feltrinelli must have feared the worst on reading these instructions. He did not understand Pasternak's behavior. If only they
could meet in person!

Pasternak no longer wanted to know about contracts; and the
idea of creating an alter ego to whom everything might be delegated, while it could not stand up in practice, was an expedient
through which he thought to simplify his life. Mme de Proyart's
hyperprotective ambition completes the picture: while she saw
things differently from Feltrinelli, and she certainly did not understand him, she was nonetheless the poet's confidante.

In the summer of 1959, Feltrinelli had to come to terms with her.
He made a virtue of necessity.

The parties met in Milan on 21 July, and Feltrinelli sent off a report to Schewe, who was in constant touch with Pasternak. Under pressure from Proyart, a "theoretical" agreement was reached regarding the Russian edition of *Doctor Zhivago*. It was also agreed that she would take over the international contracts for the *Autobiography*. Proyart produced the list of the gifts of money enclosed with the famous letter that was never delivered. Feltrinelli ordered the bank to pay out the $120,000 for the persons named by Pasternak, but temporized over the delivery of the contracts. The publishing houses of half the world, led by Kurt Wolff, were worried about an eventual changing of the guard in the management of Pasternak's affairs. Feltrinelli played for time. "I am still awaiting a signal from our mutual friend," he wrote to Schewe. "Mr. Pasternak begs you to have a little patience. He will reply to you soon. Do not lose patience and do not doubt him," replied Schewe at the end of July.

I met Schewe in July 1994. He was a seventy-two-year-old who had aged well. We met in Vienna, where he lives. To judge by his appearance, one would take him for a clerk. But he spent a lifetime as a correspondent in some of the world's greatest capitals: London, Moscow, Jerusalem. He could be described as a down-to-earth journalist of the old school, a cold war veteran. He must have practised his profession with a profound dedication to his newspaper. Now, in retirement, with five years of economic survival left, as he put it, he led a solitary, secluded life. When I visited him, I didn't have the courage to ask if he had a family, a wife, friends.

Schewe did not hide his nostalgia for the period in his life that began in April 1958, when the publisher Axel Springer sent him to the Soviet Union as a correspondent for *Die Welt*. "If I played a part in the Pasternak affair, it was thanks only to Feltrinelli, who needed a safe contact in Moscow, and Springer gave my name to Inge, Feltrinelli's wife."

Olga Ivinskaya describes him with affection in her autobiography, speaking of him as a "trusted and devoted" friend, able to ease tensions even when the temperature was rising fast, and Schewe, for all those years, remained very attached to Olga and her daughter, Irina. Of Feltrinelli he says: "He was all I wanted to be and was not." He recalls the encounters with Pasternak in Olga's house, over the hill, where the poet would arrive from the wood: "It's as if I can see him now. He would come toward us almost at a run, until he was breathless, and he would embrace us and he would be the only one to talk (with me, he spoke splendid German with a Marburg accent), and he would tell us all he had seen, heard, or received."

I got straight to the point and asked Schewe about 1959: what was going through Pasternak's mind? And the Feltrinelli–Proyart dispute? "The atmosphere surrounding Pasternak and his family became explosive after the Nobel. Conditions became incredibly harsh when he was deprived of any chance of earning a living. To say nothing of the press campaigns, police surveillance, and continual fear of making a mistake." The situation was made worse by the poet's naïveté: "He was a real child, incapable of disappointing or saying no to all those who, perhaps even in good faith, attempted to climb aboard the *Zhivago* bandwagon....Olga had to protect him all the time."

The journalist had a clear recollection of the approaching turbulence among Feltrinelli, Proyart, and Sergio D'Angelo. Pasternak suffered on this account: "He was a generous man, not greedy at all. In his good moments, when he was not afflicted by depression, he used to joke about the money he had outside the Soviet Union and, like a real Russian aristocrat, he liked to make gifts, always with the impulsiveness of a young boy."

And the rubles smuggled into Soviet territory, what did Schewe remember about that?

I took in sums on Feltrinelli's behalf, seven or eight times, for a total of about a hundred thousand rubles. Obviously this involved the risk of arrest and heaven knows what else, even though I sometimes had the impression that my guardian angels let me get on with it, considering that, out of caution, I never took in sums that were too large at any one time.... I think that Ruge also made cash deliveries in Feltrinelli's name.

At a certain point, Pasternak and Ivinskaya thought of getting Irina out of harm's way by having her marry a Westerner, thus guaranteeing her the right to leave the country. Irina could have married Schewe himself; but, although she was fond of him, she would not hear of it.

"It is a great sorrow for me that F. and J. P. have not found any common ground," wrote Pasternak to his French friend Hélène Peltier on 21 July 1959. The total power of attorney conferred upon Proyart failed to remove the burden of the management of his works from the poet's shoulders. For his part, Feltrinelli felt he had been punished for no reason. "I am for all of his projects, I would never refuse him anything," Pasternak confided to Peltier. But now signing the documents sent from Milan in early spring (he had finally received them) meant annulling the prerogatives granted to Proyart.

Olga gave the impression that she was on Feltrinelli's side. Schewe quotes one of her comments: "Giangiacomo's arguments express what I have been thinking and saying for goodness knows how long."

The situation was distracting the poet from what really mattered to him, his writing. Finally, he wrote to my father and also to Proyart. From then on, Feltrinelli and Pasternak carried on their correspondence in German.

Early August 1959

Dear friend,

Contrary to my habit of writing to you in French, this time I am writing in German, because this missive will be read by our mutual German friend, who in this way will be better able to judge the clarity of

my text, together with the sense and the usefulness of my decisions.
My friend, I owe you and Mme de Proyart exactly the same apology.
The confusion I have created around you and between you is an insult to Madame as it is to you. Of all this I am guilty, both with regard to Madame and to you. I have no need to give you new proof of
my unlimited faith, of my esteem and admiration. Today more than
ever, I am prepared to repeat: granted that I am in some way the
one who wrote the novel, you are and remain the sole creator of its
pilgrimage around the world, of its destiny and of its success. Must
I perhaps again add how great and spontaneous my enthusiasm
and gratitude for all this must be and is? I have no wish to deny the
fact that I received your letter and the contract almost a month past.
Forgive me for the delay, with which I have probably caused you
profound vexation. Forgive, too, the sincerity with which I now
make my confession to you with open heart. I have put off terribly
reading your mail because I expected that it would cause me worries
far greater than those I effectively encountered on leafing through
it today—but at the same time, roughly a month ago, I finally got
started on a work that seemed about to see the light—and I dared
not run the risk of putting to flight with gloomy thoughts the work
that had barely begun, before it had firmly rooted itself in my existence. I want to outline this letter right away. It will not be possible
to exhaust all the arguments here. I have an hour left in which to
finish it and in which to dash off a few lines to Madame de Pr. My
efforts of today must therefore be aimed solely at ensuring that we
may both rest easy in spirit once more.

That you are not just a business genius but have also shown
yourself to be a gentleman whose feelings for me are cordial and
disinterested is also known to Mme de Proyart, who will never deny
this. When, two years ago, I began to confer full powers upon
Madame, I did not mean by that to limit my trust in you. You certainly cannot have thought such a thing! But which of us could have
imagined then that the world would have shown such great interest
in us? Would it not have been ridiculous presumption on my part
if I, at that time, had burdened you not only with the contract for
the novel but also with an infinity of other commitments? It was
not possible to foresee so much success (from a commercial standpoint, not from that of my secret amour propre. This is why I delegated Mme de Proyart to take care of the *Autobiography,* of the novel
in Russian, and the poems, etc.—an additional task to be seen as

complementary to my relations with you, and not as my imposing a
limit or a barrier upon you.

What follows is addressed partly to you and partly to Mme de Pr.
You will understand the reason for this at the end.

I have reread Feltrinelli's letter. I was wrong. He is not threatening
anyone with anything. It is my duty to defend him. He did not resort
to such low methods. But he is right. I have confused the issue beyond measure and I stand guilty before him and above all before
you. Forgive me, therefore, both of you.

What are my wishes? (The same as ever, but for brevity's sake I
will not talk of the past and shall limit myself to the present and the
future.) I want the marketing of my present and future works to
enjoy success abroad without let or hindrance, in all editions, original and translated texts, adaptations for cinema and radio, etc., etc.,
and I want this marketing operation to be set up, managed, directed,
and supervised by Mr. Giangiacomo Feltrinelli of Milan, my principal publisher. For this reason, therefore, I agree to all the ideas and
proposals made by him and drawn up in contractual form, despite
the fact that I am legally unable to sign contracts, this being one of
the many states of necessity in view of which I delegated Mme de
Proyart to be so kind as to act in my stead with her authority, her
advice, her reputation, and her signature. In standing in for me, in
my eyes she has become a person who has the same unconditional
faith in Mr. Feltrinelli as I do, a sort of moral support for his ventures, always so remarkable and fortunate.

How did I see Mme de Proyart's role as my substitute? I thought
that if Mr. Feltrinelli had had need of my opinion (of a consenting
opinion, not a veto), he could have asked Mme de P. If he (not I)
found it useful to make me an annual statement of accounts, he
could have turned to Mme de Proyart, without even telling me
about it, given that at present all these issues are for me impossible,
inaccessible, and indifferent. Finally, if Mr. Feltrinelli (he not I)
wished to make deductions or payments in my favor (I have need of
them), he ought to consider Mme de Proyart as the proprietress,
without even informing me. May Madame forgive me for having reduced her responsibilities so much and for the informal way I asked
her to act in my stead, but it is a question of being Pasternak for Feltrinelli, in the rare cases in which he may have need of me, the way

one needs another person when one's own person is no longer enough.

My wish is that Mme de Proyart, with her goodness and her friendship for me, and Mr. Feltrinelli, with the strength of his experience, savoir faire, talent for inspired and fortunate ventures, and generosity, will constitute the two poles of this bifurcated plenipotentiary mandate, or, should this be impossible, to kindly come up with some other system of power of attorney and regulation, geared to the state of powerlessness in which I find myself, which both must understand and which must inevitably be respected. [...]

Be so good as to copy all this part written in French for Mme de Proyart, and send it to her at rue Fresnel, Paris XVI. I wanted to do this myself, but the need for haste is such that I do not want the letter to arrive late. One more thing. Nothing is needed here. Mr. D'Angelo's suggestion that he might help me was made during an acute crisis, which now seems to have passed. I can promise you nothing regular, nothing statutory. I trust you more than I trust my conscience and my memory. Nothing is recorded, and you will see no receipts. If money arrives, it is used up and only the gratitude that derives from it is not forgotten and grows. All the rest slips my memory. But do not even think of transferring everything here, it would be folly. Mme de Proyart is there to help you with this. Accept, I pray you, my feelings of deepest admiration, gratitude, devotion, and friendship.

Yours, B. P.

I am sending this without even rereading it.

This letter represents a final attempt to settle a dispute that so far had resisted resolution. Feltrinelli, relieved by this reconfirmation of Pasternak's faith in him, was convinced he had the problem solved. He took a plane for Paris but was rebuffed at Proyarts' home in rue Fresnel.

Milan, 25 October 1959

Dear, most esteemed friend and master,
I certainly take no pleasure in thinking back on those recent days and on the unfortunately fruitless talks in Paris! Mainly because I have the feeling that all these complications deeply disturb and irritate you, and also because it seems to me that for the first time I have not managed to carry out a task entrusted to me by you. In any

case, please forgive me if today—something I shall do again next week—I write to you on matters that I am the first to admit are rather distressing.

I have shown Mr. Pr. the letter you addressed to me (of which I have sent you another photocopy), and I have done all I could to make possible the union you hoped for. I even committed myself in accordance with the wishes of Pr., to ensure that a) Mme de Proyart will have the right of veto over all ventures and negotiations regarding the performing rights (cinema, television, etc.) to *Doctor Zhivago* and that b) I shall, naturally, provide Mme de Proyart regularly with financial statements.

In exchange for this, I requested: a) a contract for the Russian-language edition of *Doctor Zhivago* (in accordance with our epistolary agreements); b) a contract regarding the subsidiary rights to *Doctor Zhivago* (with the above-mentioned limitations); c) a contract (in conformity with the contract already drawn up for *Doctor Zhivago*) for the *Autobiography*; d) a formal option for the marketing of your future works.

All this was opposed due to lack of time in which to check out the documents, the absence (for the first week) of Mme de Proyart, and continual objections to the limitations of the powers of attorney mentioned in your letter, to the point that I began to feel certain that the Proyarts did not want any agreement, until such time as they might try to trick you into contradicting what you have told me in your letters. At that point I broke off the talks.

This, unfortunately, is how things stand: there are two ways of viewing your power of attorney—your interpretation, expressed very clearly in the letter you sent to me, and that of Proyart.

Proyart's interpretation differs from yours not only in terms of the role and responsibilities held by the Proyarts or by me concerning all publishing matters, but also in terms of the fact that the Proyarts believe themselves to be, as I see it, not only your representatives but also the "proprietors" of all the rights. And in their capacity as "proprietors" they deal with me with an eye to their own interests, respecting your will solely when your will coincides with that. *Please read the note at the end of the letter right away.** This state of affairs proves that the *pouvoir bifurqué* you hoped for does not and cannot work! The task you entrusted me with, to see to the marketing of your works in the West and to defend them from the attacks of speculators and pirates, has been made impossible, or at least arduous, now and in future, by the power of attorney you vested in the

Proyarts. Impossible, because the Proyarts refuse to make available the contractual documents you prepared–arduous, because they understand nothing about publishing and the related legal problems (to become an attorney in the publishing field requires years of highly specialized training, of which Mr. de Proyart has none).

If I am to continue acting as principal publisher, we need to find a completely different solution. I have talked at length about this with my attorney, Mr. Tesone, dwelling in particular on your problems of security, on your wish to publish and market your works without let or hindrance all over the world, and on how we can respect our commitments to you in this regard. We have come up with certain ways and means that demand determined decisions on your part–but I shall go into all this in more detail in my next letter, on the basis of documents (which are being prepared).

And now let's talk of other things!

Did you receive the books? Do the overcoat and pullover fit? What do you think of *The Leopard* and Durrell's book? Your ideas and opinions interest me very much indeed. Can you read Italian?

I would so much like to introduce you to the work of one of our young Italian writers. At present there are no translations of Testori, and I also fear that the best parts would be lost in translation.

What is new and important today in Russian literature? Could you let me know something about this? There is a possibility that I may come to Moscow with an Italian state delegation, within the ambit of cultural exchange agreements due to be endorsed by Italy and the USSR in the near future. I have already taken the first steps in this direction. Do you think that, once I get to Moscow, I may come to visit you, or will you be obliged at that very moment to accept an invitation to the Caucasus? Forgive me for the lengthy letter, but it was really necessary to say everything! Do not deny me your friendship. Yours sincerely,

                                        Giangiacomo Feltrinelli

*The Proyarts' attitude toward me is not the work of Mme de Proyart but only of her husband, who, being an attorney, is well aware where his interests lie. Mme de Proyart does not have so much as a smattering of legal knowledge, and has to submit all negotiations and legal interpretations to her husband. That she is not wholly in agreement with her husband emerges from the following example: recently she showed me one of your letters that her husband had forbidden her to show me!

That year, Schewe had taken his vacation when the summer was already almost over, and he did not return to his job in Moscow until mid-October. He delivered a few presents to Olga, who in turn alerted him to the fact that a letter Irina had sent to him, when he was on vacation, was intercepted by the Soviet authorities. Two tough-looking men had visited Olga, leaving her in no doubt that Irina would do well to stay away from him.

That Schewe was under surveillance was beyond doubt. All foreign correspondents were; and he, in his improbable guise as a secret agent, had to keep a low profile and not expose himself to excessive risks or make any overly bold moves.

Schewe made haste to get in touch with Pasternak, and on Sunday, 24 October, thanks to Olga's good offices, he obtained a meeting at the house in Peredelkino. They talked for a good three hours. "I don't understand why my friends cannot reach an agreement, surely there must be a way," he said, going straight to the point. "I am too poorly versed in contractual matters."

"The whole story," Schewe wrote to Feltrinelli, "is causing him enormous grief and is undermining his ability to concentrate on his work."

The work consisted of a few translations from which he would have earned a little income. When Pasternak mentioned the play he was thinking of writing, he struck Schewe once more as "a man full of strength and hope." "Even though here in Russia it will go the way of *Doctor Zhivago*," he heard Pasternak say, "they will hang on to the manuscript for an eternity, checking it over and over again, and in the end nothing will come of it."

As far as possible trips abroad were concerned (there were rumors of a visa for Belgrade or Warsaw), Pasternak would hear none of it, and Schewe advised Feltrinelli to forget any thoughts of adventurous encounters.

As far as Schewe was concerned, that Sunday in Peredelkino, with

the sound of fresh snow crunching underfoot, the important thing
was Olga's determined stance in favor of Feltrinelli: "She is one
hundred percent on our side, and is exerting all her influence over
P." Olga confided to Schewe that they were receiving a continuous
flow of correspondence from France, drafts of documents, letters of
intent for signature, and also a copy of the Gallimard edition of *Doctor Zhivago,* complete with a dedication written by Mme de Proyart.
All this *Papierkrieg* once more caused Pasternak to lose heart, and
on Olga's advice he imposed a four-week period of silence: there-
after, he did not reply to any further correspondence from Paris.

The time had come to make the right move and to take a chance:
Feltrinelli wanted to clear things up, even at the cost of pushing
Pasternak, and he sent off a new and definitive contract for signature. "It is my last-ditch attempt to come to an agreement and spare
Pasternak having to choose between Madame Pr. and me," he
wrote to Schewe. "Since 1956 I have borne all the responsibilities
and all the consequences, positive or negative alike. He cannot turn
his back on me now."

The text of the document drawn up by Tesone followed that of
1956, and, with a view to preserving the continuity of the original
contract, the new one was back dated. The new addition, compared to the initial contract, concerned the film rights and a commitment regarding the author's future works. The remainder is
made very clear in the accompanying letter.

Milan, 13 November 1959

Dear and most esteemed Boris Pasternak,
Doubtless you have no desire to deal at length with the Proyart-
Feltrinelli dispute. And that is why I shall address the matter very
briefly in this letter. I am enclosing a draft contract, which I pray
you to sign, for the following reasons:

1. This is a contract to all intents and purposes complementary to
   the one signed by us in 1956. We have added some riders as per
   the instructions contained in your last letter dated August 1959.

2. The contract is to be seen within the purview of the power of attorney you conferred upon Mme de Proyart. Do not gainsay that power of attorney!

3. This contract will certainly be recognized by Madame Pr. (Unfortunately, your August letter was not deemed an authoritative statement of will, a fact that has caused the distressing present situation, which makes it necessary for you to intervene on all counts once again.)

4. This contract will prevent all further future misunderstandings with Madame Pr.

5. This contract does not mean choosing between Madame de Proyart and me (a choice that has struck me at times as inevitable!). It involves no injustice or indelicacy in anyone's regard.

6. This contract integrates Madame de Proyart's power of attorney as far as the film rights are concerned. These rights are not included in her power of attorney. In order to make a film, today or in twenty years' time, a contract must be signed by you—this contract.

7. I pledge NEVER to make this contract public, even in the event of legal disputes. The advantageous aspect of this contract lies in the fact that it enables out-of-court settlements for legal disputes that would normally require a lawsuit. Without this contract, in my capacity as representative of your interests, or with a view to defending your interests, I would inevitably have to appear before a court, or drag others into court. A public suit aimed at challenging the power of attorney (which is less common in private bargaining) would put you in great difficulty. You might withdraw the power of attorney. If you do not do this, you will always be, as far as your government is concerned, fully responsible for every move made by the holder of that same power of attorney!!!

8. I would be very glad if I have managed to give you a clear picture of the situation and if I have persuaded you of the advantageous aspects of this contract and of the need to sign it. Otherwise I would be greatly saddened. I will not bore you now with thousands of explanations. Warmest good wishes,

Yours, Giangiacomo Feltrinelli

This enervating and staccato correspondence was made more complex by the arrival of a new letter from Pasternak, who had not received the last two from Italy. This letter has been lost (it was not in the safe), but it must have brought good news: Feltrinelli was extremely happy about it. He took pen and paper to write a reply, perhaps a little on the sentimental side.

Milan, 19. 11. 59

My dear Boris Pasternak,
You cannot imagine how much joy your latest letter has given me! (It crossed mine in the mail.)

I was glad to hear about you and your work, even though unfortunately the underlying tone of your letter was extremely sad and depressed. It gave me enormous pleasure to learn that you are once more concentrating on a great work and that in future you will no longer have to do translations. Naturally I will send you regular "deliveries" through our friend H. But may I advise you, for reasons of diplomacy, not to neglect translations altogether?

I am waiting most anxiously for *Blind Beauty*; the title is splendid. But it would be better if not too many people knew about it at present, otherwise it might cause an enormous song and dance and disagreeable publicity for all of us, don't you think?

The reference to the "humiliating concessions" you have made distressed me greatly. I am proud of you and full of admiration, for the faith you have in yourself, without lowering yourself to any compromise.

If only things here in the West could be organized in such a way that you would have no further reason for sadness, or any need to worry about all these matters!

Unfortunately, my Christmas presents will not arrive until after the festivities, since our friend H. returns to M. only in early January. Please give him a list of ALL the books you are interested in. Wishing you all the very best, your most devoted

Giangiacomo Feltrinelli

On 5 November 1959, Schewe sent to Milan a close-up of Pasternak, taken at Peredelkino on Sunday 25 October. He thus fulfilled a promise. In exchange, Feltrinelli sent off a photo of himself and Inge for the poet. On that same Sunday at Peredelkino, photos were also taken of Olga and her daughter, but the two women thought they had not come out all that well. They decided to take other photos on the next occasion.

In the meantime, Olga had let slip important secrets that Schewe reported, within quotation marks, in his correspondence with Feltrinelli. Pasternak feared that the clash between Feltrinelli and the Proyarts might lead to a trial and a public scandal. In the Soviet Union, his position was still perilous, the atmosphere surrounding him was only slightly easier, and his public exposure threatened to spark a new crackdown, perhaps a definitive one. Feltrinelli's reassuring letter of 23 November was not long in arriving, via Schewe: "Under no circumstances shall I allow it to come to a trial between Mme de Pr. and me."

Another secret was even more serious: "The Grand Old Man [Schewe's and Ivinskaya's nickname for Pasternak] feels that he is getting old." "He is often tired. He would like not to feel forever under the knout, always working on new translations to earn a few rubles. He would prefer to concentrate entirely on his play. But he could do so only if he were completely self-sufficient."

Schewe noted:

> The Grand Old Man has recently received various proposals from people who have offered him large sums in dollars, deriving from the income from *Zhivago*. They have promised to convert these sums into rubles and make them available to him in Peredelkino one way or another. Olga had her say in the matter: "I think it would be better if everything were to remain exclusively in Giangiacomo's hands. We can trust him. We are afraid of involving other people in this business. In any case, they all want a share of the money!"

These words were transcribed for Feltrinelli and sent off, together with the photograph of the Grand Old Man, on 5 November 1959.

In early 1959, D'Angelo began writing to Pasternak, offering to help him gain immediate access to his money. He maintained that he could bring the money into the Soviet Union without any risk. In September he had written to Olga telling her of a meeting he had in Paris with Jacqueline de Proyart, who suggested that he take the money directly to Pasternak. D'Angelo advised Olga to ask for $100,000, for any eventuality.

Looking back, it is not easy to judge what happened. Fundamentally, it was a matter of helping an important friend who had been reduced to living on a subsistence level. Nevertheless, and such is the way of the world, some people in Italy blamed Feltrinelli and Feltrinelli alone for the consequences.

That November, despite the fact that Feltrinelli had sent off a few more "sandwiches" (the word he and Schewe used to refer to the consignments in rubles), and despite other "sandwiches" that were sent off immediately afterward, Pasternak decided to accept D'Angelo's proposal. "Thanks to his inner strength," comments Schewe today,

> Pasternak had always thought he could live for three hundred years, tolerating with ill grace birthdays, bunches of flowers, and anything else that might remind him of the passing of time. Perhaps that very winter, as he neared seventy years of age, after all the emotions, he realized he was coming to the end of his life. Such a sensitive man could hardly have failed to notice that his strength was ebbing. And so, living as he was in conditions of terrible hardship, and knowing that he could draw on a great deal of money held abroad, he must have thought, "Let's have it here, as much of it as possible, now, right away..." This would have been tricky under normal circumstances, let alone at such a particular moment.

> Peredelkino, by Moscow
> 6 December 1959
> I hereby delegate the undersigned, Mr. Sergio D'Angelo to withdraw one hundred thousand dollars ($100,000) of my royalties for the uses and purposes he shall communicate and explain to two other persons in whom I trust, Mme Jacqueline de Proyart and Mr. Giangiacomo Feltrinelli.
> B. Pasternak

At the same time, the poet sent a request for ten thousand dollars to be paid to D'Angelo, perhaps as a sort of commission for the hundred-thousand-dollar operation. In the space of three months, Feltrinelli transferred both sums to D'Angelo.

It may be useful here to attempt a purely economic balance with regard to *Doctor Zhivago*, up to the point of Pasternak's death. If we add the cash gifts requested by the author in his letter of 2 February 1959 to the more recent payment made through D'Angelo, we get $235,000. To this we need to add an unspecified sum for the purchase of rubles to be transferred to Moscow. Considering that the initial sales of the rights for Germany, Great Britain, and the United States ought to have brought in $150,000 for publisher and author alike, it can be presumed that a good part of the rights income for the years 1957 and 1958 had been distributed while Pasternak was still alive. Unfortunately, the author of the most adventurous and unexpected of best-sellers, at a time when best-sellers really were best-sellers, was able to enjoy only a laughably small part of those profits.

Christmas 1959, as is only right, seemed to have brought a truce, at least in the correspondence between Pasternak and his publisher. The poet received an average of more than thirty letters a day from all over the world, distracting him from his theatrical work. He felt it his duty to reply. Moreover, letters full of concern were arriving from Paris: the Proyarts had probably sensed the danger in a new agreement between the author and Feltrinelli.

To sign or not to sign now became the real problem for Pasternak. On the one hand, his signature would have definitively cleared up a matter that had been troubling him for too long, a matter he wanted to be rid of; on the other hand, two further problems might arise. The first again concerned Mme de Proyart. There was a risk of dispute arising over the management of the mandate in the period in which she had acted as his agent. The

second fear was indeed a source of great anxiety: if the new contract was binding for the author in future too, then there might be
a repetition of what happened with *Doctor Zhivago*. For example,
if the play *Blind Beauty* were published, the Soviet authorities might
consider the fact a deliberate repetition of Pasternak's intention to
deal directly with a foreign publisher. And this would mean a new
scandal. For the Soviets knew that a contract was lying on Pasternak's desk. How they knew remains a mystery.

On his return to Moscow (with his "sandwiches") after the end-
of-year vacation, Schewe wrote to Feltrinelli, begging him to use
all precaution in the exchange of letters and advising him, for
the future, to set up "safe" meetings in some European city. "In the
corridors of power, and this is certain, they know that I am the
middleman," he informed him.

Pasternak and Olga too were nervous: "They believe that they
are under surveillance and even that there are microphones in the
walls."

Between the end of January and the beginning of February,
many meetings took place at Peredelkino with Schewe, and, despite everything, there were moments of great serenity. The poet's
reassurances, which Schewe later sent on by letter to Feltrinelli,
were clear. Feltrinelli was not to worry, Pasternak's faith in his
publisher was undimmed; now it was his turn to propose a way of
clearing matters up and, without a doubt, Feltrinelli could count
on *Blind Beauty*.

But was he doing the right thing in signing the contract? Wasn't
it too great a risk?

Pasternak signed it, but then he decided to wait and think it over.
On 20 January 1960, he wrote that he was tired of the situation.

20 January 1960

Dear friend,
I have come to know of your new plans regarding the extension of
my rights, the placing of the management of my literary affairs

more firmly in your hands, and of the complete assignment of all
that I have written and will write in the future. I agree. I was ready
to sign the contract. I had even signed it when I suddenly noticed a
problem. I am fully in agreement with your idea of backdating the
contract and of drawing it up in the form of a rider. I have no need
of your reassurances, I know perfectly well that you would never
abuse this simulation for the sake of form. But is it possible that
someday, without your knowledge and against your will, this backdating may lead to embarrassing consequences for a number of
persons—Mme de Proyart first and foremost—because of a series of
documents from the period between the backdating and the present
time? Allow me to quote some passages from your letter.

2. The contract is to be seen within the purview of the power of
   attorney you conferred upon Mme de Proyart. Do not gainsay
   that power of attorney!
3. This contract will certainly be recognized by Madame Pr.
   (Unfortunately your August letter was not deemed an authoritative statement of will, a fact that has caused the distressing
   present situation, which makes it necessary for you to intervene across the board once again.)
4. This contract will prevent all further future misunderstandings with Madame Pr.
5. This contract integrates Mme de Proyart's power of attorney
   as far as the film rights are concerned.

etc., etc.

You are right on many counts. But arrange things so that I come
to know all this from Madame; in other words, sort out all these old
problems in the light of this brand-new concept together with her;
guarantee her a safeguard against all possible abuses of your supplementary clauses, indemnify her if there is any compensation to
be made, royalties to be paid, or cases of nonperformance regarding
any obligation you or I may have toward her. In short, arrange
things so that in the part concerning Madame your proposals will
be acceptable to and desirable for the person who is my friend and
agent and who (as you yourself will see immediately, at the end of
this letter) is a nobly altruistic and valued ally in all circumstances.
I shall write to Madame, so that she may know that my wishes correspond to yours, namely that I am wholly in favor of the clear-cut
division of functions between the two of you and of the concentration of all ventures and of all effective powers in your hands. But do
not forget that once your new rights and your new ventures are

under way, I shall not be setting up an office in my home in which
to receive your letters containing even the slightest details of your
activities, to take decisions or to reply to you. I will not be involved
in anything. I must not be disturbed or prevented from working. But
there will always be serious cases in which you will have need of
my representative, my alter ego, who will need to be informed of
something or other or whose opinion will be required. As far as I
am concerned this alter ego can be none other than Madame, my
agent, my deputy or substitute.

I hope with all my heart that all will now proceed in accordance
with the spirit and the terms of your contract. Help me to ensure
that it may be concluded. And (pray do not be offended) free me of
the need to neglect my work and to write long letters. Yours,

B. Pasternak

In April 1960 Pasternak relieved Jacqueline de Proyart of her
mandate as proxy, with attestations of extreme gratitude. Up to that
month, *Doctor Zhivago* had sold 156,000 copies in Italy.

Schewe returned to Moscow in late spring, and only then was
Feltrinelli able to write the poet a different kind of letter, one that
no longer touched on those issues that had risked ruining their relationship. Unfortunately, it was late in the day.

Milan, 15 May 1960

Dear, most esteemed Boris Pasternak,
Unfortunately, the absence of our mutual friend H. S. these last few
months has interrupted our correspondence. Naturally I now take
the first opportunity to send you with this letter, and also directly,
through H. S., my warmest greetings. I have many things to tell you.
The new Russian edition of *Doctor Zhivago* will be ready at the end
of the summer. The text has been revised by Madame P. and it corresponds to the original manuscript, which is in Paris. I hope you
are in agreement. In conformity with the wishes expressed in your
letter (in the letter I received through D'Angelo), I have transferred
to our friend the same D'Angelo $100,000 of your royalties, and I
hope that by now you have received this sum, or at least a part of it.
In any event, let me have, through H. S., a few words of confirma-
tion. This would please me and put my mind at rest. *Doctor Zhivago*
is now selling slowly but steadily. In the fall it will come out in a
paperback edition, at the price of 700 lire (instead of 3,000 lire for

the hardback edition). We shall be printing another 30,000–50,000 copies. For some time· now, a paperback edition has been distributed in America. In Rome, a lawsuit is dragging on between two film companies and us (it is a trial concerning the *Doctor Zhivago* copyright).

Here it is spring, or rather summer. It is hot, people are thinking of vacations, at the seaside, in the mountains, or abroad. Only here in the publishing house is there fervent activity. We are already working on the forthcoming Christmas books, and in part on the spring 1961 schedule. Great literature is thin on the ground. At present in England and in the USA everyone is talking about *The Leopard* (the book I sent you at Christmas in the German edition). In France, *Le dernier des justes* (a book on the persecution of the Jews) has been a great success. Camus, the only representative of the in-between generation of whom one might have expected something, has unfortunately died in an automobile accident, as you will certainly have heard. The other great protagonists of the literary scene haven't produced anything particularly new. The young French writers of the nouvelle vague are trying to develop their school further–but they have run aground on a quasi-sterile experimental formalism, despite the fact that their early work represented a search for new ideas. Something really new–the result of a combination of the evolved classical form with a content that goes beyond the stereotyped "I love you, you love another man, and the other man loves another woman, who in her turn loves me unrequited"– is not to be found. In this, a highly negative role has been played by the French political scene, the endless colonial war in Africa, waged for years with unprecedented brutality, the internal divisions in France over the sense or the absurdity of this war, de Gaulle's taking of power, and the rejection of the democratic system (de Gaulle himself has been unable to find an "issue" in Algeria, neither peace nor war, the blackmail to which the whole of France is subjected by the army, which wants victory over the Africans and to impose its power over the metropolitan territory, all this has sundered the *élan,* the backbone of youth. The Fourth Empire is the age of compromise, of money and intellectual poverty.

In Spain, where writers have been living for twenty years under the dictatorship of Franco and the Catholic Church, perhaps the novel is entering a phase of growth. After the great disappointment of 1945 (we all hoped that the end of the war would also be the end of Franco), the Spanish are rebelling once more and have found their "outlet" (even though this is forbidden in their country) in literature. In Italy, there are two literary movements: the fundamental feature of the first is formalism, which leads to literary acrobatics, the other uses literature as the instrument of a sociological representation. Any attempt to write a novel with a hero, with ideas, with a treatment of the problems facing the individual, with a profound humanity, is rejected almost on principle.

But all this talk had made me stray from the focal point of my letter. How are you and your family? How is your health and your work? All of us are expecting so very much from you, and from your next work!!!

With my warmest and sincerest best wishes,
Giangiacomo Feltrinelli

Not even a week was to go by before Feltrinelli found himself reading a news item that rocked him. Here is his reason:

22 May 1960

My dear, most esteemed Boris Pasternak,
I had barely sent off my letter of the fifteenth, when I received, alas, a reply to my queries.

I was deeply distressed to learn from the newspaper of your illness, but my worry over your state of health was allayed somewhat by learning a few days later, again from the newspaper, that you had got over the crisis. I hope you are in good hands. Should you need a doctor from here, let me know right away, and I shall do everything to come to your aid. There is no need to add that, should you need medicines or goodness knows what else, you must let me know immediately.

Do not deny me, I beseech you, the chance to help even in this most difficult moment.

A thousand good wishes and warmest greetings.
Yours,
Giangiacomo Feltrinelli

Schewe did not manage to deliver this last letter; Pasternak was in the hospital and died on 30 May.

In a letter to Proyart, six months previously, Pasternak had expressed the wish that Feltrinelli might pay any price to keep his body out of the hands of the Soviet authorities. He wanted to be buried in Milan, where Olga would have watched over his grave. But the funeral was held in Peredelkino; the Italian publisher was persona non grata and there was no chance of a visa. Schewe went to the service. The reports of his standing silent and composed alongside the coffin strike me as plausible. To a colleague who had elbowed his way through the crowd, Schewe apparently said: "Yes, I know, I am not taking notes or photographs...but I am burying a friend.

Bombarded on all sides, Feltrinelli dictated a brief press communiqué: "The death of Pasternak is a blow as hard as losing a best friend. He was the personification of my nonconformist ideals combined with wisdom and profound culture."

Olga Ivinskaya gave the signed contract for *Doctor Zhivago* to Schewe and asked him to take it to Milan.

In 1959 Feltrinelli published translated versions of *The Rain King* by Saul Bellow, *Out of Africa* by Karen Blixen, *The King's Mother* by Kazimierz Brandys, *Aleph* by Jorge Luis Borges, *The Setting Sun* by Osamu Dazai, *The Ginger Man* by J. P. Donleavy, *The Promise* by Friedrich Dürrenmatt, *Howards End* by E. M. Forster, *Homo Faber* by Max Frisch, *The Habit of Loving* by Doris Lessing, and *Portrait of a Man Unknown* by Nathalie Sarraute.... "There was a moment in which Feltrinelli was an Italian publishing house only because its head office was in Milan. I don't think any other Italian publisher received more manuscripts from abroad than from Italy," wrote Valerio Riva. And, more recently, Michele Ranchetti: "We were a benchmark for all the publishers in the world, who looked to us to point the way forward."

Toward the end of the fifties, Feltrinelli traveled the world and, with the exception of the Soviet Union, all doors were open to him. During a visit to London, the press called him a "miracle worker." A British journalist followed him from one appointment to another for an interview: "I managed to talk to him only when he was dashing off to the Reform Club, where he made Sir Stanley Unwin wait for over twenty minutes. This is something that an English publisher would not easily allow to happen."

But Doris Lessing received an invitation to breakfast at the Ritz: "In those days, they had yet to invent the 'working breakfast,' but during the meeting we discovered that neither of us usually took breakfast. All we had was coffee and orange juice. [...] "I was struck by his vitality. In fact vitality is often associated with celebrity."

In the late fifties, Feltrinelli, barely thirty-three, sported a big black mustache.

6

Now I will have a word with Ingelein. We understand each other straight off. I invite her to have a drink with me, assuming the tone my mother and I reserve for great occasions. She is ready to tell me many things. Her contribution is crucial; a party to this story and one of its leading figures, she has never given in.

She has no trouble remembering the important moments, the encounters, the clashes, the journeys, who was there and who was not, what the newspapers carried. In theory I could start with questions and take notes. But we can do without the charade. She can tell me by herself.

When did the sixties, when people thought anything was possible, begin?

The sixties were the story of the magic carpet; everybody talks about it, but only a few saw it land on their doorstep. I was one of those few. Someone briefly opened the door, and for a second I saw it. It was bright red, but maybe I had got hold of the wrong end of the stick, taken chalk for cheese. It would be nice to be able to understand times past, but in reality there are only different times for

people who are always the same. "No period of the past is so unknown to us as the three, four, or five decades that separate our
twenties from those of our fathers." This is how an important Austrian author put it.

For Giangiacomo Feltrinelli the sixties began on Via Andegari,
where he brought together family, business, the publishing house,
and also his important library. "Here, in this old house, in the center of Milan, where my father lived, to whom at this time my
thoughts turn with infinite gratitude, for all the things he allowed
me to do and to have done." These were fitting words with which
to inaugurate the premises of the Istituto Giangiacomo Feltrinelli.
It was 25 March 1961. Alongside the education minister there was
the empty seat reserved for Togliatti, who was invited but was busy
elsewhere.

On the birth of Carlo Fitzgerald Feltrinelli, the fourth floor was
completely inundated with flowers. Even the bathrooms. It was a
real party, and the cheering went on and on. From the Agnelli family to Pietro Secchia, half of Italy sent telegrams. Secchia also took
the trouble to come in person. His friendship with my father dated
back to the old days in politics.

The odd thing was that when Feltrinelli left the PCI, he was considered a right-winger, but the man he stayed in touch with was
Secchia, the hard-liner of the party, by now merely a senator. One
might have suspected a strong political bond between the two, but
as far as Feltrinelli was concerned, the internal life of the party
was no longer of burning interest. Contact with Togliatti was frequent but indirect (and concerned only the activities of the institute), while Secchia was a friend and they saw each other from
time to time.

Upon the conclusion of the customary round of congratulations,
the "strong man" of the Resistance movement confided in his
secretary–chauffeur, who was waiting for him in the car: "Goodness

knows why they chose Fitzgerald as a middle name for their son. It can't have anything to do with the American president, can it?"

Enrico Filippini, a young German scholar destined for success, felt a wind of change blowing through Via Andegari. He was to write about it a little later in a scintillating society piece:

> One day the walls of the publishing house changed color: they all became fauves, cadmium yellow, traffic-light red, dark green; perhaps Inge had a hand in this: the young man had understood that now one went about subversion in a different way, and that gestures had to become more radical and less conventional [...].
>
> Economically speaking, being a publisher means having a lot of money at your command and being prepared to gamble with it, or not having any at all and wanting to make lots of it. In the latter case, the results are often harmful to the public; the former requires you to have at least some good reason, for example, a belief that culture is very important, worth the effort of getting up every morning at murderous hours, working twelve hours a day, committing yourself to lunch discussions, dinner discussions, travel discussions, living with misfits and neuropaths, stirring up a bit of a social whirl, hitting the headlines.... The young man spends his days, and sometimes even his nights, in a cadmium-yellow office full of books, ashtrays, Mies van der Rohe armchairs, and photographs; he drives his car at alarming speeds, spends weeks aboard his yacht on the North Sea, Friday evenings he leaves with his wife and son for a castle perched above the village of Villadeati, and there he dreams up and discards book series, projects, contracts among hunting trophies, a real Finnish sauna and a swimming pool, amid books on Italian history and books on sexology, quality paperbacks and avant-garde novels, and magazines in four languages. [...]
>
> The young man started his business in the gloomy fifties, cold war, neorealism, immobility, and at that time he dressed as a neorealist, a woollen vest and any old shirt: *commitment*.... His latest image is frankly better: light-colored clothes, striped shirts, stupendous ties.... And it is not a matter of fashion, it is a matter of culture.

Feltrinelli was usually at work by seven thirty. It was a good time to write letters or perhaps hold briefing sessions with his

colleagues. The family apartment was on the same floor as the office. "At that hour the publishing house was deserted and strangely
silent," recalls the philosopher Paolo Rossi, "whereas normally
one was caught up in a highly charged atmosphere." The door of
Feltrinelli's office was open, and visitors would find him not at his
desk but in the armchair beside the window (on the right as you
went in). On the floor there would be books, newspapers, mail,
notes, and an open pack of Senior Service cigarettes.

In this room, when the offices were bustling with activity, Tina
would fix the rhythm of appointments. Sometime in early 1962, Feltrinelli met with the critic Cesare Garboli to work out the details of
a contract for a new edition of Dante's minor works that Garboli
was to edit for the Universale Economica series.

Garboli recalls the scene in his book *Falbalas*:

> Feltrinelli was sitting on the other side of the desk, and he was ask-
> ing me about my work on Dante. "These minor works, are they in-
> teresting?" I do not have a ready wit, unfortunately. My instinct is to
> lend assistance, not to strike. I think that the intention behind Fel-
> trinelli's question was to discuss or to examine the advisability of
> reprinting works that were already so well known. Moreover, the
> physical presence of a person, the event that unfolds when we are in
> the presence of a person in flesh and blood, in short the theatrical
> power of reality, prevails, in me, over all other faculties and throws
> everything into crisis, I cannot defend myself; it is more powerful, so
> to speak, than my mental strength; and I let myself be invaded be-
> cause it strikes me as fair to honor reality and its sudden right to
> exist. For a moment, I doubted that *Vita nuova*, the *Convivio*, and
> the *De vulgari eloquentia*, the works that are, in my view, the proof
> of the existence of reality, nay, the proof of my very existence, were
> "worth republishing," works worthy of reappearing in public and of
> being readmitted to a cultural circuit. Never have Dante's minor
> works emerged in such bad shape as they did from that meeting.

Something of the kind must have happened on other occasions.
While many heard Feltrinelli talk competently about books and
culture, others like Garboli recall him as "ignorant as a friar's
heel." Perhaps both versions hold some truth.

"Do you read a lot of books?" I once asked him toward the end of the sixties. He replied that he read plenty, but not an excessive amount.

In an article for *King* magazine, Feltrinelli provided a few witty definitions of his business. He said that publishers can be defined in thousands of ways, that they are unlikely to change the world (a publisher cannot even change his publisher), that they must not take themselves too seriously, and that they have absolutely nothing to teach anyone. "Publishers," he maintained, "are handcarts, people who go around with the sign Printed Pages for Sale, they are conveyors of messages [...]. Knowing nothing, they must know everything, everything of use."

The basic idea was that publishers must shoulder the responsibility of selecting what is desirable for people to read, thereby providing "necessary" books with an outlet. He felt that those who read are richer; that they are more independent, can orient themselves better; and that there are many things they ought to know about. The old decor inherited from the provincial academic tradition is not of much use, its wood paneling, its pompous and backward-looking erudition. New instruments and new languages are needed: "because everything must and will change."

But Feltrinelli was not a publishing Barnum who chose books by leaping through a ring of fire. The famous morning sessions in the deserted office served to direct and plan series like the Philosophy of Science library created by Ludovico Geymonat in 1960; the Library of Clinical Psychology and Psychiatry series directed by Gaetano Benedetti and Pier Francesco Galli; the Fisb (*I fatti e le idee. Saggi e biografie*) library; the Mathematics Series inaugurated in 1963 by Lucio Lombardo Radice and Edoardo Vesentini; and the History of Science library edited by Paolo Rossi and Libero Sosio. There were many innovative books guaranteed to shake Italian readers out of their parochialism.

From the Philosophy of Science to the History of Science, on leafing through the catalog between the two series that were born at each end of the decade, one sees a clear attempt to think of contemporary culture as an intrinsically scientific culture. But what fields of knowledge were covered? Logic and mathematics, naturally, but also psychology, anthropology, social sciences, and literature–philology, linguistics, and semiotics.

In a preface to the famous book by Charles Snow, Geymonat wrote:

> Today, no one can be so blind as to fail to realize that the existence of two cultures, as different and as far apart from each other as the literary–humanistic culture is from the scientific–technical culture, constitutes serious grounds for a crisis in our civilization; it marks a rift that grows deeper from day to day, and threatens to become a real barrier to comprehension, deeper and more pernicious than any other subdivision.

To narrow the gap between the "two cultures" was, in brief, the theoretical basis of Feltrinelli's publishing plan.

"It was an adventurous 'home-grown' operation," says a witness who wishes to remain anonymous, "piloted by enthusiasm, without deference for tradition. Compared to other publishing houses, Feltrinelli did not pursue a 'cultural policy'."

It burned with its own fire.

To exercise my memory, I will talk about the four trees.

On the first, we would stay hunkered down and silent. There were deer all around, and it was usually Christmas. I described this one already.

The second is a cedar of Lebanon more than sixty feet high that has been flourishing since Napoleon's day. A lightning strike mangled its top, but this is merely an aesthetic problem; the bark is incredibly resistant. There are many things to be discovered beneath the cedar: animals' lairs, ravines, car racing tracks, hidden lives, roots that disappear into the ground. Where its shade ends, the lawn begins. The lawn is the English-style lawn of Villadeati, and in the summer the Bermuda grass runs wild. My father's nicotine-stained fingers would try to weed it out, and I would help him with this absorbing task. I also used to tag along when he went into the vineyard for the grape harvest, or if there was a plant to be pruned, a greenhouse to be heated, an engine to be repaired, or a swimming pool to be cleaned. Saul Bellow maintains that algae used to grow in the pool (as they do in the Adriatic). He talks about this in a short story. They are not algae, Saul, but needles from the cedar of Lebanon, and I would float along with them through a life without shadows. One foggy morning, I saw my father leave, not down the main drive but along the path that runs through the shade of the big cedar. My days were no longer to be so peaceful.

The third tree boasts the biggest cluster of magnolias I have ever seen. I won't say anything about the white flowers, everything is sweet on the shores of Lake Garda, even the tomatoes in the pasta sauce. That house (the "Bavarian mausoleum") is in reality a labyrinth in which it is easy to get lost among the corridors and the anterooms. There are mirrors, stairways, billiard tables, baldachins, and even a bunker dug by the Germans. The emergency telephone handsets hang down in the darkness. In the village there is talk of ghosts, but there is the warmth of our lunches in the kitchen and the veranda steps are the perfect place to sit and chat. From here, we can look at the lake, and Monte Baldo with its topping of snow is like a Japanese postcard. Once a day, the tourist excursion boat passes. The local guide explains that this was Mussolini's last residence and that the famous Doctor Zhivago also lived here.

The fourth tree isn't really a tree at all. It is perfectly straight, with stays instead of branches. The *Eskimosa* is a hull about sixteen meters long and is based in Porto Ercole. The boat is named after Ingelein, who has high cheekbones like a Laplander or an Eskimo. The white cap with the black visor and the garnet red band looks like a Danish student's cap, but on the captain it looked like a skipper's cap. If the captain had been merely a blend of impetuosity and impatience, he would never have tolerated all the things you need to do to keep the prow straight. The engine was never used; if there was no wind, you could always play chess in the cockpit. On coming into harbor, the sails were kept hoisted until the last moment and the final maneuvers were silent.

Everybody has had something to say about Cuba. In the early sixties, no matter how far away you were, you had to reckon with Fidel Castro. For many, he was synonymous with a dangerous extravagance that soon became an obsession for them. In his *Age of Extremes,* Eric J. Hobsbawm wrote:

> Probably no head of state during the brief century [...] had a more enthusiastic and impassioned audience than this bearded man in the crumpled camouflage uniform, who always arrived late for political rallies and then spoke for hours, uninterruptedly, communicating his rather confused thoughts to the attentive and consenting multitudes, of which I too was a part. For once revolution was experienced as a sort of collective honeymoon.

The early sixties witnessed the last act of the old colonial powers. The outcome of the Suez crisis (contemporaneous with the Hungarian uprising) accelerated a process that was already well under way in Asia. Now it was the African countries' turn to fight for freedom.

These were issues that interested Feltrinelli, both as a publisher and for their political importance (the two things coincided). The first signs or symptoms are to be found in a letter he sent to Ben Barka, the leader of the Moroccan Union Nationale des Forces Populaires, and another sent to Sékou Touré, the president of the Republic of Guinea. Guinea had been independent since 1958. In the summer of 1962, Feltrinelli went first to Nigeria and then to Ghana to attend the Accra conference, the only publisher to do so, I believe. Promoted by the Ghanaian president Kwame Nkrumah, the conference was one of the first international meetings of "non-aligned" politicians. The theme was nuclear disarmament. Representing Italy was Lelio Basso, an authoritative figure of the socialist left. The British Labour Party peer Lord Kennet, who was also present, today observes with some amusement that, in all likelihood, the whole thing had been organized by the Ghanaian president for reasons of personal prestige.

Feltrinelli had been working as a publisher since 1956, when he published a translation of *Outlaw Africa* by the Jeansons, a French couple. The book was considered to be the theoretical bible of the nascent anticolonialist movement in Europe. Publication of *The Algerians at War*, a report by Dominique Darbois and Philippe Vigneu, came in 1960. A copy of this book was dispatched to Havana: it was Feltrinelli's first contact with Castro, who sent his thanks. In 1962 Feltrinelli brought out another book by Francis Jeanson, *Problems and Perspectives in the Algerian Revolution*. Jeanson had been unable to find a French publisher, but Feltrinelli had a French version printed and distributed in France under his own imprint.

Juan Goytisolo's novel, *The Surf*, was banned in Franco's Spain and hailed in Italy as the finest work produced so far by the new generation of Spanish writers, very close in spirit–we read in the blurb–to Pasolini's *Ragazzi di vita*. The book was launched in February 1961 in a theater in Milan, accompanied by the screening of a documentary on the conditions facing domestic migrant workers in Spain. The film had barely begun when a group of ex-paratroopers, subsequently stopped by the police, interrupted the event by throwing smoke bombs. The Madrid press picked up the story, denouncing the provocative nature of the event and speculating on the meaning of the incidents. Feltrinelli's response was simply to send two functionaries of the publishing house to Barcelona, ostensibly to protest and deny but in effect to distribute his books in Spain. Nothing came of it, apart from a certain outcry in the local press. The Italian publisher's name, however, became taboo in those parts, which also, and more important, afforded him ready access into the circles of the intellectual opposition.

In Europe, the problem of the freedom of the press was now seen in a new light. As far as Feltrinelli was concerned, the picture was grim. In Italy, every other month his books were banned by public prosecutors who appealed to the courts to lay down the law. In France, the publishers and writers who had denounced the crimes perpetrated by the military were put on trial, as in *Deserter,* a book that told the dramatic story of a young man who had refused to fight in Algeria. In West Germany, in the fall of 1962, the *Spiegel* case exploded like a bombshell when the defense minister, Franz Josef Strauss, accused the weekly of having violated state secrets and engineered the arrest of its publisher, Rudolf Augstein.

After having sent off dozens of telegrams to half of Europe, Feltrinelli drew up a letter of condemnation to be sent to the German ambassador in Rome. It was signed by, among others, Giorgio Bassani, Paolo Grassi, Alberto Mondadori,* Elio Vittorini, and Eugenio Scalfari.† The confidential affairs office of the Italian Ministry of the Interior also took an interest in the matter: who had allegedly supplied *Der Spiegel* with the sensitive documentation? Feltrinelli, of course! Feltrinelli versus Strauss, NATO's principal ally in Europe. Fascinating but unlikely: my German source does not corroborate the story.

To complete the story of the growing threat to the freedom of the press, we should add the preemptive censorship employed in socialist countries, where the few publishing houses were state-owned, a fact that prevented the publication of certain works a priori. In Spain, publishers had to submit their manuscripts to the offices of the Ministry of Information, which sent everything back with cuts, marks in red and blue pencil, and an accompanying note on paper with no letterhead, saying yes or no.

---

*(1914–76). Journalist and publisher.

†(1924–). Law graduate, important journalist and writer, Scalfari founded *Espresso* and *La repubblica.*

With the Algerian crisis at its peak, the Istituto Feltrinelli offered asylum to two or three political refugees or "deserters," just as the conviction that determined action on the issue should be taken was coalescing in political and intellectual circles in Milan.

On 1 November 1961 various newspapers ran a paid appeal, which provides a good indication of the political climate and of just how much was at stake:

> For seven years the forces of French conservation have been waging a ruthless war on the Algerian people. A people is being oppressed and exterminated because it is demanding freedom, independence, and social justice.
>
> Some 800,000 dead is the bloody toll of this war: men, women, and children have been killed in the fighting, butchered and tortured in the course of roundups and police operations.
>
> 1,500,000 Algerians languish in the concentration camps of North Africa.
>
> Tens of thousands have been imprisoned in France for years.
>
> In order to defend their economic interests against all the interests of the French people, the colonialist forces are opening the door to fascism and military dictatorship.
>
> By riding roughshod over the traditions of the Enlightenment and democracy, French conservative forces and some military circles are a threat to democracy; they are a hotbed of intrigues against democratic and progressive forces in Europe.
>
> The freedom of the press is seriously threatened in France. Algerians and French citizens are being persecuted and hunted down with methods that will remind world opinion of those employed by the Nazi-Fascists. Citizens of Italy, it is necessary–on this, the centenary of the Unification of Italy, mindful of the traditions of freedom of our Risorgimento, and of the traditions of democracy and progress expressed by Garibaldi and Mazzini–to support the Algerian people in their struggle for independence as well as the democratic and progressive forces within France today.
>
> Their struggle is our struggle. Italians, we ask you to make a strong expression of indignation against the fascist forces at work in France and against the war in Algeria.

The first signatories were Basso, Feltrinelli, Grassi, Piovene, and Vittorini. Academics and intellectuals were swift to follow their lead.

In the meantime, in France, the United Socialist Party led by Pierre Mendès-France and the left-wing Catholics of Témoignage Chrétien were facing a delicate situation. The end of the war in Algeria made it imperative for France to return to its democratic traditions. It was necessary to reverse a process that was exploiting the emergency to make steady inroads on parliamentary democracy. From France there came requests for political, intellectual, and even economic solidarity.

The network of those who supported these appeals provides a good definition of Milan of that time. Gilles Martinet (one of the founders of the PSU) wrote to Feltrinelli, who agreed to ask for the support of his writers, of publishers like Alberto Mondadori, of business people like Roberto Olivetti, and of journalists like Italo Pietra. A similar task fell to Paolo Grassi, who, apart from the world of the theater, drew in the socialists and the backers of his Piccolo Teatro. Aldo Bassetti also had a list, as did the bookseller Vando Aldrovandi, who involved the publishers Einaudi and Lerici and the representatives of the great industrial families like Giulia Devoto Falck and Giulia Maria Crespi.

This was the Milan accustomed to popping into the well-known Bar Biffi for a plate of risotto al salto and a glass of good wine. The journalist Eugenio Scalfari says that at least once a week he would find himself at the same table with the banker Renato Cantoni and Giangiacomo Feltrinelli.

It is not true that Feltrinelli always backed demonstrations, appeals, or requests for help. He had learned how to make himself respected and how to dissociate himself from knee-jerk activism. When Giovanni Pirelli and Rossana Rossanda, sure of his willingness, took it for granted that he would help with the preparations for an exhibition in the name of the Committee for the Birth of the Algerian Nation, he replied: "I am sorry, but I have no intention of paying a share of the expenses involved in setting up the exhibition. I certainly would not have refused to contribute to this fine initiative had the request been made in a politer fashion. Seventeen years in politics ought to have taught you that you cannot act by 'decree.'"

After the death of Pasternak, Olga Ivinskaya and her daughter were arrested. They were sentenced to the labor camps: eight years for Olga, three for Irina. Olga was arrested in mid-August 1960, Irina in September.

During the month of June, about half the hundred thousand dollars requested by Pasternak had been taken to Moscow by fiduciaries of D'Angelo. A married couple, the Benedettis, arrived by car, traveling on tourist visas, with no problems at the border. In the trunk of their car was a suitcase full of rubles, almost half a million in all, but the banknotes had recently gone out of circulation and were hard to change. The couple had not taken even the most elementary precautions. There were witnesses to the delivery of the money, and Olga went right out and bought a brand new motor scooter for her youngest son...too much for even the most tolerant of police forces.

A few weeks before, while Pasternak was still alive, the Garritano family (Garritano was a correspondent with *L'Unità*) had also brought a large sum in rubles. The sender was again D'Angelo. In that same period, the couple was asked to send Feltrinelli an envelope with the receipts and a will drawn up by Boris in Olga's favor. Although the Garritanos had tried to present Feltrinelli in a poor light on more than one occasion, Olga appealed to them to take those papers to Italy. (Schewe was not in the Soviet Union at that time.) The Garritanos told Olga they planned to leave for Rome the following day, but they went off on a trip to the Caucasus instead and lost (or allowed someone to take) the documents. An "imprudence," says Garritano today, but he says it as if it was still an open wound.

After the Garritano incident, Olga broke off relations with everyone except Schewe and Feltrinelli. To them she sent desperate

letters, worried about what might happen to her, fears that were
soon to prove well founded. When the secret police arrested her,
they searched the house and found a letter in Italian in which she
was advised to communicate only with Schewe. Feltrinelli had already tried to put her on her guard as far as D'Angelo was concerned. "Unfortunately," says Ivinskaya in her autobiography,
"owing to the circumstances (and often our imprudence) we dis-
obeyed Feltrinelli's warnings and continued to write to dear Sergio.
We were to pay dearly for this." Many years later, shortly before
she died, Olga talked to me. She spoke about Pasternak, herself,
Feltrinelli, D'Angelo's emissaries, the suitcases full of banknotes,
the letters, the haste, and all the moves prompted by fear.

The events in Moscow in the summer of 1960 again reverberated
around the world. Feltrinelli sent off a communiqué to the press
agencies: "It is my opinion that Olga Ivinskaya is not responsible
either for the transfer of the sums or for the destination of those
same sums. The order to make the transfer was made by Pasternak
alone, he himself said that it was immaterial whether the rubles
were handed over to him or to Ivinskaya." The communiqué also
clarified the matter of the rubles that came from funds at Pasternak's disposal in Western bank accounts and the role played by
D'Angelo (whose name was not mentioned) in the transmission of
a part of these funds to Moscow.

Not long after, a third-rate weekly, whose political affiliations
lay in the murky area around the right wing of the Christian Democratic party, unleashed a barrage of accusations against Feltrinelli. He was accused of having deliberately betrayed Ivinskaya,
leaving her at the mercy of the Soviet police. Feltrinelli commented
to Schewe: "It is a provocation so base, it leaves you breathless with
anger." The articles were apparently orchestrated by the former
Communist Reale and by D'Angelo himself, who was soon to become the US correspondent for *Fiorino*, a magazine belonging to
the same publishing group. The suspicion that D'Angelo and Gar-

ritano, for reasons of their own, were connected with someone in America or (more probably) in Russia crept into the correspondence between Feltrinelli and Schewe.

Feltrinelli and Schewe kept in touch in order to record all information coming from labor camp 385/14. There, five hundred kilometers from Moscow, the wind was so strong that you had to walk backward. Olga had to be helped. But how? By provoking a new head-on clash with the Soviet authorities? By soliciting a protest on the part of the international community? Or, instead, by tackling the problem from another angle: by seeking what little chance there was of talking, making a deal?

After the breach between Feltrinelli and the PCI (December 1957), Del Bo had always been the one to maintain contacts with the central office of the PCI. He was scrupulous about this. He wrote a letter to Alicata, the Minister for Culture, in which he referred to the activities of the institute. But the letters were too vague, and Alicata complained about this. With Togliatti, on the other hand, the approach was highly deferential. Del Bo had written to Togliatti, congratulating him on his essay on the formation of the Communist leadership between 1923 and 1924. Togliatti's contribution, which was to be published in the third volume of the series, contains an important new battle cry: to reconstruct the history of the PCI as an integral part of Italian national history. That Togliatti's piece was published in the *Annali* of the Istituto Feltrinelli was a signal not to be underestimated.

Regarding Del Bo's plans to visit Moscow, Togliatti had sought the advice of Alicata, who gave his opinion on this at the end of 1959:

I believe that we ought to point out to our Soviet comrades the advisability of reestablishing contacts between the Institute of Marxism–Leninism and the Feltrinelli Library. However, Del Bo must be made to understand, in an appropriate manner, that without our intervention such contacts would be impossible to organize, at least for the time being, given the reservations that those in charge of Institute of Marxism–Leninism have concerning Feltrinelli's activities overall.

In 1960, with the deepening scandals over *Doctor Zhivago,* it became impossible to take matters any further. On 15 September 1960, the economist Piero Sraffa noted this remark made by Del Bo: "On account of Pasternak, the Soviets want nothing to do with Feltrinelli either as a publisher or as an institute." But in 1961, after the Soviet visit to Milan, Del Bo's trip to Moscow finally received the green light. He was accompanied by the historian Enzo Collotti. Late that summer, for almost two weeks, the Italian delegation was the guest of the Institute of Marxism-Leninism, and the meetings proved cordial and highly fruitful, especially concerning the opportunities for exchanging documents. Collotti recalls that General Boltin (a famous military historian), his chest laden with medals and accompanied by an honor guard, was waiting to greet the Italian delegation at the foot of the airplane steps. It cannot be that far from the truth to suppose that Del Bo used the situation, and his skill in diplomacy, to sound out the possibility of a conciliatory solution to the Ivinskaya case. According to Collotti, who was not supposed to know anything about it, the Pasternak question was in fact one of the principal reasons for the visit.

Some weeks after Del Bo's return to Italy, the second important episode of the year occurred. Feltrinelli decided to hand over to the Soviets, that is, to the administration of the Marx–Engels–Lenin Institute, some of the original letters received from Pasternak during the turbulent months following the publication of the novel. What was the sense of this gesture? He explained this himself to Pospelov: "There is no need for me to tell you how important these papers are to me from a human standpoint. But I deprive myself of them willingly if my decision may be considered a step toward bringing this affair to an end."

Feltrinelli and Del Bo attached great importance to this initiative. The envelope containing the letters was handed over to Secchia with precise instructions. On 11 October, Del Bo urged:

Make sure that T. takes the envelope with him and delivers it personally to Pospelov. I believe this to be extremely important. Should T. feel that it is unsuitable for him to take it, give the envelope back to Leonardi and we shall think over our next move here in Milan. Agreed? Do not try other ways. Thank you and interpret Giangiacomo's words as a concrete step in everybody's best interest.

"T." obviously stands for Togliatti, who from 14 October was in Moscow for the 22nd Congress of the CPSU. On 12 October, it was Feltrinelli's turn to write to Secchia:

I hope that this gesture of "unilateral disarmament" on my part may lead, when a suitable occasion arises, to a consideration of the possibility of alleviating the lot of Mrs. Ivinskaya and her daughter: as well as easing my mind, a pardon or a reduced sentence that might lead to their release would also offer the Soviets an advantageous way of ending the polemic with intellectual and political circles in London and Paris, a polemic that might otherwise drag on for a long time. Perhaps it may be possible to draw the Soviets' attention to the fact that, should international politics enter a phase of détente in the near future, they might do something for the two Ivinskaya women as part of the variety of acts and gestures to be made. I would be really grateful to you if you would intercede, directly or indirectly, in this regard. I enclose for your attention an English article containing some statements made by Surkov, whose style is unsuited to a polemic between a Soviet personality and the Western world.

Secchia wasted no time in replying:

I have received the envelope, which I immediately had delivered to the person we agreed upon; in fact I was lucky because I was able to speak to him of the matter right away. Your gesture and your initiative were appreciated both by me and by him, and we hope that the friends to whom your gesture is addressed will also take things in the desired spirit.

To what extent these "friends" actually did appreciate Feltrinelli's move we do not know, but from spring 1962 onward vague hints began to circulate about the possibility that something might be

done for Olga and Irina. And in fact, Irina was freed just before
the summer, after serving half her sentence. Was this the effect of
the diplomatic mission entrusted to the good offices of Secchia
and Togliatti? Perhaps. This is what Feltrinelli wrote to Schewe on
2 July 1962:

> My feeling is that what little I have managed to do for the liberation
> of O. and I. ought not to be made public, especially with regard to
> Irina. There have been contacts between the Party here and the
> Party in M. Perhaps I have done the Russians a favor by handing
> over the documents you know about. But Irina must not know this.
> All the Russians have done in relation to the release of Irina and
> perhaps, before much longer, of Olga, they have done of their own
> free will, without pressure or negotiation. We have to save their face,
> and it would be better if the girl knew as little as possible of the
> background.

As part of his attempt to secure Olga's release, which occurred
in 1964, Feltrinelli also put pressure on Fidel Castro, whom he met
in the beginning of that year. At least, this was what Olga told me.
She was never to meet my father.

As soon as Olga was freed, she took steps to support herself and
her daughter by having cash sent from the West. I have been unable
to establish whether this aid, now tolerated by the authorities, depended on "what little" Feltrinelli had been able to do previously.

In early 1964 Feltrinelli and Metro-Goldwyn-Mayer came to an
agreement for the film version of *Doctor Zhivago,* on the basis of a
flat fee of $450,000. The first drafts of the contract mention ten po-
tential directors: Federico Fellini, Luchino Visconti, Vittorio De
Sica, David Lean, Carol Reed, Elia Kazan, Stanley Kubrick, Billy
Wilder, Peter Ustinov, and Joseph L. Mankiewicz. The choice fell
immediately on Lean. The Italians insisted that the treatment,
screenplay, and dialogues be based on Zveteremich's Italian translation. The idea behind this was to prevent any errors contained in

other translations from "misrepresenting or distorting the author's ideas in a way that might lead to their being attributed with a meaning and a political orientation that was not in conformity with his will." This was how Feltrinelli put it in a letter to Carlo Ponti.

Many years later, I called Ponti in Los Angeles to learn more. He did not have fond memories of the long and difficult negotiations. In that rasping voice of his he said: "Right from the start, the plan was to have David Lean as the director and, as for Feltrinelli, he didn't give a damn, all he wanted was the money."

Whichever way things went, the Americans did their best to create a product that would satisfy even the most sophisticated viewer. The winner of five Oscars, *Doctor Zhivago* broke all records in Italian cinemas, showing for six hundred days. It is still the seventh most popular film of all time. "It was the tops as a commercial and an artistic film alike," says Ponti. "Yet," he continues, "Feltrinelli didn't even come to the premiere, to the great chagrin of the executives at Metro who wanted his opinion, but he didn't give a damn, he didn't give a damn for anything or anybody."

They initially thought of going on location to a certain part of Yugoslavia, the only country conveniently close to Italy's eastern frontier. There, moreover, it would have cost less to hire extras. Feltrinelli delegated the attorney Filippo Carpi de' Resmini, who was a trusted friend as well as his cousin, to handle film-related business from Rome.

Filippo, who was a kind of uncle to me, would always tell the story of how he, Carlo Ponti, and Ponti's wife, Sophia Loren, visited Marshall Tito's summer residence to champion the cause of the film. Tito received them on the pier, he was cordial, and a real gentleman with Sophia, but he hedged over the proposals made by the tiny Italian delegation. Better to let the matter drop.

Ponti denies the episode. He had known Tito well for a long time, the Yugoslav supremo would have immediately given the

film the green light: but he did not want David Lean, considered to
be too much of an anti-Communist. Ponti came up with a splendid
anecdote: through the embassy in London, the Soviets sent a letter
to Lean, inviting him to travel all over the Soviet Union. Once he
got to know the way our people lived, they said, he would no
longer wish to direct a film based on *Doctor Zhivago*.

So Omar Sharif with his mustache and Julie Christie with her
limpid gaze went off to Spain with Lean, where they had a whole
neighborhood of Moscow reconstructed. The film was shot on location in other countries too. There is a photo of the set in Finland,
with Feltrinelli meeting Yuri Zhivago in the snow.

More or less at the same time, shortly after Olga's release, Feltrinelli made official contact with the Soviet authorities and in particular with Professor Volchov, the president of the College of
International Jurists of Moscow, the official representative of the
Pasternak family. This was an important development: for the first
time it was possible to sit around a table and deal in a conventional
fashion. After going to considerable lengths to sound out the real
intentions of the parties, the Soviets made a first visit to Milan and
named their own Italian representatives. For his part, Feltrinelli
produced a statement of the proceeds from *Doctor Zhivago*. At
first, especially after the film, the Soviets' aim was to secure a tacit
agreement that would solve, solely for the past, an exclusively economic problem. Feltrinelli's position was different. Here is the text
of his letter to Professor Volchov during the summer of 1966:

> It seems to me that the time has come for frankness and loyalty, all
> the more fitting by way of a tribute to the memory of the late Poet. I
> cannot forget that, solely because Pasternak gave me a mandate to
> publish and market his work, he was obliged to endure the harshest
> condemnation and persecution, which profoundly embittered the
> last years of his life. Nor can I forget that for this reason alone he was
> expelled from the Writers' Union, banished from the literary com-
> munity, publicly accused of treachery and disloyalty toward his na-

tive land, and even induced to disavow the fact that he had ever assigned me the task of publishing his great novel. [...]

All this belongs to the recent past, a past that lives on in everyone's memory, a past that, unfortunately, we have yet to recover from. But I believe that times will change and I am certain that you, too, as a man of honor, will agree with the need to avoid proceeding any further along this line [...] with the mere presentation and the settlement of an economic dispute related to the publication of the book. [...]

The time is therefore ripe, in my opinion, for all of us to take a more open and straightforward step forward, including those who at the time showed no mercy to the noble figure of the late Poet. Moreover, I feel that I would be betraying the faith that the late lamented author had in me were I not to take the trouble to make—unfortunately, by now, only to his memory—at least those (minimal) amends due to his qualities as a man, a citizen, and a writer.

To this end, I maintain that it is indispensable to dispel the pall of secrecy that has until now hung over my relations with Pasternak and finally to emerge—as we say here—into the light of day. I am therefore authorized to propose to you, in the name of the publishing house represented by me, the stipulation of a standard publishing contract with the Poet's heirs, which may define the past and at the same time obtain all the appropriate blessings, approvals, and authorizations on the part of the various competent organizations, associations, and bodies in your country. With the express support, in any event, of the Union of Soviet Writers and through those forms of publicity that can be reasonably discussed and agreed upon.

It took a good three of four years to reach an agreement, regarding the past, the future, and Olga, who, formally, had no right to anything. The Soviets made several visits to Milan, where they learned to wind spaghetti around their forks, amused themselves, and discussed business. The talks were very long and very tough. Professor Volchov never went anywhere without his fountain pen, with which he claimed to have signed death sentences at the Nuremberg trials. But in the course of one endless afternoon, he hurled it against a wall in a fit of rage. That pen was his pride and joy, and he broke it beyond repair.

The dealings finally led to a handshake: the Soviet State Legal Advisory Office would receive a six-figure sum in dollars (but their clients, the heirs, were to receive much less, I fear). A final calculation was reached by deducting what had been transferred to Pasternak during his lifetime (the Legal Advisory Office accepted the principle) as well as the considerable expenses incurred in the management of the copyright. A standard contract was to bind the parties (Olga Ivinskaya included) for the next twenty years. After so many battles, this was for all parties the logical if not the ideal conclusion to the negotiations.

In 1989, in Moscow, the attorney Tesone renewed the rights to *Doctor Zhivago* and struck a deal for the first publication of the novel in Soviet territory. It was the time of perestroika. In accordance with the terms of the 1970 contract, the rights were freely available. The magazine *Novy Mir,* which was supposed to have published the book thirty-five years before, was ready to do so now. Only four words were requested in the copyright line: "© Giangiacomo Feltrinelli Editore Milano."

After the Soviet Union collapsed, I met Olga Ivinskaya shortly before she died. She was bedridden but had seen that there would be no lack of vodka and cigarettes for our warm meeting. Then she wrote me a letter about Feltrinelli and Pasternak and about two stars that meet in space like the stars in Lermontov's poem. The day after our only meeting, I made a visit to Peredelkino, which my father would have loved to see.

Andrei Voznesensky sent off a collection of his poems to Boris Pasternak when he was only fourteen. It was in 1946. As in a dream, the master replied, granting the boy his lifelong friendship. Andrei was also to become aware of the name "Feltrinelli." This happened a few months after Pasternak's death, when the world was picking up such speed that in Moscow people were suddenly talking of "Jack" (Kerouac), while in London Andrei himself was all the rage. "He has taken off like a rocket in the starry firmament of poetry," wrote the *Observer*.

Voznesensky's encounter with my father was in Paris (late 1961, early 1962?), while the meeting in the Kremlin, the one in which Khrushchev interrupted Voznesensky's speech, occurred in March 1963. Voznesensky recalled these events in January 1997:

One day they called me at my hotel in Paris, and a honeyed voice told me that Signor Feltrinelli had come to meet me.

This was my first trip abroad. I was in ecstasy over the way the most important French newspapers (*Le Figaro, France soir* and *Le Monde*) had greeted my poetry readings; I had literally lost my head.

A black limousine with shades drawn was waiting for me at the corner. A snakelike smile played on the face of the silent man who was to accompany me. It seemed like a scene from a thriller. I don't remember where I was taken, perhaps it was a villa in the suburbs or a secret apartment. We sat down in the lounge to wait.

And then, impetuously, he strode into the room. Tall, with a tennis player's build, slightly curved shoulders, in a gray suit. In his eyes shone a sad and frenetic light. But the most striking thing was his mustache, curving downward in the style favored by Ukrainian terrorists. [...]

I sensed in Feltrinelli a certain adventurous passion that is dear to me. A current of reciprocal liking began to flow between us. He played the part of the one who likes to set universal principles ablaze, and I was a legendary figure in the stadia of Moscow. [...] We spoke briefly of *Zhivago*, and he toyed with his mustache, curling it, as he told me, in tones of wonder mixed with disgust, of the episode in which that syrupy hyena Surkov had gone to visit him, presenting himself in Pasternak's name, to ask him to stop the publication of the novel. Feltrinelli offered me a lifetime contract for the world rights to my work. Until then, I had never signed a contract: Soviet law prohibited direct contact with publishers. And now the chance had presented itself! I accepted, but only for the Italian rights. I was behaving like a consummate actor, knocking back the whisky in one gulp. He offered me an incredible advance. I don't recall now, but for someone like me, who had never received a cent from publishers, it was a mind-boggling amount. I was dumbstruck. I refused. The silent escort grew even more silent at this brazenness on my part. "So how much do you want?" Plucking up my courage, I went for a figure that was ten times higher. This, I thought, was how one deals with publishers. Feltrinelli paled, and dashed out of the room. The escort shot me a glance over the rims of his glasses, doubtless thinking something like "Just listen to this crazy Russian!" I said to myself: "Andryusha, now you've blown it!"

Three minutes later, the door was thrown open; Feltrinelli came in with a calm but determined expression. He said: "OK. How would you like to be paid? By check, or would you prefer a draft to be sent to your bank?" "No. I want it all right now. In cash!" In those days I didn't even know what a check was, while in practical terms, as far as the Soviet authorities were concerned, having a bank account meant you were a CIA agent. "OK, OK," said the whiskers, looking at the ceiling, "but in that case you'll have to come to Italy."

And so I perpetrated the second crime. Soviet citizens could not ask foreign consulates for a visa directly. This was possible only through Moscow, after a special commission had vetted the request. But I went to the Italian consulate in Paris, and three days later there I was in Rome. Imitating an American accent, I told the cab driver: "Take me to the best hotel." The luxurious hotel in Piazza di Spagna was swarming with Americans and wealthy cardinals. I knew that I was going to have to spend all the money in one week. I was positive that, on my return to Moscow, the road to Europe would be closed to me forever. And so I bought fur coats and jewelry for all my friends. I set to drinking myself to death, and, when I left the hotel, I forgot a drawing by Picasso that someone had given me as a present.

[...]

It was not long before the punishment arrived, in the form of Khrushchev brandishing a raised fist in fury. "Voznesensky!" he yelled. "Get out of this country! You have done nothing but slander our system; you are trying to provoke a Hungarian uprising here! Go off to your friends abroad...." The hall of the great assembly room in the Kremlin resounded with a babble of voices: "Shame! Shame! Get out of the country!" And all this because I had said that Lermontov, the genius Pasternak, and Akhmadulina belonged to one direct line of descent. Which made the secretary general hit the roof. For Khrushchev, not long before, had defined Pasternak as a pig that shits in his own trough, and now this one here says he was a genius! That windbag Khrushchev just couldn't appreciate straight talk. Feltrinelli was a straight talker.

I don't know whether the great leader had found out, from my dossier, about my criminal association with Feltrinelli. The vitriolic articles about me made no mention of it, but as far as I am concerned, it was the real cause of the accusations. "Now Shelepin will prepare your passport!" yelled the atomic power.

Shelepin, the minister of the KGB, blurted out: "You didn't come to the Kremlin in a jacket and tie but in a pullover. You are a beatnik!" No one in the room knew what a beatnik was, but everyone shouted in chorus: "Beatnik! get out of this country!..."

Thinking they would not find me, I took refuge in one of the Baltic countries. I would spend hours lying down in the woods, looking at the sky overhead. At a certain point, on a dead branch outlined against the sky, I saw a tiny slow-moving figure. I recognized it: it reminded me of a mustache.

I am certain that Feltrinelli's pleasure in publishing Jack Kerouac's *The Subterraneans* increased when the book was confiscated because of its presumed obscene content. Barney Rosset arrived from America in his capacity as the original publisher of the work, and Kerouac sent a letter to the judge (who was from Varese, I think), admitting that he had not so much as a smattering of law, but knew the foundation of jurisprudence: "The judge is always right!"

And Testori's play *Arialda*? It was the same year and the same fate: "Highly offensive to the common sense of decency, for the turpitude and triviality of the events considered." Visconti was working on *Rocco and His Brothers,* all too freely based on Testori's novel *Il ponte della Ghisolfa.* Visconti came across a copy of *Arialda,* and, enthusiastic, he had it staged by Paolo Stoppa. At the premiere in Milan, the company had to stop the performance. The theater resounded with whistling, shouting, and insults. Feltrinelli jumped to his feet, facing the infuriated crowd: "You provocateurs, cut it out, you provocateurs!"

Many other Feltrinelli books were being examined for obscenity. In particular, Selby's *Last Exit to Brooklyn,* with his stories of "perverts," and Henry Miller's two *Tropics.* My parents had met Miller in Italy on various occasions. In the publishing house there was great enthusiasm for them, but it was impossible to publish the

*Tropic*s in Italy. With a trial inevitable, Feltrinelli asked some eminent psychiatrists to demolish the paradigm of "obscenity," that elusive whiff of corruption that according to the lawmakers causes irreparable psychological damage.

This time, Feltrinelli did not manage to convince Tesone, the lawyer in the Pasternak case, to whom he gave a copy of an invaluable little book, *The Trial of Lady Chatterley,* so that he might prepare himself for a trial of "unprecedented dimensions in Italy." The two men argued bitterly. Tesone felt that Miller's *Tropic*s represented too much of a risk, and he tendered his resignation. Feltrinelli continued doing things his way. But with a difference... *Tropic of Cancer* began to circulate in 1962, in a Feltrinelli edition printed in Bellinzona and kept in stock in the Gondrand warehouses in Basel. A notice on the cover said "Paperback edition for foreign sale only, the publisher prohibits its export and sale in Italy." This served to prevent confiscation, but—as the accountant Pozzi recalls—"we had the books transported from Basel to the Maison di Livre Italien in Nice. We would go by car to pick them up and return to Italy via the customs post at Ventimiglia carrying two to three hundred copies. We brought the books into Italy and sold them under the counter, but not in Feltrinelli bookstores." The bookseller Bertini sold them: "I picked up some *Tropic*s at the 1962 Frankfurt Book Fair. Feltrinelli made me pay for them. He wanted a check. 'If you end up in jail, that's your fucking problem,' he said to me." On his way back, Bertini avoided Switzerland and crossed the border at the Brenner pass. But the customs men stopped his Lancia Appia series 3, perhaps because the load made it look a bit down on the springs. "The trunk was full of *Tropic*s, mixed with foreign publishers' catalogs. I told them I had come from the Frankfurt Book Fair. I thought I'd had it. 'What a lot of books on cancer,' said the customs man. 'Yeah,' I said, 'it's a nasty business.'"

"Thanks for all you are doing. I take my hat off to you Italians for having been so professional, thanks for being so understanding,"

Miller wrote to his publisher and to those who had worked with painstaking determination on the translation and editing.

When the author visited Gargnano, Feltrinelli, knowing Miller's habits, had a Ping-Pong table set up under the big magnolia, and there some hard-fought matches were played. The *Tropic*s, in a single volume, were not officially published in Italy until 1967. A new trial was ordered. But times had already begun to change.

On the evening of 13 February 1965, Nanni Balestrini, the editor and poet, was walking down Via del Corso, in Rome, on his way to a show. A small local theater was presenting the first night of an adaptation of Rolf Hochhuth's *The Deputy*. When Balestrini got there, he found five jeeps, an armored car, and two police vans: no one was allowed in, the show was prohibited. Scuffles followed, and the young poet was frog-marched off by the cops, the soles of his shoes dragging along the ground. It was at that point that he spotted his employer arriving, dressed to kill, in the company of Mary McCarthy. Mustache to mustache, he heard Feltrinelli yell at the cop: "Let him go, he is one of my associates." The captive was freed. The prohibition of the show caused a scandal because the police action was so brutal. The audience was made up of Italian critics, but also of foreign observers. The minister of the interior had to issue an apology. Two days later, the show was staged in the warehouse of the Feltrinelli bookstore on Via del Babbuino.

The Deputy was an indictment of Pope Pius XII's failure to speak out against the Nazi atrocities, and a savage critique of the moral and political responsibilities of the Catholic Church. Feltrinelli believed strongly in the book. "*Doctor Zhivago*, Hochhuth's *The Deputy*, and the experimental work of the Italian avant-garde," he wrote in the catalog published to mark the house's tenth anniversary, "were episodes in the same battle for freedom of expression against any power that held the analysis, criticism, or creative work of a poet or a scientist to be offensive to legitimate ideals, illustrious men, or glorious traditions; for nothing is ever

absolute and untouchable, nothing is ever beyond historic or literary criticism."

To celebrate the anniversary of the publishing house, they
threw a big party at Gargnano in the summer of 1965. Grisha Von
Rezzori turned up with Anita Pallenberg, the girlfriend of Keith or
Mick of the Stones.

Other publishing excitement began in Palermo in October, in
the form of a spin-off from an experimental music event. It was an
era in which conferences were becoming "interdisciplinary," the
idea being that various languages might in some way coincide.
Why not extend the scope of the weeklong event in Palermo to include a discussion of the new literature? The idea arose from an
off-the-cuff suggestion made by Filippini, and the young poet-
editor Balestrini had gone to work on organizing it. The cry
"Everybody to Palermo" shook up Italian intellectual circles.
Overnight a sleeper "avant-garde" was born.

The concept of "the open work" was no longer a question of
mere poetics, it became a concept for operating at all levels of a
complex society. And it called for writers capable of using diverse
disciplinary languages. This was Group 63: enormous eclecticism
and the maximum of innovation, where what counted, even more
than results, was attitude. The discourses of the establishment
(wasn't that how they put it?), those of left-wing conservatism and
conservatism *tout court,* began to betray a sense of uneasiness for
the first time. The general climate was changing, but the change
did not become obvious until literature was affected, and literature
became the place where all these changes converged.

Group 63 was foreshadowed in 1956, with the foundation of the
magazine *Verri* run by Luciano Anceschi (Giangiacomo's first
tutor). The group of poets known as the Novissimi gravitated to the
magazine: it was no longer possible to write a certain type of poetry.
And Anceschi's teachings were attuned to the moment: phenome-

nology plus structuralism seemed to catch the very point of the century. Then, three years later, Umberto Eco wrote an essay titled "L'opera in movimento e la coscienza dell'epoca," which was later included in his book *The Open Work*, published by Bompiani in 1962: the phrase became the watchword of the culture of the sixties.

The name Group 63 was borrowed from a German precedent, Group 47, with which the Feltrinelli publishing house already had dealings. The similarity with the German group lay in the method. The authors held public readings of their works, they refuted tradition, prized innovation, accepted the consequences of aggressive, destructive, even self-destructive debate: a novelty as far as Italian Arcadia was concerned. But there were also parties, dances, gatherings around the pool, brawls, exhibitions, and concerts.

The idea of forming the group came from Via Andegari, but the headquarters were in the bookstore in Rome's Via del Babbuino. It cannot be said that Feltrinelli had exclusive rights to Group 63, but (along with Bompiani) it was its principal outlet in the world of publishing.

However, as the novelist Alberto Arbasino put it, as a publishing house "Feltrinelli had the luxury of possessing two souls." His was not only the house that had published the misunderstood *Leopard* and the series directed by Giorgio Bassani but also the young writers who defined Bassani and Cassola as the Lialas* of 1963.

Was the literary world of the fifties really "boorish, smothering, and triumphally smug" (as the young writers believed)? And as for the "provincial fuddy duddies" in Feltrinelli's Roman offices on Via Arenula, unable to repeat the miracle of *The Leopard* every year, were they really so many "spongers"? On the other hand: did the "theoretical glaciation" (as the older generation would have it) of Group 63 really exact tolls? Did their writing represent the funeral

---

*Liala. Pseudonym of Amelia Negretti (1897–1997), successful author of romantic novels (an Italian Barbara Cartland).

offerings of our literature? And when Feltrinelli sacked Bassani, did
he think that by so doing he was celebrating "one of the blackest
days in Italian literature"? He broke into Bassani's desk drawers at
night and had his office sealed off. And raised his voice when Bassani showed up late the following morning. But this did not mark
the advent of some kind of literary terrorism, some bookish St.
Bartholomew's Night. Feltrinelli justifiably demanded that his
staff, his offices, his archives, his writing paper, and his salaries not
be used to divert his authors toward other publishers. Bassani had
become so disenchanted with the new wave in literature that he
had begun to move his authors away from such contamination. He
was never to admit this; all he said he did was to take issue with
the "so-called" Group 63.

In Feltrinelli's view, the books produced by the avant-garde were
a necessary part of the house's soul. This was why a special series
was created for them: *I materiali*, launched in 1964. Edoardo Sanguineti, a writer who was ahead of his time, recalls that the publisher kept a low profile and left his writers to get on with things.

Fratelli d'Italia (1963) was the emblematic work of this moment
in Italian literary history. Its publication was opposed by the very
man in charge of the series (Bassani), who disliked its chaotic
blend of genres, found that it lacked what he called the "filter of
memory," and could not bear either its virtuoso passages or its
fragmentary nature. In a press communiqué, Feltrinelli cut internal and external disputes short: "I have no wish to get involved in
the row over the novel. In my opinion, what Alberto Arbasino has
produced is, first and foremost, a book, which some will read as a
novel, others as nonfiction, and perhaps others again as a pamphlet or a collection of newspaper articles."

In his next book (*Paese senza*), Arbasino reflected at length
upon his time with Feltrinelli:

Giangiacomo was typically shy and aggressive, highly puritanical,
capable of bursts of good humor but incapable of relaxing. Needs,

none. Desires, out of the question. He had some typically upper-middle-class traits: the habit of assessing—directly and without any beating about the bush—the economic side of operations, right down to the managerial affectation of taking pencil and paper and making spot calculations of costs and proceeds; of changing the subject to ask polite questions about things that interested the other party whenever the conversation languished; and of fearing that people came to him only because of his money, which resulted in a reserve that made it hard to forge simple relationships. But the managerial tone would disappear instantly when he left the office for a lunch or for the weekend: as if he had determined to draw a sharp distinction between Business and Private Life. [...]

Through the continuous restlessness and the many enthusiasms that followed, one sensed above all an enormous vivacity, an inexhaustible capacity for exuberance. I remember, for example, his long-cultivated plans for a *History of Taste in Twentieth-Century Italy* (which was never written because I went off the idea), and his enthusiasm for colored paper napkins and games, which the various Feltrinelli bookstores were full of for some time.

As far as working together was concerned, my recollection is that the planning and preparation of a wide variety of extremely different books, the professional meetings, and the face-to-face talks were extremely efficient and competent. There were moments of irony: Rizzoli never stole an author from him, he would say, smiling, because otherwise Feltrinelli would have evicted the Milan soccer team—of which a member of the Rizzoli family was then the owner—from their offices on the ground floor of Via Andegari, an address that Rizzoli very much wanted to keep. And even though Feltrinelli surrounded himself with associates who were more experimentally oriented than professional, so much the better for the future: for the dust jackets of my most adventurous books they would choose a Fra Galgario or a Cy Twombly. [...] Around 1962, when the manuscript of *Fratelli d'Italia* was ready, Giorgio Bassani (who was in charge of the fiction series) was against it because the novel struck him as a disordered and scandalous jumble of fact and fiction, and moreover he feared that it would be interpreted only on the basis of gossip and polemic. All Giangiacomo said was: any blame will be taken by the director of the series when he discovers and endorses nonsense. But if the nonsense is the work of an author who is already well known, all the blame falls on the author.

The brawling excursions of the *Fratelli d'Italia* were perceived in many quarters as a social slander on a national level. Feltrinelli said:

This book is a product of this society, and is no better and no worse than that society: perhaps for the first time, a certain [section of] society has seen itself in the mirror. I understand the surprise, but I am surprised by an indignation that smacks of bad faith. We are all what we want to be, and why be ashamed of what we are and of what we want to be? [...] In the novel Arbasino describes places, habits, expressions, and events common to a certain section of Italian society. I mean to say that blend of café, literary, and theatrical society, in short the snobbish world of the Milanese and Roman intelligentsia. Intelligent, unconventional, sometimes cynical. And sometimes presumptuous and arrogant.

The shade of the big cedar of Lebanon welcomed Arbasino for the launch of *Fratelli d'Italia*:

Villadeati, with the local wine and salame and grappa, was an extremely pleasant "high place" of conversation and relaxation in springtime and in the fall. [...]

There, we still have an ever more distant recollection—for almost all of us are dead—of a crowded September party, and a great rustic Sunday lunch, in an Italy that was still carefree, with a youthful and highly urbane Milan that today may seem a mixed grill cooked up between the Urbino of Baldassare Castiglione* and the salon of the Countess Maffei. [...]

But at Villadeati on that Sunday now as distant as *Gone with the Wind*, the village band was in the loggia playing traditional Piedmontese dance music, and all Milan was there, Giangiacomo handed out the sausages and the chicken to Wally Toscanini,† who was sitting on the lawn saying, "How delightful, how delightful"; Giannalisa and Inge, dressed in red, were chatting in German from a tower to a balcony; and Pietrino Bianchi was gazing ecstatically upward and exclaiming "All right, this is how the Italian cinema should have been, this is how *La notte* should have been made"...

---

*The author of *The Coutier* (1478–1529).
†The daughter of the orchestra conductor and a well-known socialite in Milan.

And then Pietro Ferraro flew low overhead in his plane, dropping leaflets bearing good wishes for Giangiacomo and Inge, messages that wound up even in the plate of sweets I was sharing with Ernesto Rogers...

Milan was proud to be the technocratic capital of the new Italian capitalism. There were two hundred art galleries, and conceptual artists stayed in the Torre Velasca* with wall-to-wall carpets and trilingual secretaries. The mothers of my pals in kindergarten talked of Christmas safaris in their red Morris cars; the driest among them commented on the death of that decrepit old Communist Pope John XXIII. Camilla Cederna† watched over us all with the care of a subversive entomologist.

On the second floor of Via Andegari, above the head office of the AC Milan Football Club, were the guest apartments for friends of the publishing house.

I have to mention the role played by Inge Feltrinelli, because here she was the leading lady. She says she was inspired by Gottfried and Brigitte Fischer's accounts of their home in Berlin, before the Nazi period, where people like Thomas Mann or Albert Einstein would drop in for a coffee.

Almost fifty years later, the guest apartments were intended to be something similar and the guest book is a fascinating list of a variety of internationally known names. Examples? The spring-summer tour of 1965: Ernesto Sábato, Robert Maxwell, James Baldwin, George Sadoul, John Polanyi (Nobel Prize for Chemistry), Gregory Corso, Max Frisch, and Ingeborg Bachmann.

The friends. One very dear to me was Roberto Olivetti. Very much part of those years, Roberto was the son of Olivetti founder

*Milan's first skyscraper.
†(1911–97). One of the most caustic pens in Italian journalism. An editorialist with *Espresso*, she was the author of *Pinelli, una finestra sulla strage* (Feltrinelli, 1971) and of an inquiry that was to lead to the resignation of Giovanni Leone, the president of the republic.

Adriano Olivetti (who died in 1960). My father had been on friendly
terms with Olivetti senior. At this point a 1958 document from the
archives of the Interior Ministry comes in handy.

> On the occasion of a book fair in the Canavese area, Giangiacomo
> Feltrinelli went to Ivrea, where he had a long and fruitful talk with
> Adriano Olivetti. The two left-wing industrialists hit it off; judging by
> what they said later, they understood each other very well and laid
> the groundwork for a joint venture. The meeting was largely the
> work of Olivetti, who at his own expense had organized a book fair
> specifically to showcase Feltrinelli's publications and had ordered
> the city to be festooned with banners bearing the name Feltrinelli in
> large letters. The Milanese millionaire was touched by this and
> hopes with all his heart that he may have the strength to leave the
> PCI [...].

In the early sixties Roberto had thrown himself into the family
business, armed with a sincere enthusiasm for electronics and the
new technologies.

Feltrinelli's friendship with Roberto led to his becoming less of
an outsider in the social world of the Italian upper class. Giangiacomo had been a guest in the Agnelli home, but there was nothing
for him there; much better to sit barefoot on the pier at Porto Ercole, or to take a winter sauna and a cold plunge at Villadeati; even
better still was the impetuosity of two rich, handsome young globe-
trotters of the same age consumed by curiosity about a world in
which distances were becoming irrelevant. What's more, Anna
and Inge were friends, they became mothers, there was me, there
was Anna's daughter Desire, we had a life in common.

Roberto had no luck at Olivetti. The family shareholders gave
him no respite, he was too far ahead of his time, stubbornly obsessed as he was with microprocessors (the term had yet to be invented). After resigning from his most important posts, and after a
spell running the Edizioni di Comunità, he financed the Adelphi
publishing house and *Espresso* magazine.

He had realized, I think, that the timing of ideas can be out of phase with the timing of individual lives. I have always thought of him as a wise and ironic man. He took my upbringing very much to heart, helping me over the most difficult moments (the seventies and eighties), and was always close to me, even when he learned he had the lung cancer that was to carry him off at fifty-seven.

The ingredients of the Italian "economic miracle" were, first, integration with the European market, the first government of the center left, the labor unions moving toward unity, the new Christian Democratic power structure, and the PCI ever more assimilated. And, above all, a development plan based on the automobile and the consumer society. Then around the mid-sixties, there was the first talk of recession and the end of the miracle.

Feltrinelli observed this transformation of Italian society with ideas that were not entirely clear. The publishing house had been in existence for a decade and, given the nature of the enterprise, absorbed enormous energy and resources. Success and prestige were not lacking, but its size was by no means comparable to those of the great publishing companies. At a certain point, Feltrinelli embarked on talks in a bid to buy into the weekly *Espresso,* perhaps with a view to giving his own group a new importance. But in the end they could not agree either on a price or on who the majority shareholder ought to be.

What has been said about the publishing house also holds for the Feltrinelli Institute. By that time it was acclaimed all over the world, but it was the kind of venture that it is hard to sustain privately. And in Italy there is no point counting on the solicitude of public institutions.

In 1964, Feltrinelli gave serious consideration to the idea of selling the library. In the meantime, he put it "on ice," as he said in a letter to the historian Edward (E. P.) Thompson: closed the service to the public and cut both staff and research programs. There were a few contacts with the Milan town council, but it soon became evident that the only potential purchasers able to guarantee costs and continuity were outside Italy. From the United States both the Harvard University Library and the Hoover Library of Stanford University made inquiries; the historian Ernst Nolte wrote from the German Federal Republic; and Michael Bernstein sent out feelers from Paris. In Great Britain, Thompson, who also informed his government, tried to find a European or, better still, a British home for the Milanese archives. The name of the omnivorous and already very powerful publisher Robert Maxwell also came up.

Apart from these signals, numerous offers were made to purchase individual collections held by the library. But Feltrinelli had no intention of selling things off piecemeal, and, in any case, the idea was to keep the fruit of so much hard work in Italy.

Mysterious rumors began to circulate about what was going on at Via Andegari. Rossanda opened a file and found out as much as she could. Her report to Togliatti, dated August 1963, was brief and worried. She spoke of the sacking, in her view on "political" grounds, of many associates of the publishing house and the institute on the grounds of temporary closure. She suggested the possibility of calling for industrial action. (In contrast with this, the last part of her report is wholly concerned with the situation within the Einaudi publishing house: she saw no problems there.)

Feltrinelli had Del Bo reply to Togliatti, who was following the affairs of the institute closely. The Communist leader talked of the matter in alarmed tones during his last meeting with Piero Sraffa, in July 1964. Sraffa had been in touch with Del Bo for some time. Nenni, then the deputy prime minister, sent a worried letter, in the name of "socialist culture." When rumors of the closing and sale of the library became more insistent, Togliatti decided to step in personally. He wrote to Raffaele Mattioli, one of the most powerful figures in Milanese financial circles, who had always been on very friendly terms with my father. The letter is dated 23 July 1964, and it begins with a sanctimonious lie.

Dear Mattioli,
I have never had occasion to write a letter to a banker. I do not know, therefore, if I will manage to express myself in a pertinent manner. The matter concerns the Feltrinelli Institute and its fate, both of which should be close to the hearts of all Italian scholars. My opinion, formed through fairly direct contacts, is that intervention of a certain urgency is required. But I do not think it advisable to take any steps to exclude Feltrinelli from his position as head of the institute. The institute ought to be transformed, in my view, into a foundation, without our changing either the name or the founder. Having done this, however, it will be necessary to guarantee annual running costs. I believe that you too are familiar with the figures. Now, don't you think that this sum could be put together through a commitment, at least for a certain number of years, on the part of a group of banks or the like? This is the problem I would pose you, considering that the solution I have suggested might be well received. But perhaps you know more about it than I do! If possible, keep my opinion in mind. And accept my best and most cordial wishes.

Togliatti

The leader of the PCI, who died a few weeks later, was never to receive what must have been a difficult reply to write.

During 1964, Feltrinelli had come to the point where certain decisions had to be made. What to do? Raise the stakes, seek new alliances, or give up certain business activities? Havana provided a good argument in favor of carrying on as before.

Selling and marketing books in Italy has never been easy. The fault lies with the schools and the lack of libraries, and the statistics have always been enough to make you blanch. Then there is the bromide that books are good for us, that they make us better people, and are even good for our health, a notion that publishers tend to endorse even before they call in the marketing teams. In reality, reading takes time and effort, and when we overdo it, it

leaves us "blind, consumptive, stooped, and dyspeptic," as Valerio
Riva would put it.

Around the mid-sixties, however, there was talk of a small "Italian bookselling boom." It was one of those moments when everything in the book trade seemed to be changing. The technological
revolution, paperbacks on sale at newsstands, distribution networks, the advertising departments: was "family" publishing finished? Were we really moving from "the consumption of literature
to the consumption of books"? Were books to become pieces of
merchandise like so many others? These were the issues that concerned the more traditional publishers.

How to encourage the spread of literature in Italy? In the course
of a television debate with Valentino Bompiani and Livio Garzanti,
two of the biggest publishers in Italy, Feltrinelli insisted on the role
of paperbacks and complained about the lack of time for reading:
his idea was that the working week had to be reduced. With these
same issues in mind, he replied to his colleagues Einaudi and Mondadori from the pages of the *Corriere della sera* (2 August 1964). Einaudi was betting on the development of municipal libraries, while
Mondadori saw new possibilities in installment plans, mail-order
sales, the creation of book clubs, and other commercial initiatives
outside the traditional channels of distribution. Feltrinelli wrote:

> For some time now, I have been trying to drop any preconceived no-
> tions, asking myself if it is true that the worst way to sell books is
> through bookstores.
>   You know that I am still young and a little impetuous: I like to
> gain firsthand the experience I need for my work. So I turned myself
> into a bookseller; I went into bookstores to see how they sold books,
> who bought them, who paid for them, and who (alas) bought them
> on credit or (worse still) merely leafed through them. I tried to put
> myself in the bookseller's shoes, but never forgetting that I am a
> publisher. I made some interesting discoveries: the foremost among
> them is that the criticisms often leveled at bookstores are based on
> hearsay, unjust, groundless, and perhaps even defamatory.
>   In Italy over these last few years, many new things have been in-

troduced (I introduced some of them). I thought we needed a revolution in the way books are displayed, and in the choice of stock. In
my bookstore on Via Manzoni, in Milan, I am not afraid to display
the same book in two or three different places, to show books face-
on rather than spine-on, to put the price tag in clear view above
each book, or even to present books inside those wire baskets green-
grocers use to display fruit and vegetables.

But of course there are more than just Feltrinelli bookstores [...].
In Milan alone, there are 250: It certainly cannot be said that the
network is inadequate.

Staffing has also improved remarkably in the last few years.
There are still no schools for booksellers, which exist, for example,
in Germany and Holland, but there are already young booksellers
who are not content merely with learning publishers' catalogs by
heart. Of course, if we had a modern school for booksellers, many
of our problems would be solved: and I wonder what costs more, a
gigantic advertising apparatus with complex customer administration and heavyweight public relations organizations or a good
school that might produce fifty new booksellers a year, all armed
with new ideas and a modern approach.

In June 1966, thirty years before the buzzing cyberworld of ama-
zon.com, a journalist from *La Nazione* asked Feltrinelli what he
thought the bookstore of the future might be like. The reporter jot-
ted down a confused jumble of things he had never heard of before: bookstores like jukeboxes, without books, only keys and
buttons. You go in, choose a title, and press a button. A machine
hooked up to the nearest printing works transmits the order. The
order, forwarded to the warehouse, comes to the punched tape
containing the text of the book selected. In a twinkling, an enormous offset printer prints out and sends the chosen books to the
bookstore in the typeface, language, and binding required. "Or perhaps in the cheap edition, with the pages bound along the top
rather than at the side, designed to be thrown away after reading."

The Feltrinelli bookstores went through their most important
phase of development during the early sixties, by which time people
had a clearer grasp of how a chain of bookstores can develop on a

large scale. The first experiments, which had been made since 1957, served as a general rehearsal for gathering information on sales and market trends. Compared to traditional family-run bookstores, the ones in which a counter separated the customer and the bookseller in his dark-gray dust coat, the Feltrinelli stores were already revolutionary: no schoolbooks, stacks of paperbacks, and the catalogs of the best publishers displayed face-on.

Around 1960, Feltrinelli came up with an idea for self-service kiosks; he had them constructed in Germany. Several were set up in Milan and in various seaside resorts, but, as they were not licensed to sell newspapers, it wasn't long before they failed. The experience did bequeath many ideas regarding the optimum exploitation of shelf space when, between 1963 and 1965, the second generation of bookstores came along.

Once he had changed the top management of the bookselling company, Feltrinelli began the search for larger premises, in busy city-center streets. The future mayor of Bologna, Renato Zangheri (who collaborated with the Feltrinelli Institute), accompanied Giangiacomo through the streets of his city in order to calculate the flow of potential passing trade. The historic nucleus of the most important Feltrinelli bookstores began to take shape: in the shadow of the two towers in Bologna, on Via Manzoni in Milan, on Via del Babbuino in Rome, on Via Cavour in Florence (with the blessing of Mayor La Pira). Each store had a history of its own bound up with the personality of the bookseller chosen to run it.

Feltrinelli tried many ways of drawing the public. In Florence, they offered roasted chestnuts. In Milan, a barefoot Joan Baez dropped in. In Bologna, he put new books on sale and set up the first big meet-the-author events. And in Rome, "it seemed as if all of the city's cultural life had gravitated to the triangle formed by Cesaretto's trattoria, the Plinio gallery, and the bookstore on Via del Babbuino," recalls the bookseller Carlo Conticelli.

Also in Rome, the bookseller Franca Fortini has this to say:

A bookstore with a pinball machine: naturally it was Feltrinelli who
had had it installed, and when he came here, the first thing he
would do was to start playing with this thing, either for fun or to let
off steam. They took the pinball machine into the back room, but
even the distributor couldn't believe his eyes. In 1965, pinball was at
best something you found in a few bars patronized by really young
people. You would see the machines at the seaside in summertime,
or in some country places.... And alongside the pinball he put the
Coca-Cola stand, a dartboard, lots of posters on the walls, and he
even had them put in a really beautiful jukebox, like something out
of some wild-west saloon, all chrome-plated and full of records,
rock, the Beatles–who were just getting big. [...] The high-school
kids would come in and start dancing. The Feltrinelli bookstore was
the first discothèque in Rome. It was a scandal, these fourteen- or
fifteen-year-old kids dancing in the store to the music from the
jukebox.

Feltrinelli also "raided" London; he came back with badges and
all the latest gimmicks: Marilyn made up to resemble Mao, silver
belts in the form of snakes, ties, grass-green miniskirts, mock-
leopardskin hats. All this merchandise was dumped in large wickerwork baskets, as in the street markets, by the bookstore cashiers.
He had a parking sign made with the message "Make love, not war"
on it. And what about the famous spray can "Paint your cop yellow"? When the Rome police came to confiscate the cans, they took
it out on Concitelli, the manager. "So you want to paint us yellow,
huh?" they said to him. And he: "For heaven's sake, it's only a joke.
My cop could be my boss, or my wife." But a prosecution followed,
and a report on the matter was sent to the Ministry of the Interior.

Feltrinelli did not go hunting for memorabilia only on Carnaby
Street. He also went to Milan's arty Brera district. There was a boutique there run by a young blonde who sold pop clothes and art-
nouveau bric-a-brac. He was smitten by her straight away and
invited her to dinner.

———

In January 1966, my father met Luigi Barzini on a New York
street. One crossed over to the other sidewalk; the other pretended
he hadn't seen anything. Benedetta, Barzini's younger daughter,
was in town on her own account.

Very beautiful and anorexic, Benedetta had stopped feeding herself in the conventional fashion when she was fifteen. In 1958, she
had been taken to a clinic in Zurich, then to Geneva and Paris.
When she was able to do without an IV, Feltrinelli took her with
him to Via Andegari. "I'm going to look after you now," he said, but
despite his sincere desire to protect her, he didn't manage it well.
"It would have been too painful: my illness was the visible sign of
a suffering he too had known," says Benedetta today. Moral: the
girl found her way by herself. In 1963, a chance photo for *Vogue
Italia* opened the door to the United States and to the court of Irv-
ing Penn, for whom she worked for a couple of years. Benedetta
was the only one able to compete with the black models, being
from the Mediterranean and therefore exotic.

In January 1966 Benedetta was twenty-three. On the night she
met her half brother in New York, they decided to party. Benedetta
suggested she introduce Giangiacomo to Andy Warhol. "I was incredibly proud: for the first time, I was going to take him to a place
that was my place." Andy was there, in his studio; they chatted,
and Feltrinelli was planted in front of a cine camera for a ten-
minute filmed sequence. I found some frames from the session in
a book by Warhol and Gerard Malanga. The publisher of *Doctor
Zhivago* alongside Lou Reed, Nico, and Sally Kirkland.

I don't have any clear memories of my father in Milan, either in
the office or at home. Of course, I cannot forget when he rushed to
the dentist's when I had a problem with the anesthetic, or when he
dressed up as Santa Claus for me and my friends, or the look on his
face when I made a foray into his office. But I don't have many domestic memories. Only extra-domestic ones.

My parents didn't have much of an ear for music. While my

mother's favorite social occasion was a ball, my father was fond of
folk music, the songs of the Resistance, the Kurds, the Guate-
malans, the Mexicans....So, close to the fireplace, on the fourth
floor at Via Andegari, a high-quality German record player, angular
and elegant, was in evidence. And there were the slim spines of the
rows of records: a little classical music, a lot of modern material. I
mean to say, records on the Italian "Sole" label, the anthologies
produced by Folkway Records, the Columbia Library, Cisco Hous-
ton, Leadbelly, Big Bill Broonzy...But also *Aftermath*, Françoise
Hardy, *Sgt. Pepper*, Coltrane, Jannacci, The Rockets, *Lotte Lenya
Sings Brecht, Bringing It All Back Home* and Mina. Popular music
for all tastes and in all genres. Together with the songs of the
Spartacists. *Sgt. Pepper* was my father's favorite record.

. What aroused my curiosity, though, was the sleeve of *Bringing
It All Back Home*. I discovered it when I was no longer a kid. I'm
referring not to the songs but to the sleeve. The copy on the shelf
bore a mysterious dedication written in blue ink in the top right-
hand corner: Für Giangiacomo von Manuela. There is also a date:
"16.3.66." As for the photo in the center of the album, better to describe it in the words of Robert Shelton:

> Daniel Kramer's cover photograph, shot through an edge-softened
> lens, is an essay in symbols. Dylan fondles his cat—named Rolling
> Stone. Behind him, albums by Von Schmidt, Lenya, Robert John-
> son...Elsewhere, a fallout shelter sign, a copy of *Time*, a nineteenth-
> century portrait. Just left of center on the mantelpiece is Dylan's *The
> Clown*, a glass collage he made for Bernard Paturel from some bits
> of colored glass Bernard was about to discard.

In all probability, the "essay in symbols" was an entirely acci-
dental creation, just as it is purely the product of imagination to
think what I thought, and still think, of the photograph on *Bringing
It All Back Home*: it looked as if it had been taken in our house,
in the very room where we sat down to chat, next to the record
player. I recognize everything. When Manuela gave the album to
my father, on 16 March 1966, perhaps he listened to it (a present

from Manuela gets listened to at least once), and nothing was missing: the fireplace, *Time,* sofa, fallout shelter, album, portrait (nineteenth-century, and fifteenth too), collage, pieces of glass, "electricity"... You can make the comparison to this day: thirty years have gone by, and the fireplace is where it was, pretty much the same, with a few more books and a few less symbols.

In that room, as a child, I found a community I didn't think strange, because I was already used to it. Later, and very slowly, I associated many faces and voices with the elements of real life. Like the man who called from the airport saying he was Henry Kissinger. It was Kissinger indeed, then a brilliant professor at Harvard.

But to return to the record, there was a song that fitted the film perfectly. In fact, it was the sound track of a film, from 1966. I have seen only excerpts of *Un homme et une femme* on television: the director was Lelouch, the stars Jean-Louis Trintignant and Anouk Aimée. And I don't even know the title of the song, it is a kind of French-style samba, smooth, feminine, sexy. Every now and then, they still air it on the radio, and it's like rediscovering my old orange beanbag: the one I used to lie on to stare at the herd of adults at the trough.

In 1966, the atmosphere in Milan's exclusive G. Parini high school was electric. *La Zanzara,* the school magazine, had run a survey that escaped the headmaster's attention. The girls and boys at the school had been asking questions about the use of the birth-control pill. Nothing unhealthy about that, but it was enough to have three students put on trial. The case became a national scandal: speeches from prosecuting attorneys, rivers of ink, a full-blown battle... One Milanese bookstore acted as a sounding board for the event, and one publishing house published a detailed account of it. "Mr. Feltrinelli, could we ask you the question that everyone is talking about these days? Why are you taking part in the Italian youth movement?" "Ask me something more specific, I've been talking since eight this morning and I need to warm myself up."

In Florence, high school girls had to wear black smocks to school. During a public meeting on the *Zanzara* case, following speeches by lawyers and teachers, two likable youngsters took the floor. They introduced themselves: "We are students at Parini." Their presence embarrassed the few or the many who were not yet aware of the news. Yet, not far from there, Don Milani's* kids were already locked in a public struggle to defend their right to avoid military service. In Rome the death of Paolo Rossi (a socialist university student and a victim of neo-Fascist violence) became a problem at the government level; the social sciences faculty at the University of Trent was in an uproar...It was getting more and more difficult to ignore the youth.

Just before the summer, the town council of Florence launched an event called British Week. At the bookstore on Via Cavour they decided to exhibit Penguin books; the baskets were full of London-made knickknacks imported by Feltrinelli, and the manager, Valerio Bertini, hired Mal and the Primitives, an English band with a regular gig at the Piper Club in Rome. The idea was to have them do a show in the store every afternoon, from six to six thirty, just to pull in a few people. But on the first night, the act went so well that Mal had to give a few encores. The following day, they turned up the amps, and things got a bit more complicated. The din made by the band could be heard as far as away as the Duomo, and traffic was blocked by the hundreds of kids on the sidewalk outside the bookstore.

For the last day of British Week, it was decided to hold an out-and-out happening, still among the books and the shelves. Surprise visitors included the unconventional singer Patti Pravo as well as

---

*Don Milani, a dissident Catholic priest, was an ardent champion of the underprivileged and their right to an education. His book *Letter to a Schoolteacher* became a cult book in the student protest movement.

Inge and Giangicomo. The party went on until four in the morning.
"It was a triumph"; Bertini recalls that in one week they sold almost everything, books and other things. What was left in the
storeroom was engulfed by muddy water: on 4 November Florence
had what turned out to be a historic flood.

The day on which the Arno broke its banks and Ponte Vecchio
risked collapsing, the bookstore was damaged too: the floor was
covered by two and half meters of a stinking blackish mass that ruined everything. The few books that survived swelled up on the
shelves. They needed a pickax to knock down the shelves. Pozzi,
the accountant, rang from Milan: "How are sales?" Bertini swore.

On 6 November the only vehicles on the streets were ambu-
lances, army jeeps, and an armored car with the president of the
republic on board. The bookstore staff tried to free themselves
from the mud. Feltrinelli made a surprise dash to Via Cavour. He
was on foot, in mountaineering dress and bearing a bulging backpack, as if he were arriving from a mission across the enemy lines.
How had he got through? Had he come by train? Of course not! He
had managed to somehow slip through the net and the barriers,
arriving aboard his Citroën Ds as far as Via San Gallo, less than a
hundred meters from the store. The car and the backpack were full
of ham sandwiches, milk, antibiotics, gas lamps, wax polish for the
shelves, various disinfectants, pasta, rice, and rags. He appeared at
the head of the stairs leading down to the basement full of sludge
to ask for a preliminary inventory of the damage. Before leaving
again, he thanked the staff one by one.

Giuseppe Zigaina is an excellent and well-known painter. Looking at his pictures, you can understand why he never left Friuli.
Karstic, lunar, lagoonal landscapes, sometimes with tree stumps,
other times with sunflowers, they are still his obsession. The house,
on the road that leads from Cervignano to Aquileia, is the same: in-
teriors with lots of woodwork, the smell of paints in the rooms, the

curved lawn. According to Giorgio Bocca, Feltrinelli used to practice throwing hand grenades on that lawn. Most people come here
to relax, to look for mosaics, to go to Zompitta for barbecues or to
Sistiana to eat fish.

Zigaina has chosen a kind of exile rather than lose touch with
his roots. He draws his inspiration from the evocative quality of an
epic land, rugged frontier country that has often been fought over.
Sometimes I went with him well beyond the chimneys of Umago,
on board the *Oedipus Rex*, a former fishing smack he bought in
1969. Before that, Zigaina had the *Istanbul,* a sloop in which he
nearly drowned along with Maria Callas when she was playing
Medea on the lagoon.

Zigaina was a great friend of Pasolini, from the days in Casarsa,
just after the war. He was also a great friend of Giangiacomo, more
or less at the same time. With him he shared the excitement and
the heated debates over the first exhibitions in Milan, the conversations with Vidali, the construction of the House of the People in
Cervignano, the abortive attempt to open a Feltrinelli store in Trieste, and many other things.

One day, Peppino talked to Feltrinelli of Pasolini: he might be the
right man to direct the new poetry series. But some backed another candidate, and Feltrinelli could not make up his mind, or
changed it, and the series did not get off the ground. Pasolini, who
had perhaps already been contacted, was disappointed, which
boded ill for his sole encounter with Feltrinelli. The meeting took
place in the early sixties, in the summer, at Cervignano; in Zigaina's
house. The host was tense, the atmosphere between the two guests
frigid. A little white wine was required. Zigaina: "Pasolini was in a
bad mode, his shyness did the rest. Giangiacomo, I was sure, had
no great liking for Pierpaolo."

But with the wine, the atmosphere became more relaxed, and
the talk began to flow. At a certain point Feltrinelli started in
on the story of a dream he had had the night before, which he

recalled clearly. He told of how he had found himself in the jaws of an enormous tiger. Pasolini immediately said, "A castration complex!" According to Zigaina, that was the end of the evening. Giangiacomo was mortally offended, and the two men never spoke again.

I no longer recall on which boat we went out on the lagoon with my father and Peppino: the *Oedipus Rex* or the *Istanbul*. It must have been a year, or at least some months, before the winter of 1969. It was my first visit to the island of Anfora. It was enormous fun brushing the waves while hanging from the deck by a belt; a great day. My father introduced me to the young woman from the boutique in Brera, saying she was his fiancée, but no other explanation was forthcoming. We returned at sunset, to the calls of nocturnal animals. On the lagoon, Peppino said, folks say little.

From a certain point onward, at the publishing house the climate was one of permanent revolution: "What youth is against, we are against," and young people were more and more agitated. In the editorial office, there was talk of passive resistance, the abolition of the internal combustion engine, world famine, the structure of the Italian family, libidinal neuroses, White Papers, and Latin America.

Feltrinelli's reasoning was taking a steadily apocalyptic turn. The capitalist world was on "the brink of eruption," and revolution was smoldering beneath the ashes.

Authors were aware of the new climate. Arbasino again, from *Paese senza*:

> In 1968, I was working on two books that were rather too literary (*Super-Eliogabalo* and *Sessanta posizioni*) for the house's image, by then heavily politicized and ideological, and I told Feltrinelli that I thought the books were unsuitable and he might be embarrassed by the contrast between them and his pamphlets. But he wanted them, despite everything: in fact there was a great and moving embrace, followed (both of us were embarrassed) by a kiss.

Mario Spagnol left the team for Mondadori; Valerio Riva got a separation by mutual consent in the summer of 1968; and when Filippini announced his departure, Feltrinelli pointed a gun at him. It all finished in a farewell drink at the bar of the Hotel Continental. The reins of the editorial department were now in the hands of Giampiero Brega, who had returned to the fold after a spell elsewhere. He was a versatile man, in the French manner (a rare bird here in Italy), and highly cultivated. His roots were in the PCI, but he was attracted by the most advanced theories of contemporary Marxism. He curbed and refined Feltrinelli's political impetuosity, kept the product lines broadly based, and watched over the publishing house's various souls.

Between 1967 and 1969, Feltrinelli published Castro (*Funeral Oration for Ernesto Che Guevara*), Chairman Mao's *Little Red Book*, the strategies of General Giap, the speeches of Ho Chi Minh, Dutschke's students, and Althusser's readings of *Das Kapital*. They were joined by Lévi-Strauss, Jakobson's linguistics, the poetic texts of Schönberg, Peter Brook's notes on theater, Panofsky's *Dürer*, Harry Stack Sullivan, and Eugen Bleuler. Other popular publications were the Genoan chef Nino Bergese's cookbook and a manual on LSD written by a variety of authors. The purely literary offerings ranged from the new Tom Wolfe to Don Backy, from James Baldwin to the Feltrinelli K350 series of thrillers. But the real phenomenon came from South America: Asturias (the Nobel Prize winner), Sábato, Vargas Llosa, Fuentes, *A Hundred Years of Solitude*. The Italian Enrico Cicogna was the first person in the world to translate Gabriel García Márquez, in 1968. The novel was not left-wing, but it oozed "magic realism," the ethic of miracles. One edition followed another; the response was overwhelming, and the newspapers for the first time used the term "cult book." One of the many reprints came out with a band bearing a quote from the publisher: "One of the best books I have ever read."

In 1967–68 the situation was still under control. Feltrinelli spent more time on the road than in Milan, but he always came back knowing his own mind. He still liked making books. As he explained in an article for *King*:

> I define myself as a publisher [...] explain myself in relation to the profession that has taken up ninety percent of my time for fifteen years. [Yet being a publisher] resists definition, or rather it may be defined in a thousand ways. List all those who have made a fortune by publishing books and make another list of all those who have squandered a fortune by doing the same thing. In contemporary publishing, the former are as numerous as the latter: I am thinking, for example, of Ernst Rowohlt or Gaston Gallimard on the one side, and of Kurt Wolff on the other. Rowohlt and Gallimard have made fortunes, their publishing houses are both economic and cultural fortunes: Wolff, the man who discovered almost all of contemporary German literature before the Great War of 1914–18, has lost his shirt a number of times, but culturally speaking he was always right.
>
> The term "fortune" has acquired a meaning that is no longer merely economic but something subtler and more ambiguous, a meaning that is, not very metaphorically, political. So let's forget the idea of publishing fortunes on a business level: the behemoths with half a million titles, fifty copy editors, a dozen low-quality magazines for intellectual servants or servile intellectuals, a printing works with super machinery provided by American aid, an intimidating bureaucracy and a "literary prize purchasing department." It is pointless trying to explain how such organizations work, [and in any case] the creation of such a monster is far from my intentions. I hope my publishing house will flourish economically, but I cannot help remembering that it sprang above all from a mirage, from a desire that I hesitate to call cultural only because the word "culture" strikes me as too big to be continually brought into play.
>
> So let's say this: I am pursuing a fortune in the second sense. I am trying to provide a publishing service that is perhaps wrong in the here and now, in the contemporary historical context, but will nonetheless, I am almost prepared to bet, be proved right in the historical long term.
>
> *Guevara's writings are necessary.* In the mixed-up universe of books, of communications, of values that are often pseudo-values, of information (true and false), of nonsense, of flashes of genius, of folly and of apathy, I refuse to join the ranks of the upholsterers of the world, the packagers, the painters, the producers of the superfluous. Since the deadly proliferation of printed paper seems to be

depriving publishing of all sense and purpose, I hold that the only way this business can be restored is by something that, despite fashion, I do not hesitate to call "morality": necessary books exist, necessary publications exist. No matter how paradoxical this may seem, I, as a publisher, fully subscribe to what Fidel Castro has called "the abolition of intellectual property," and that is the abolition of copyright: this measure serves to ensure that Cuba may have the necessary books, the books that Cubans need. But even in a situation of "private intellectual property" there are necessary books. [...] In the universe of Western letters there is a genre called the novel. Many say it is dead, many say it is alive: people write novels, read them, buy them.... My suggestion is that certain novels are dead and others alive: the living ones are the necessary ones. Living novels are the ones that capture changes in the world's intellectual, aesthetic, or moral awareness, a new sensitivity, new problems, or that propose a model for these new levels of awareness, or that explode the superstition about the unchanging identity of human nature, or that propose new paradoxes. This is why I published Pasternak and Velso Mucci, Parise and Gombrowicz, Lombardi and Fuentes, Vargas Llosa and Sanguineti, Balestrini and Selby, Porta and Henry Miller...the very heterogeneity of these pairs of names strikes me as vital and amusing. This is why I am publishing the young writers of the avant-garde.

There are political books, or, rather, books about politics. Many testify to a failure to take political action. Others accompany a concrete political act, an act that the public wants and has to know about. Recently, in three or four days, the bookstores have sold an entire and considerably large print run of a little book containing some essays by Ernesto "Che" Guevara: I would have agreed to publish this book even if it had not sold, because Guevara's writings are necessary. In fact I am publishing a little series (Documents of the South American Revolution), made up of books written by authors who are not as well known as Guevara and consequently sell less: I am publishing them all the same because young people want them and because it is right that they have them.

Breaking the breast barrier. A German journalist once wrote that I had gone from political commitment to pornographic commitment. Although I am a supporter of so-called disengagement and call pornographic only what strikes me as repugnant but not what may violate an ordinary—or at any rate petit bourgeois—rhetorical code, I applaud the bombardment of recent magazines that has achieved this amazing result: the breast barrier has been broken, and now you can show a naked breast on a book cover. Of course, this is a microrevolution, but we must make those revolutions that it is possible to make. Also, a small revolution can lead to a bigger one.

I don't want to give the impression that I am a man who sees publishing from a pedagogical standpoint, who feels he has something to teach. A publisher lives under the bombardment of printed paper in a world that has become smaller and devoid of frontiers, and he is glad of that: from the bombs that fall on his desk he must choose the ones to throw back so that they may explode in the minds of readers. He is surrounded by collaborators, who, because they are intelligent and sensitive, are often temperamental: during office hours, he must use all of himself and especially his eyes and nose.

A publisher is a person who spends money to buy titles, to pay royalties, to pay the production costs and the general costs needed to publicize books. Therefore he deals with people who handle money, with banks, with accountants, with data-processing centers.

The publisher is a vehicle for ideas. The books he publishes must then be sold. Therefore he has to have a sales apparatus, and the technical problems are many.

Can a publisher change the world? Or at least change the world of books? Certain books do make a difference [...]. My dream, which I hold to be the major factor behind that "fortune" I mentioned earlier, is the book that lays hold of you, that throws things out of kilter, that does something to the people who read it [...] that amid the confusion of everyday life sounds a note that will still ring out when the nonessential sounds have died away.

Is it a good thing for women to wear long skirts, or would it be better if they wore short ones? Did the German social democrats do well to join the Great Coalition? Why did Senator Merzagora resign as president of the senate? Is the birth-control pill a good thing or a bad thing? What is the ultimate meaning of science for man? What are the prospects for the labor unions in Italy? Would it be better to do this book typographically or lithographically? Can we pay this advance? What is Italy's position in the European Common Market? Is it possible to make a psychoanalytic analysis of the fad for buttons, slogans, and badges? Is the new publishing favored by the Red Guards? Can the culture industry be justified? What are students reading and what do they think about? What is the minimum

wage? What is the social function of obscenity? It appears that the
Bolivian General Ovando wants to sell the *Diary of the Che Gue-*
vara for $250,000: is the publisher still a publisher or a financier of
the war of oppression? Is black power rising in the United States?
Will it stamp out bellicose imperialism? Is the unrest affecting Italian youth a purely physical malaise, or is it political and rational? Is
there any hope?...

I admit: a publisher has nothing to teach, he does not want to
catechize anyone, and in many ways he knows nothing. And I
admit: a publisher, if he is not to be ridiculous, must not take himself too seriously. He is handcart, a man with a sign saying "Printed
Paper for Sale," a vehicle for messages. He is, to paraphrase this
McLuhan that everyone is talking about, a promoter of messages
that are also massages. And at the same time he is nothing, a mere
meeting place where messages are received, rerouted, and transmitted.... Yet: the right messages must be received and rerouted,
and writing that rises to the level of reality must be received and
transmitted. And so: the publisher must throw himself headlong
into reality, even at the risk of drowning. Knowing nothing, he must
make everything known, everything that is of use and makes
people more conscious at different levels. In this sense, "fortune"
acquires a real meaning, it becomes a horizon, a triumphant and
unfettered life.... And so: a publisher is nothing, he may think of
himself as a mere handcart, but a publisher must also approach his
work on the basis of a very risky working hypothesis: that everything, really everything, must and will change.

The Edizioni della libreria series made its début with a circular
personally endorsed by Feltrinelli in May 1967. It was intended for
his nine bookstores, in nine different cities. "Our Milan bookstore
has prepared a series of remarkably interesting political pamphlets. In many ways, this is a necessary adjunct to the party's publicity material on some particularly urgent topics. These are
documents and texts necessary for the political training of militants." The pamphlets were usually short and sold at an average
price of 250 lire; in other words, next to nothing. The first concerned Italy: Secchia's speech before the senate against the reform
of the public security law, and Terraccini on the same subject.

Hard on the heels of these came the series Documents of the South American Revolution: Che Guevara (*We Need to Create Two, Three, Many Vietnams*), Régis Debray (*Revolution within Revolution*), the resolutions of the Central Committee of the Cuban Communist Party (*We Accept Our Revolutionary Responsibilities*), Camillo Castano (*Ten Days in Guatemala*), Douglas Bravo (*Guerrilla Warfare in Venezuela*), and others, on Brazil, Puerto Rico, Argentina, Chile, Peru, and Bolivia.

New series rapidly appeared: on Africa, Asia, the Italian debate, the problem of southern Italy, and the student struggle. A hundred or so titles in all. The standard print run was four thousand copies. Big sellers were *The Blood of Lions* by Edoard Marcel Simbu (on the guerrilla war in the Congo) and *School for the Students*. Feltrinelli differentiated "militant" production from the publishing house's programs, perhaps in order to maintain a certain equilibrium, perhaps in order to make the message more incisive. As far as he was concerned, those little books had become the most urgent thing.

In August 1967 he also published the first number of *Tricontinental*, a bimonthly produced by the Organization of Solidarity with the Peoples of Asia, Africa, and Latin America.

It all began during the Havana Conference in early 1966. In Europe, this event had been largely ignored, but it was important. For the first time, there was a meeting that included six hundred delegates from the neutral governments of Africa and Asia, from the Communist countries (USSR, China, Outer Mongolia, North Vietnam, North Korea, and Cuba), and from international Communist organizations (the World Federation of Labor Unions and the Federation of Democratic Youth). The assembly proclaimed the need for "a global revolutionary strategy to counter the global imperialist strategy." *Tricontinental* was the new organ of information, made in Cuba, with English, French, and Italian coeditions.

"The duty of every revolutionary is to make revolution." The magazine was aimed at those who were in agreement with this: articles on the death of Lumumba, the oil wars in the Middle East, Ho Chi Minh writing to Johnson, struggle and victory in Laos, the speeches of Che, news from the black power movement in the States. Of particular interest was the third number (December 1967). The cover featured a fresco by Sebastiano Matta, there were pieces by Jean-Paul Sartre (reflections on the Russell Tribunal), on the Debray trial in Camiri, and then, halfway through, *Palestina: comandos "Tormenta."* For the first time, a journalist (unnamed) had managed to meet the leaders of Al Fatah, the group that had given a revolutionary character to the Palestinian cause. From Damascus, they took him by jeep to the secret encampment.

Following the Six Days' War (June 1967) and the occupation of the Gaza Strip, there were 350,000 new arrivals in the refugee camps. The Arab world (not always united) opened its eyes. No more handouts from the United Nations; "the aggressor is a tool of American imperialism!" The men of Al Fatah repeated the slogan to the correspondent from *Tricontinental.* They were seated on bunks, in a little room, among maps, rifles, and uniforms. Outside, the yelling of the instructors could be heard. One of them, Abou Ammar, expressed himself with "serenity and maturity": a hard face, a generous expression. When he took off his military beret, he revealed a pronounced bald patch. He stubbed out his cigarette on the muddy toe of his boot. Suddenly he said: "There are no wars without deaths, but it is preferable to die killing the enemy and knowing that final victory will be ours rather than to wait for a slow, inexorable death, sitting beneath a tent in the desert."

Since February 1969, Abu Ammar, or Yasser Arafat, has been the leader of the Palestine Liberation Organization. I don't know exactly when, but it was in the fall of 1967 that he granted Feltrinelli his first public interview.

7

It seems that in the early sixties men and women emerged from the Stone Age, ready to give meaning to words like "independence," "sovereignty," and "self-determination," even though they had yet to work out an ideology for those terms. It was a new vision of the world: all peoples could decide for themselves, no more oppressive systems, full rights for all the new names in the great address book of the world.

All the lonely people, where do they all come from? In order to answer this question, books had to be made, translated, and sent to the stores as fast as possible: investigations written by journalists with guts, with photos supplied by the adventurous paparazzi of war. Understanding "the other" in order to understand ourselves. Politics as the highest form of human endeavor. Through politics, people thought, we can understand everything. It followed that no goal was unrealizable.

Many of these people have now become more realistic; politics has not achieved everything. How naive the watchwords of that time now seem. The disorderly armies of the peoples had no room to maneuver. Perhaps we are all more realistic now, as a dramatically shrinking future looms over a terribly tense present.

Feltrinelli's Cuban adventure can be divided into two phases. The first, between 1964 and 1965, was spent in the hunt for a great book, the memoirs of Fidel Castro. The second, from 1967 to 1970, was another matter altogether.

The Castro book was to be the big new scoop. A major international best-seller, like *Doctor Zhivago*.

A few days before Feltrinelli's editor Valerio Riva left for Cuba, John F. Kennedy was assassinated. The first news, sent out by a Dallas radio station, was that the Cuban secret service was responsible. At that moment, Castro was never at greater risk of being eliminated. Amid the total chaos of that late November 1963, the world rocked on its foundations.

What to do about the plans for the memoirs of the *Lider Maximo*? Carry on, give up, or postpone them? Shall we go to the center of the action or sit in hiding and watch what happens? Riva argued with the travel agency, but he left for Cuba all the same, via New York and Mexico City. Hot on his heels, via Prague, came the Cuban journalist Carlos Franqui.

More than a year before, Juan Goytisolo had introduced Franqui to Riva during a conference of the European Writers' Community held in Florence. The former editor of the daily *Revolución*, for which he was now a correspondent, Franqui wanted to propose a European edition of Castro's speeches. He was taken to Milan, where they told him they wanted an authentic book of memoirs, beginning before the Sierra Maestra and perhaps ending with the Cuba of the missile crisis. After I don't know how long, Franqui let it be known that something could be done. This was followed by much coming and going between Italy and Cuba in order to gather documentation and draft a first outline to be put before the author. Riva and Herberto Padilla acted as ghostwriters.

The results of that preparatory work were taken back to Havana by Franqui. He was also carrying $25,000 hidden in the lining of his suitcase. It was the advance for Fidel Castro Ruiz.

Riva's journey lasted longer than predicted. After stopping over in New York, he spent a week in Mexico City. It was not easy to obtain a visa from the Cuban embassy there. This had been tried earlier by Lee Harvey Oswald.

When Riva finally landed in Havana, on 9 December, the nightmare began. There was no one waiting for him at the airport. Franqui, who should have preceded him, did not show up. When questioned, Riva declared that he was the guest of Fidel Castro and had come to persuade him to write his memoirs. It was the most inopportune moment for cobbled-together explanations, without so much as a scrap of official paper and after a suspicious stopover in New York. The faces around him darkened.

Riva described his first night in Cuba in a letter to Feltrinelli dated 20 January 1964:

> I couldn't understand what had happened. I was without a passport and confined to a hotel room on the twenty-second floor of a skyscraper from which you could see the poorly lit city. The paint was peeling slightly, and the room was dirty. There was no soap in the bathroom: the air-conditioning did not work very well, and a draft played directly on my neck. I spent most of the night pacing up and down the room, wringing my hands and wondering what was going to happen the next day.

The next day, luckily, Franqui arrived. His return to Havana had been delayed by a technical problem with his plane. Seven days stuck in Prague, where he had almost lost his dollars.

Franqui was in a tricky position in Cuba. After the revolution, he had been the most outstanding figure in the cultural information sector. A Trotskyist with a passion for the avant-garde, he had often argued with the Communists in the columns of *Revolución*. His star began to wane after the birth of *Lunes,* a cultural supplement printed by his paper and edited by a first-rate writer, Guillermo Cabrera Infante. The editorial staff was stricken by a painful case of "castroencephalitis," and the supplement had to close. The official excuse was that there was a paper shortage.

Recently, Franqui had spent a lot of time outside Cuba. He had left his family in Italy. This had not passed unobserved.

Again from Riva's letter:

> That his wife and children remained in Italy could mean that Franqui has returned to Cuba but with reservations: that in reality he has already decided to go into exile and that he has become more attached to the publishing house than to the revolution. It would be serious if those people received an impression of this kind. Serious for Franqui, who would certainly be forbidden to leave the island; serious for the book, because in the situation we find ourselves, with $25,000 already paid out, without a signed contract, with a manuscript made up of things that are very well known but not entirely unpublished either (and the only unpublished material concerns the guerrilla war), the suspicion that we are at the center of a maneuver that is in some way counterrevolutionary could spell complete disaster.

Despite these worries, for Riva the days passed tranquilly enough. It seemed like a typical holiday in which nothing much happens. Of Fidel there was not a trace. Celia Sanchez, his right-hand man, let Franqui know that the commandante was perhaps on a trip, and that Franqui would hear something within a few days. In Cuba, keeping people waiting is a ritual, especially when it is a matter of a meeting with the leader. Riva describes it all very well:

> There is a curious custom in Havana. When Celia Sanchez tells someone that Fidel will call him for a meeting, the fortunate mortal must lock himself in his hotel room, with the telephone near to hand, and wait for it to ring. The call may come at any hour of the day or night, but I think this is a legend. My call, for example, came at seven in the evening. The designee must be at his post when Fidel calls. If Fidel calls and does not find you, you might as well pack your bags and go. You are on the blacklist. The role, rank, or fame of the person singled out for the "great honor" is of no importance then.

After three weeks, Riva was more and more demoralized as X hour did not come. On New Year's Eve, to raise his spirits, he decided to organize a little private party. But at the crucial moment they called the hotel to tell him to rush straight over to Franqui's house. Castro was expected any minute.

Three long American cars arrived at high speed. The first entered the courtyard of Franqui's house, I saw that it was full of soldiers armed to the teeth [...]. The left-hand front door of the second car opened, and out stepped a big man wearing an old beret at a crooked angle. He had a short beard, a broad face, and a nice smile. "Franqui!" he yelled, and he moved forward to embrace him. I stepped forward with my hand outstretched and said: "At last, how are you? I'm happy to see you." He took my hand, turned toward Franqui, and said: "This is the Italian, I suppose?" Franqui said: "Yes, this is Valerio." "Well, Valerio. Welcome to Cuba. And forgive me: I should have come before but I couldn't. These are terrible times." He shook his head and dragged me into the house. He sprawled out on the divan and immediately said to Franqui: "You know, Franqui, I've read the book, it's really wonderful. I never thought it would come out so well. I gave it to some other people to read: they all say it's marvelous. I'm really happy. You've done a good job. Do you think we can add anything? I have material that perhaps you're not familiar with, you might take a look. [...] There's only one part, about the battle of Santa Clara: I didn't write that at all: it was Che. People ought to be told. I don't want them saying that I steal. Why don't we get someone to do a thorough job on that story?" Franqui put in a word: "True. [...] Either Fidel tells the story or that episode is out: there's no arguing about that." I was worried Franqui might launch into a discussion of the guerrilla war: he says he has no memory, but he can even remember the number of matches he used in the Sierra Maestra. In the meantime, I was studying Fidel: he has a strange half-falsetto voice. Sometimes his tone is shrill, sometimes soft and suave. Using his right hand, he continually played with his paratrooper's beret, adjusting it over his forehead, over his ear. He kept crossing and uncrossing his legs. [...] He is fat, with a belly and a big backside, but seen from close up he gives an impression of youth and strength. The beard looks as if it has been stuck on: the skin of his face is soft, smooth, childlike. His features are kind, pleasant, not military at all. He is forever excusing himself, listens with attention and composure, and never interrupts. [But if] he has an idea in his

head, it is not going to be easy to persuade him to change it. If you
tell him something he doesn't want to hear, he simply doesn't hear
it. He uses the same tone as before, but kindly, as if it's his fault he
forgot what you just said to him a moment before. Money was mentioned, but all he said was: "Yes, yes, thanks." [...] I showed him your
report on the planned contracts, the photocopies of the letters. Franqui spoke to him about Frankfurt and of the good job we had done. I
said we should add things and that the most important part was between 1961 and 1963. But Fidel wouldn't be persuaded: he made it
very clear: "I don't want to touch it. If I touch it, I'll ruin it. At most,
I'll write a preface, because I want people to know that this is your
work and that I don't come into it." It was awful. [...] Then I had a
brainstorm: in New York I got Mike Bessie to write me a letter. I ran
to my briefcase, took out the letter, showed it to Fidel, and began
talking to him about America and of the interest that his book would
arouse there. He read the letter carefully and said: "Obviously these
gentlemen see the matter from a commercial point of view. They are
thinking of the money they can make, because I am well known in
America and a lot of people will buy my book. However, it might be
a great trick, you see, to use this book to show them how things
really are and that I am not the ogre the newspapers make me out to
be." His eyes glittered, and he raised his left fist: "It would really be
a good joke. To use this book to take them from the rear," and he
made a gesture with his outstretched hand, energetically, as if sticking something into someone. "Because the people of the capitalist
world don't know me at all. [...] Let them find out, let them read:
something will stick. And not just what the newspapers say. They
can take this book home and keep it. Now it is decided: I must throw
myself into this." I began to insist again on the need for new material. "But I don't have the time," he said, "you have no idea how
many things I have to do in a day." I know that he also does pointless
things, that he wastes hours and hours trying out tractors, kids' bi-
cycles, new types of rifles, seeing how much milk can be squeezed
by hand from a cow's udder [...]. "We can use a tape recorder," I suggested. The idea struck him. "Right," he said, "that wouldn't be so
complicated." Franqui explained to him that a tape recorder often
gives good results: more liveliness, more immediacy.

Well played, Riva, you've done it. But the author was left with a
last doubt:

"So, how does this tape recorder work?"

In those same hours, a Soviet delegation led by Nikolai Podgorny was arriving in Havana. Preparations had to be made for Castro's imminent journey to the Soviet Union, where he was to make a long-term trade agreement. It was about sugar. Cuba was going to supply millions of tons of it to the Soviet Union: a permanent market for the national product.

Riva has another anecdote: as soon as Podgorny got off the plane, the first thing he asked Castro was: "Can we have the rights to your book of memoirs?" Castro shrewdly replied that he would ask Feltrinelli.

Feltrinelli's schedule: departure for New York with Inge on 30 January 1964, one day in the Big Apple, then Washington, for a two- or three-day stopover, and then on to Havana via Mexico. The planned stopover: ten nights. Feltrinelli explained all this to the American consul when he went to ask for the State Department waiver. He also told the diplomat about Castro's memoirs: the draft text written by the ghostwriters contained a lot of propaganda and not much analysis of the facts; more work was still necessary, especially for the period 1959–63. Feltrinelli also wanted to spend time in the United States: "to get to know firsthand US policy with regard to Latin America and Cuba in particular." To get a "balanced" view of the situation.

On 22 January, the US embassy in Rome telegraphed its opinion to Washington:

> [Feltrinelli] can get to Cuba without having to pass through the United States. The information and the points of view that he could obtain during his brief visit to the United States could favorably influence the way he handles Castro's memoirs, while denying him entry could give rise to a negative judgment of the US position on Cuba and Castro. In short, we see nothing to gain and much to lose by refusing to give him a transit pass.

Riva was perplexed by Feltrinelli's plans. In Latin America, you are well received if you come as a European who is offering a new

opening; but you will be detested if you arrive as a friend of the
United States. He urged:

> Always travel as if you were a normal tourist and not like some jit-
> tery international conspirator. [...] As I have already told you, for-
> eign news can have peculiar repercussions here: if you make
> particular statements, I cannot answer for the welcome you will
> find in Cuba. Despite everything, we are still on the razor's edge,
> since everything always depends on Castro's mood. So be very care-
> ful. There is no mediation, it is impossible. At present the United
> States have taken a hard knock, their hands are tied for the immi-
> nent elections, but it is hide-bound types like Goldwater who are
> calling the tune. The Americans will be making no pro-Cuban
> statements, at least not until the president has been elected. [...] So
> it's a waste of time. What's more, in Cuba they don't want to hear
> about America.

In New York, Giangiacomo and Inge spent the day with Sanford
Greenburger, the agent who spotted talent for the publishing house.
In Washington, the principal contact was Henry Brandon, the correspondent of the *Sunday Times*. But the program also included
meetings with Charles Murphy, the senior editor of *Fortune*, and
with Ben Bradlee of *Newsweek*, as well as a visit to the physicist Leo
Szilard. Szilard had spent a long time in Italy and he knew Inge,
who had introduced him to Giangiacomo. He was the man who, together with Einstein, had written to Roosevelt warning him that the
Nazis were on the verge of acquiring atomic power.

On the night of 5 February, a plane landed, a sweetish scent
wafted in through the open door, and Mr. and Mrs. Feltrinelli were
in Havana.

In early February 1964, my parents experienced all that the capital can offer interested and important tourists: Tropicana & Bode-
guita; Hemingway's house (old Renée set the table); the heroes of
the Revolution (Haydée Santamaría); Bola de Nieve, the most
amazing voice in the Caribbean; and the city's intellectuals. I imagine a lot of crushed ice beneath the palm trees, sunbathing, and the

moon hanging over the famous horizon. The Feltrinellis were
lodged in a government villa with garden and pool.

In the meantime, Italo Calvino, who had just married Chichita,
was treading the threadbare amaranth carpet of the Habana Libre,
a hotel straight out of the movies and a symbol of the time when
Havana really was the navel of the world. The writer was making
his first return to the country where he had been born. He had
been invited by La Casa de las Américas, on the suggestion of Julio
Cortázar. On the evening of 10 February he was scheduled to give
a public reading from *The Road to San Giovanni*. Amused for
some reason by Calvino's presence, Feltrinelli could not attend the
soirée because at nine thirty Fidel arrived at the government villa.

The first meeting was exploratory. Castro was expecting someone with the aplomb of an old millionaire, a powerful international
publisher. He began to talk "business," sounding out the possibilities of mediation for the import of chemical and industrial products, agricultural machinery, taxis, all in exchange for sugar. He
said with great confidence that in 1970 Cuba would produce 8–10
million tons of sugar, and that the island would also be able to export cattle.

He did not notice that the Italian was about his age and not wearing spats. The Italian also asked nonpertinent questions: when
were the elections going to be held? Was mediation possible with
the USA? What was happening in Latin America? He pronounced
Spanish well but made grammatical mistakes with every sentence.
Castro slowly began to catch on; he stiffened and asked a couple of
times: "Is this really the millionaire?" To impress those present, he
replied to a question with a quotation from Machiavelli, which took
even Riva–who was present at the meeting–by surprise. Machiavelli, maintained Fidel, had often been misinterpreted.

As they talked, the atmosphere grew more relaxed and the initial coolness was transformed into liking. Castro laughed, joked,

talked, and back-slapped. Feltrinelli was almost embarrassed by so much cordiality. "Unspoiled" (in English) was the word Inge chose to describe Castro in her journal.

The conversation was freewheeling: the October crisis, agricultural production, the clichés and the tedium of the official documents produced by the Communist parties of Latin America ("Socialism must not be boring but joyous"), relations with the States and, also, *Doctor Zhivago.* Castro said that he had read it, in installments, in the *Diario de la Marina,* in Batista's time. Feltrinelli turned to Riva: "Those rats! They published a pirated edition!"

At the end of the visit, Feltrinelli noted down his first impressions:

> In my opinion, F. C. is not a Communist or Marxist because the role of 26 July contradicts all Marxist orthodox processes, because the role of the peasants contradicts those processes, because his attitude to organization does not reflect the traditional Communist definition or practice. He is a middle-class Utopian and idealist (whose Utopia once came true). He runs this country as if it were his company, his corporation (poor application of the American executive philosophy). He has to be an idealist because, as in all countries in Africa or Latin America, there is no bourgeoisie.

Castro's words of farewell to everyone were "See you soon." Naturally, no one could say when. Patience was required. Then something changed. On 19 February, Feltrinelli wrote to colleagues at the publishing house:

> Dear Friends,
> Here is the situation: after having waited for two weeks, in which we have had only one interview with the Supreme Beard,* we made up our minds to leave and let things take their indefinite course. The days passed like this (in a magnificent villa with park, palm trees, and revolutionary guards armed with submachine guns): Riva was supposed to arrive at our place every morning at eight, but he would show up at eleven thirty. Numerous telephone calls were made at eight, nine, and ten thirty, we looked for him in his

*Play on words: in Italian, *barba* can mean both "beard" and "bore."

hotel, but to no avail. Then Franqui would arrive. The stenographer was the only one to arrive at the agreed time. At eleven thirty, therefore, we would have our general meeting to go over the latest news. Almost every day, we would receive advance warning to the effect that Fidel would be coming the following morning without fail. The night before he had been watching the pelota, then he had to go interview a fisherman who had arrived from Florida, at four in the morning he had been seen at the Habana Libre talking with Liza Howard (US television), and he had gone to bed at six; at nine he had been seen visiting chickens (he is a great fan of chickens, cows, etc.), then, yes, there had been a brief cabinet meeting to decide whether to cut off the water supplies to the base at Guantanamo and so on. But tomorrow morning the thing was sure to come off. Come the following morning...So we decided to leave. But on the day of our departure, we received word from several quarters of a new evening visit. And that evening, in fact, he arrived [...] in a good mood and said, good, come to my house tomorrow at nine and we'll get down to work. We went, and we found him wearing slippers and pajama jacket and pants and naturally his beard and for two hours we got in some good work. He told us to come back tomorrow (that is today), but today he was sleeping, he had to get up twice during the night on important affairs of state and had had almost no rest. The most important fact is that we are authorized to show up every morning at nine at his house, and we no longer have to wait for him. A decisive step. When he is in a good mood, he talks willingly and a lot. But you have to keep him off his favorite subject. Which is cows. He dreams of boundless cattle farms and, with a certain sexual satisfaction, of the artificial insemination of one hundred thousand cows that in 1965 would give him one hundred thousand calves, of which 50,000 would be females that could be made pregnant in their turn (artificial insemination) in 1967 and would give birth in 1968 to another 50,000 calves, of which 25,000 would be females, and in the meantime the 100,000 original cows would have become pregnant once more...and so on, forever and ever, amen. Our hero talks all the time, to interrupt him you have to shout. He talks about everything. When he talks about politics, for example about the role of the party and of the state of Cuba, you can see that he is improvising, that is to say, he develops his ideas as he talks (it gives one a certain pleasure to think that some questions stimulate him to have new thoughts that tomorrow, literally, can determine his political stance).

So they could knock on the Comandante's door every morning. On the roof of the house there was a small chicken coop and a basketball hoop. In the breaks, Giangiacomo and Fidel would take a few shots at the basket while Inge photographed their one-on-one matches. "He has taken, damn and blast him, a certain liking for me, with the result that he will work, that is, dictate, only if I am there," Feltrinelli wrote to Milan.

They worked using a question-and-answer system. The topics were extremely varied. On the great political figures: Castro had a poor view of Truman; he had even read his memoirs, badly written and presumptuous. He admired de Gaulle's rebellious spirit but found his memoirs laughable. That man never made mistakes, he had foreseen everything, never a doubt, "a born genius." Churchill, as far as memoirs went was the best of all. On the Communist nature of the revolution: "The revolution would have been made and would have been the same even if there had not been one single Communist. Most of the middle class, and the petit bourgeoisie, are for the revolution: the party must not become a part of the state." But, right after that, on the distinction between party and state: "We expect party functionaries to be state functionaries and administrators too." On the contradictions inherent in his being a man of government and a professional revolutionary Castro responded with an evasive smile: "Yes, there are [contradictions], but in the final analysis each country must make the revolution with the men at its disposal."

These were followed by more questions on Cuba, on the "dogmatic" wing of the party, freedom in the arts, the roles of science and culture, small private enterprises, the failure to hold elections in 1959, Latin America, the characteristics of revolutionary movements, relations with the United States, the USSR, the different applications of the socialist model, the agricultural crisis in Eastern Europe, Khrushchev, and why did those socialist states that consolidated themselves become conservative?

Finally, personal questions: his adolescence, the first struggles for peace, the visa for a trip to the United States in 1949: "I still can't understand it." And women too. Feltrinelli noted: "His sly expression when I asked him what kind of woman he liked." "Refined, spiritual, sweet," came the reply.

On Cuban-American relations, Feltrinelli made an interesting note after the meeting of 24 February, which went on until four in the morning:

> Was present during a long telephone call–35–40 minutes–with Liza Howard, who had been to see Johnson. Liza said that opinions and orientation are changing in Washington. [...] She asked (in Johnson's name) the Cubans to find a way of making a conciliatory gesture. Fidel replied that they had saved the life of an American pilot who ditched his plane into the sea, and they had returned an airplane and a fishing boat. Liza asked for a statement to the effect that in September 1964 all Russian soldiers had left the island. Fidel said that there were only technical advisers, never had the Cuban government recognized the existence of Soviet military personnel on the island: in any case, he would think it over, but there was no hurry. Impression: highly satisfied, in no hurry to close the deal (as he has already said on other occasions), but has, as I foresaw, an interest in normalization.

During his stay in Cuba, Feltrinelli kept an eye on the publishing house in Milan. Suggestions, orders, advice: on the campaign for the launch of Luigi Meneghello's book, on the organization of James Baldwin's visit, on advance orders for scientific books, on buying. "Be careful not to order reprints when they are not necessary, but for Christ's sake do so when they are necessary." Moreover, he was angry with Del Bo, Filippini, Pozzi, Spagnol, and Morino: "I detest your benevolent protectiveness, your phony paternalism, and the psychological ignorance that leads you to believe that keeping me in the dark will make it easier in my mind." Spagnol wrote to him from Milan: "I knew that the Caribbean was a hurricane zone, but I wasn't aware that they were powerful

enough to disturb even the quiet waters of Via Andegari…" Filippini sent him a gem: Einaudi wanted to publish a miscellany of
Khrushchev's speeches. "An insider at Einaudi told me the reason
for this: 'So Feltrinelli has gone to Cuba? Right. Then I'm going to
Khrushchev!'"

After a month of work with the stenographer, Feltrinelli went
home. He left Riva to carry on.

At the airport, he and Inge were told that the return flight was
going to be three or four hours late. In the end, it turned out to be
six hours. To kill time, Feltrinelli dashed off a note:

> I have mixed feelings about this man: he is a sort of Garibaldi, ut-
> terly unsuited to government work, incapable of working, reasoning,
> and hard thinking. Impulsive, rhetorical. High-pitched. Ideologically
> confused. For example, on the question of party and state (and in
> practice I don't think things are the way he says they are). I think he
> is poorly informed, he confuses his polemical denunciations with
> reality. He never asks for news, he seems to me a person so con-
> vinced of himself, of the things that were learned at random and that
> stuck in his mind, of the clichés he has picked up, that talking to him
> is useless.

After the publisher's departure, work on the Castro book came
to a standstill almost immediately. Riva, who stayed on for another
two months, struggled to maintain his concentration. The author
lost it altogether. Castro was enthusiastic about the project but always had something else to do. Everything depended on his mood
swings.

Just when Castro was up and running, Franqui would make
him lose the thread with pointless questions that made him launch
into endless philosophical lucubrations. In April, Riva wrote to
Feltrinelli:

> For his own squalid little reasons, Franqui would love to get proof of
> Fidel's "cultural liberalism" from this book, and he mistakes a set of
> superficial schoolboy notions for "cultural liberalism" […]. Fidel has

no original ideas: no one asks them of him, nor does he expect to
dish them up. He has said this himself very well: his gift is political
cunning, or, to put this more kindly, revolutionary sagacity. [...] Our
man is an intellectual of action–not a philosopher or a thinker.

Franqui wanted to return to Paris; Riva, his liver and brain reduced to mush, was recalled to his homeland. The publishers–
Athenaeum of New York, Heinemann of London, and Hachette of
Paris–with whom agreements had been made were told that the
work was going to take longer to produce than planned.

In 1965, Feltrinelli returned to Cuba, again with Riva. In Spain,
he had had ten copies printed of Castro's memoirs–as a demo: the
work was not yet finished. But by that time, the book was only a
pretext for talking about politics.

Arriving in Havana, Feltrinelli found that at least one thing was
unchanged: waiting to meet the Comandante. He decided to speed
things up. He prepared a card and hung it on the door of his room
at the Habana Libre. Passersby read: "Hunger Strike." Within half
an hour, reassuring functionaries rushed to make amends, and he
was invited to Castro's home the following evening. This was when
Fidel suggested a contest to see who made the best spaghetti. His
recipe: two hens, 500 grams of pasta to be cooked in the chicken
broth, with slivers of fresh cheese.

Of this evening, and of subsequent meetings, Feltrinelli made
notes and wrote a detailed memorandum. Here are some excerpts:

As soon as we arrived–a cordial welcome–I began to talk of the
book: Fidel said it was fine but much had to be added, especially for
the postrevolutionary period. For the next three months he would do
nothing else, wanting to make an important book. [...]
    The new Soviet leaders, he said, are capable, sensible. [...] The
tension with Khrushchev sprang from the Caribbean crisis and was
not centered on the withdrawal of the Soviet troops that Cuba finally agreed to as long as they left all their armaments in Cuba. [...]
Khrushchev generously supported the Cuban revolutioni, which

otherwise would have been unable to stand up to the Americans. [...]On the missile question, a Soviet emissary asked Fidel what he thought the Soviets could do for Cuba. Fidel replied: Arrange things so that an attack on Cuba is seen as an attack on the USSR–but de facto, not in words. It was necessary to install medium-range missiles in Cuba. Fidel's impression is that his interlocutor was sent specifically to agree on this, because the missiles were then installed.

Fidel saw the missile installations as a strategic matter of the greatest importance and also as a political matter inasmuch as it would have led to Cuba's becoming a de facto member of the nuclear club. [...] Criticisms of the Soviets: The missiles were installed in the light of day in a very vulnerable position with insufficient anti-aircraft protection, especially against low-level flight. Khrushchev made a mistake in telling Kennedy that these were only defensive missiles; in fact, he deceived the American president without solving anything, because at the end of the day the photographs demonstrated that they were anything but defensive. He ought to have said frankly that these were armaments that fell within the framework of a Soviet–Cuban accord. [...] The Caribbean crisis and the withdrawal of the missiles, followed by that of the Soviet troops, could have had terrible psychological consequences for the Cuban people, who would have felt completely unprotected. [...]

But Khrushchev was still among the most courageous of Soviet leaders.

On the Sino-Soviet dissension and Vietnam. Much of Castro's original liking for the Chinese had dissipated. The Chinese revolutionary attitude in which he had once believed in fact concealed: a) exclusively Chinese power politics; b) a continuous, systematic, stubborn and irrational smear campaign against the USSR. [...]

With regard to Vietnam, the Chinese attitude was equivocal, it put a brake on Soviet aid, and tended to alienate Vietnam from the Vietcong. They ought to set aside their disagreements: the Soviets are prepared to help Vietnam, and union with the USSR would make them safe from American attack. [...] Mao is an arteriosclerotic old fool who talks with the gods. As long as he is alive, you cannot count on any changes in Chinese policies. [...]

The revolution in Latin America is certainly under way. Currently in Colombia, in Paraguay, and in Chile the situation is developing fairly rapidly. In Venezuela the guerrilla war is still developing.

Cuba's support of this movement is quasi-official. But the Cubans could not do this if they didn't have Soviet backing in their turn. Santo Domingo: the attitude of the Americans is really absurd. Bosch was certainly not a Communist, and at first the movement was no more than a military putsch. But the panic of the Americans has transformed the Santo Domingo case into a popular revolt. [...]

The most explosive situation, however, is in Africa: the Congo, Angola, South Africa, and some east African countries are on the brink of revolution. More Soviet support—perhaps indirect—is required and large quantities of arms ought to be sent to Nasser and Ben Bella. This revolutionary spirit of international aid needs developing. When there was tension between Algeria and Morocco, the Cubans didn't think twice before sending a fully equipped battalion to Algeria within eight days.

American imperialism. Fidel's stance with regard to the Americans is extremely tough and absolutely intransigent. You get the impression that, come what may: a) it is not possible to either come to terms or coexist with American imperialism; b) it must be fought with steadfast determination. You always have to shoot. If the Cubans at the time of the Caribbean crisis had not shot at the American aircraft that flew low over Cuba, if they had not shot then (counter to the opinion of the Soviets), today you couldn't even play football in Cuba without the risk of hitting some American plane.

Stalin: a madman who liquidated the flower of the Soviet general staff and of the party and who allowed the mobilization of a German army three million strong without taking countermeasures, a coward and an idiot. What we now need—says Fidel—is for the USSR, calmly and firmly, to put a stop to the effrontery of the Americans in Vietnam and in Germany.

My personal observations:

a) Fidel looks as if he has put on a little weight, but he is in very good health.

b) The country is still run like a large company: steering committees elected from above but functional nonetheless.

c) The Che Guevara crisis. After Che's speech in Algiers [The question] whether it was necessary to give priority to agriculture and the industry complementary to agriculture, or whether it was necessary to proceed to the more general industrialization that Che probably saw within the frame of reference of the particular interchange between socialist countries. The fact remains that for two months now he has

been living in the country and no longer shows up at the Industry Ministry.

d) The Cuban economic situation is much improved. In any
restaurant, you get three times more for the same price than
you would have received last year. The shops seem to be well
stocked with clothing. Trucks run on good tires. Yogurt is
abundant and cheap.

e) The CIA is concentrating on attempts to organize an internal
plot calculated to overthrow the regime from within. These
efforts lead to petty plotting and, consequently, to increased
political vigilance. Every now and then, these little plots are
discovered. News of them is not given to the press [...]. Internal vigilance is, I think, more intense now than it was
before. The army and the police are without a doubt the best-
organized and most efficient sectors in the country.

f) The screw has been tightened in the cultural field. Some
cliques have been gaining in strength and power. For example, the hold of the Writers' Union on the publishing
houses. Writers' unions should never have control over publishing houses, which should instead be run by officials or
even by individual writers, but without answering to or de-
pending on the Writers' Union.

21 MAY, 8 P.M.–dinner with Fidel in the government villa. The
topic of conversation: the homosexual problem. With disturbing ve-
hemence he said: At this time we must extol the finest qualities
of our people. There is no place for parasites (as if there were no
parasites apart from homosexuals) that concentrate in certain areas
and influence youth. Pathetic individual cases. Predictably the
target of his railings was extended from pederasts to cover intellectuals: architects, writers (e.g., del Puente), theater folk, etc., as he
developed a heroic conception–already expounded with regard to
the struggle, and discrimination against pederasty–against the (traditional) Cuban intellectuals. Ay! ay! ay! I spy dangerous clouds of
intolerance!!

A brief discussion about Perón, who from this continent looks
like a demagogue but not a Fascist, Ho Chi Minh, and Che. [Castro]
said that Che was cutting sugar cane in the west. He joked about the
problem of Che but didn't say anything. [...] It is hard both to make
revolutions and to maintain them. You have to avoid what happened
in the French Revolution, using the guillotine until there are no more
revolutionaries, or what happened during the Soviet Revolution.

These and other simplistic statements, about literature and the arts, oozing with the machismo of a puritanism allied to a profound ignorance of the sexual and psychological, ethnological and socio-logical problems that determine sexual mores and the development of the arts, confirm the impression that there has been a turn of the screw in respect to cultural and moral problems alike.

By now the business of the memoirs had become merely a con-test of ideas between a nonpolitical politician (Giangiacomo) and an ultrapolitical politician (Fidel). Feltrinelli wanted something from Castro that might be transformed into public, official deci-sions. He was expecting an exchange among equals. At a certain point in their talks, without mincing words, Feltrinelli attacked the anti-gay obsession of the Cuban authorities (and of Fidel in per-son). Two days later, the prison authorities released a group of students listed in police files under P for pederast.

The two visits of 1964 and 1965 had a powerful impact on Fel-trinelli. He spoke of them in a semiserious but sincere 1967 inter-view with Gianfranco Venè in a glossy magazine.

"In 1964, when I became Castro's friend, I no longer believed in any-thing. No type of commitment, either ideological or political. Then..."

"Castroism?"

"No, but finding yourself talking about world politics face to face with a head of state, and being in direct contact with a concrete en-vironment like the Cuban one, can change something in your life."

"For example?"

"I speak for myself, naturally. We are living in times in which we do not know how to give a content, a perspective to our anxieties. We talk of politics and we talk of it in an abstract way. [...] But not Cuba. Cuba is there, and politics is constructed day by day with im-mediate effects. And, more important, it is constructed outside the usual framework: capitalism, Soviet socialism..."

In April 1967, Feltrinelli was back in Cuba for a two-week visit. Castro took him along on a trip to Camagüey. They travelled by car at night. Riva was also with them. Although still formally with the publishing house, he was there to write a newspaper article. The autobiography was no longer mentioned.

In Havana, Feltrinelli made friends with the photographer Alberto Korda. They talked at length about Che. Korda gave him the negative of a photo taken seven years before, during the funeral for the victims of the La Coubre disaster (a cargo ship full of weapons that had exploded at its moorings). His Leica had scanned the tribune draped in the colors of mourning that was reserved for local dignitaries: it was a windy day, and two chance shots immortalized a strange expression on Guevara's face.

Korda said that Feltrinelli was pessimistic about Che's fate. No one knew that he had been in hiding in Bolivia for five months.

On 1 June 1967, Feltrinelli wrote, in English, to Lyndon B. Johnson, president of the United States of America:

Dear Mr. President,
I am a leading Italian publisher.

From time to time, my authors, because of their writings, incur the wrath of governments: as a publisher, it is my duty to do whatever I can to guarantee their freedom and to help them be heard.

Ten years ago, it was the case of Boris Pasternak, who was attacked by the Soviet Writers Association and by the League of Communist Youth. I was Mr. Pasternak's publisher at that time. Today, it is the case of Régis Debray, a young French philosopher who is the author of *A Revolution within the Revolution*. Debray was arrested by the Bolivian police at the end of April, 1967, mainly because he wrote this book. Since his arrest, little has been heard of him and he has been held incommunicado. There are rumors that he has been brought to Panama to be questioned by United States officials. Official reports from Bolivia refer to a trial that will soon be held. But this trial will be a farce since the president of Bolivia, General Barrientos, has said that (a) "the adventures of Mr. Debray will end in Bolivia" and that (b) he will ask his government to pass a law reinstating the death penalty in Bolivia.

That the US strongly supports General Barrientos is known throughout the world. American influence in Bolivian politics, in the Bolivian economy, is a determining element, demonstrated by the presence of US military personnel and military aid. The responsibility for Régis Debray's fate is therefore directly in the hands of the US government. [...] As the publisher of Mr. Debray, I ask you, Mr. President, to exert all your powerful influence for the immediate release of Régis Debray, and as a representative of a large section of Italian culture, I respectfully suggest that you fully acknowledge all the implications of Mr. Debray's prolonged detention and, worse still, his possible execution or imprisonment.

Washington did not reply. In early July there was a call from Rome: it was Luis Hernandez, the first secretary of the Cuban embassy. Hernandez needed to talk to Feltrinelli face to face. He was sent by Manuel "Barbarroja" Piñeiro, the head of the secret Liberación department and the chief of Cuban counterespionage. His internal enemies called him James Bongo.

When I went to Cuba in 1992, I visited him. Barbarroja's beard was white, he ought to have retired long ago. Would he tell me everything? He wouldn't. But we did talk for a long time on the veranda of his house. He also summoned Hernandez and another man connected with the affair.

Piñeiro had a good memory, and Hernandez also had clear recollections of his trip to Milan in the summer of 1967. He had never seen Feltrinelli before. On arriving in the guest apartments on Via Andegari, he immediately noted Feltrinelli's brightly colored necktie and the hundreds of magazines and documents lying all over the place: "Can this be the millionaire publisher?" Feltrinelli was sitting on the floor. Hernandez joined him on the carpet, and they began to chat.

Apart from a few short articles in *Le Monde,* in Europe generally and in Italy not much was known about Bolivia, the guerrilla war, or Debray. On 19 April 1967, on coming down unarmed and in civilian clothes from the Camiri hills, Debray was arrested with the Argentinean Ciro Bustos and the Anglo-Chilean photographer George Roth. Their capture gave the Bolivian military proof that

Che was in Bolivia. Debray had been sent to maintain connections with Cuba. In 1966 he had already made a reconnaissance mission to Bolivia on behalf of the Cubans. When they arrested him, he said he was a journalist, but he was tortured.

Hernandez, in other words Piñeiro, in other words Fidel, felt that a campaign of solidarity was urgently required to draw international attention to the Debray case. The Cubans proposed that my father personally follow the trial scheduled to be held in the coming weeks. (Debray's French publisher, François Maspéro, was already about to leave). Five minutes later, the decision was made. ("He has millions of defects, but he is a man who makes quick decisions," Goffredo Parise once said of Feltrinelli.)

"The only instructions we gave him were to go to La Paz." According to Piñeiro and Hernandez, there was no prearranged plan.

On his arrival in Bolivia on 9 August, Feltrinelli checked into one of the two grand hotels of the capital, the La Paz. The city was swarming with journalists who were not journalists, informers who were informing God knows whom, observers who were observing heaven knows what, tourists who were not real tourists, Anglo Chileans, Franco Argentineans, German Bolivians, Cuban Americans, and Guatemalan Danes. All bustling about but keeping a low profile. The Italian mingled with the crowd. He frequented the lobby of the Hotel Copacabana, tried to buy a map and a copy of the Bolivian constitution, booked an excursion to Lake Titicaca, and inquired about the permits required to get to Camiri. Camiri was the prison in which Debray was waiting to stand trial. In his first hours in La Paz, Feltrinelli tried to get in touch with Humberto Vázquez Viana to find out about his brother Jorge, known as El Loro. He was a guerrilla. Captured and wounded by the rangers, while still alive he had been thrown out of a helicopter flying over the jungle.

According to the reconstruction of the Cubans Adys Cupull and Froilán González, the authors of the investigative book *La CIA contra el Che* ("The CIA versus Che"), Feltrinelli apparently also met Colonel Carlos Vargas Velarde of the Ministry of Defense, who allegedly offered to provide him with proof of a CIA presence in Bolivia and of the American plan to infiltrate mercenaries and Cuban counterrevolutionaries into the country. Their mission was to carry out spoiling operations in the hot zones, in order to lay the blame on Che's "gang." A few months later, Colonel Velarde, suspected of being hand in glove with Havana, was found dead in his office.

In *La CIA contra el Che*, it is also said that the Italian publisher was approached by George Roth, the photographer arrested with Debray and suspected of being a CIA collaborator. Roth wanted to offer Feltrinelli a report on the Camiri episode.

Around mid-August, Sibilla Melega landed at La Paz Airport. Twenty years old, from Merano in northern Italy, she was the beautiful blonde who sold beatnik trinkets in her boutique in Brera. She had been on vacation in Stromboli when Feltrinelli sent her a ticket for her first transatlantic trip.

On the morning of 17 August, Feltrinelli realized that he was being tailed, and the following afternoon, at 5:30 p.m., two plain-clothes officers presented themselves at his hotel and escorted him to the offices of the DIC (the Bolivian criminal investigations department). A long interrogation and then straight to prison. The news of his arrest caused an immediate international stir. "The impact was enormous," recall Hernandez and Piñeiro.

Antonio Arguedas, then the Minister of the Interior, speaking of these matters thirty years later with the journalist Antonio Peredo, in the autumn of 1997, recalled that the tip-off regarding Feltrinelli's presence in Bolivia had come from the CIA. His arrest was the work of the head of the intelligence service, Roberto Quintanilla and the American agent Julio García, who was on the ministry staff. The interrogation was conducted directly by the CIA, but produced no results.

There was no shortage of reasons for arresting Feltrinelli, but the pretexts were risible: the $4,000 they found in his pocket, the hundreds of photos he had taken (but they were of Lake Titicaca!), the maps (but they were printed by the Istituto Geografico De Agostini of Novara, Italy), the contracts with the Vázquez Viana family (but the father of El Loro was a famous historian: the family was very well known). The suspect clung to the sound rule of saying nothing. His interrogators lost patience: "You're a Russian spy! You're an agent of Soviet Communism!"

Sibilla was in the hotel when they took him away. She was stunned. Finding herself catapulted into a drama she could never have imagined, she dashed to the Hotel Copacabana, where she ran into Jan Stage, a thirty-year-old Dane who had been hired by the Cubans to send the news from La Paz via Paris. He destroyed Feltrinelli's contacts book and notes that Sibilla had in her possession. Some days before, my father had asked Stage to see if he could do something about hiring a plane, a small cargo plane, a DC3, anything, as long as it flew. (According to Stage, it wasn't clear why Feltrinelli needed a plane. Perhaps to fly someone out of Bolivia. Whom?)

On 19 August, Sibilla too was arrested and questioned.

That afternoon, all the Italian popular press ran the story. *La Notte* of Milan: "Publisher Feltrinelli vanishes in Bolivia"; the same headline for the *Carlino Sera* of Bologna and for *Telestar* of Palermo.

The following day, the headline of the *Gazzetta di Vigevano* read: "Feltrinelli Arrested in Bolivia." The same headline appeared in *France Soir. Le Monde* was more cautious: "Regis Débray's Italian Publisher Apparently Held by Police." The feeling was that the press was responding well. Some commentators provided detailed lists of the accusations levelled at Feltrinelli: he had contravened clause C of the decree of 28 January 1957 whereby foreigners were forbidden to interfere with the internal affairs of the country. Minister Arguedas issued a statement: "Bolivia is faced by the serious problem of the guerrillas and can have no respect for those who work openly with them."

In Italy, President Saragat and Foreign Minister Fanfani intervened immediately. Thanks to them, the Bolivian authorities expelled Feltrinelli after one day and two nights in jail.

On 20 August, at 2 p.m., they took him to the airport. To return to Europe, he had to stop over in Lima. Just enough time for them to declare him persona non grata there too.

On the 21st, from the *Times* to the *Glasgow Herald,* there was a single headline: "Publisher Expelled from Bolivia." The *Kölner Stadtanzeiger* was slightly behind with the news but ventured the most accurate headline: "*Zhivago* Publisher Arrested." More up-to-date was the *Corriere d'informazione*: "Feltrinelli Also Expelled from Peru," Minister Arguedas issued a press communiqué: "If freedom and justice did not exist in Bolivia, Giangiacomo Feltrinelli would not have left the country alive."

As he was escorting Sibilla to the airport, Colonel Roberto Quintanilla took an image of the Virgin Mary from his pocket. He gave it to her. His voice carried above the noise of the jeep as he advised her to light a votive candle to the Madonna.

The political objective had been attained. The publisher was shaken by his narrow escape but euphoric at the same time. When he arrived at Linate Airport in Milan (via Lima and Madrid), he was wearing a blue pullover and carrying an attaché case. A Senior Service in his mouth, he was whisked away by a black Citroën DS, avoiding the assault of the journalists.

In Italy, there was no shortage of declarations of solidarity, but there were also those who protested against him. Some papers launched furious attacks; the neo-Fascists made their opinions clear in parliament, and in the Feltrinelli bookstores in Rome and Milan they did the same, but with sticks and cudgels. Their war cry was "Down with Feltrinelli, the agitprop millionaire."

A few days after his return from La Paz, Giangiacomo offered Sibilla a new vacation. They left for Malaga and rented a two-master to sail to Oran and from there to Algiers. The sea was rough, the helmsman got lost a few times, and when they reached their destination, the sails were ruined. Feltrinelli met Colonel Boumédienne and told him he was planning to go to Rhodesia. There was some guerrilla action going on in the border regions. An increasingly agitated Sibilla persuaded him to drop the idea and go back to Italy, this time by plane.

During his North African trip, Feltrinelli found the time to write two long articles on his Bolivian adventure, which were published in Italy in early September. It was a hallucination more than a factual account. In his piece for *Espresso,* he denounced the slaughters perpetrated by the Barrientos regime, the wretched conditions of the peasantry, and American interference. His report concluded: "There is no doubt about it: another Vietnam has begun." But a few weeks later it all came to an end at the village of La Higuera. Colonel Quintanilla had Che's hands amputated and preserved in formaldehyde: they were the proof that he no longer lived.

In May 1972, Minister Arguedas (who in the meantime had abandoned the CIA for the Cubans) was to issue a surprising statement. He said that in August 1967 Feltrinelli had offered the Bolivians a ransom of $50 million for Che, in the event of his capture. The CIA said that the deal was out of the question. True or false?

In January 1968, Feltrinelli returned to Cuba once more, for a three-week stay. This time he was accompanied by Enrico Filippini, who was to recall the trip in an article for *La Repubblica*:

I went with him to Havana for the "Cultural Congress," which was
the last episode in cordial relations between Castro's regime and the
European intelligentsia. On the plane he did nothing but write.
"What are you writing?" I asked him. "Articles for *La Sinistra*." *La
Sinistra* was the monthly founded by Lucio Colletti, bought and later
scuppered by Feltrinelli. In Havana they gave us adjoining rooms.
He asked me never to close the door, and said that he would do likewise. Once I went into his room. He was sleeping on the floor, on a
pallet made of newspapers next to the bed. I had gone in to suggest
that he make a few publishing contracts: one with a really old an-
thropologist called Ortiz, who had written a fantastic book called
Africanía de la musica cubana, and another two with certain young
sociologists from the Cuban Institute of Books. "You sign them," he
said. "But my signature has no legal value," I said. "It doesn't matter." I observed him wandering the corridors of the Habana Libre. I
heard him make a speech in Spanish that only an Italian could have
understood. I understood: he wanted to let the Cubans know that his
function as a European publisher had ceased, that he thought of
himself only as "a fighter against imperialism."

During his stay on the island, Feltrinelli worked on an essay on
the Italian situation called "Guerrilla Warfare and Revolutionary
Politics." When he returned to Milan, the Italian secret services
obtained a photocopy of the documents. How did they do that? Mi-
crofilm at customs or a mole on Via Andegari? In his text, Feltrinelli offers a few examples of the "vanguard strategies," with
examples from South Vietnam and Venezuela, that were needed to
orient the future struggles of the Italian working class.

There are three possible strategies, he said, two wrong ones and
a right one. The wrong are the "revisionist" concept, inspired by
the PCI, and the Trotskyite concept of an "armed revolutionary insurrection in the future" (which opposed the PCI's cautious strategy in appearance only). The correct line was "the use of systematic
and progressive counterviolence." "Political guerrilla warfare
must develop as the fundamental strategic element in this current
phase of the struggle of the Italian proletariat": against class power
and against the authoritarian system. Resistance against coup at-

tempts from the right, an application of "foquism"* and the internationalist character of the struggle were all necessary to the
success of the Italian radical left.

The Italian secret service considered Feltrinelli's ideas unoriginal if not downright comical. But from then on, their surveillance
of him became even more obsessive.

Late that spring, an urgent invitation arrived from Havana. They
didn't say what for, but it must have been important. When Feltrinelli landed, he learned that Castro wanted to give him and
Maspēro a copy of Che's Bolivian diary, which had been smuggled
out of La Paz by Minister Antonio Arguedas: this was Operation
Aunt Victoria. Holed up in a little villa in Vedado, Feltrinelli translated the text in a couple of nights.

The diary was to come out in Italy in 1968 (before Maspēro's version), and the rights were sold for no charge to the publishers of
half the world. At that time, the Dutch publisher Rob van Gennep
resembled Che a lot: "I read the news of the diary's publication in
the international press, and I sent a telegram to Milan to find out if
I could have a copy of the manuscript. Within forty-eight hours, I
don't know how, I received it, without an accompanying letter. I
rounded up ten journalists, and in one night the translation was
ready. Ten days later, we had sixty thousand copies of the book in
the bookstores. It was a huge success."

The same thing happened in Italy. The cover of the Italian edition
bore the legend: "The proceeds of this publication will be donated
entirely to the revolutionary movements of Latin America." Questions were asked in parliament. Feltrinelli printed thousands of
posters from the negative of the famous photo by Alberto Korda
("Che in the sky with jacket") and had them hung in his bookstores.
The image flew over every city square on the planet. Much later, a

*Reference to a guerrilla tactic. Sporadic hit-and-run attacks are seen as the
metaphoric equivalent of lots of "little fires" that, theoretically, will one day unite
to form the big blaze that is revolution.

victim of lean times, Korda was to say that if he had asked for a percentage on that photo, he would have become a millionaire.

An embassy colleague of Luis Hernandez, Andrés Del Río, was bemused when Feltrinelli handed him a suitcase full of banknotes: Del Río did not know what to do with all that money, and so the suitcase was transformed into a bank deposit amounting to over half a million Swiss francs. The name of the account? The functionary still remembers it: Río Verde.

8

When the signs came, they came as a surprise to everyone. The golden age of postwar prosperity was losing its luster in the year 1968: the crisis facing De Gaulle, the Prague Spring, the *Little Red Book,* the *White Album,* Tommy Smith and John Carlos raising black fists to the sky, *Butch Cassidy and the Sundance Kid* in the cinema, an explosion of wage demands around the world, further cracks in Sino-Soviet relations, guerrilla warfare in the Third World, and the struggle at Nanterre, 22 March 1968. For the first time, you could count for something at the age of twenty, and sixty-eight meant the student revolt that was almost never limited to the schools and colleges. Above all, there was Vietnam: the inelegant swaggering of defeated imperialism. Vaster and more indefinite questions were emerging, a new anti-capitalist awareness in a West already in its third general crisis, a dry run for what would later be called globalization.

What is certain is that the world had never before witnessed events like those in Paris in May 1968, when an alliance of students and workers brought both the city and industrial production to a standstill for almost a month.

In Italy, the watchword was still "national reconstruction," the third Moro administration was in power, and the center-left was finally eclipsed. But from the end of 1967 (student unrest in Turin, and not only there) to the autumn of 1969 (labor trouble in Turin and everywhere else) there was a crescendo of unrest. The right to schooling for the children of migrant workers, no more piecework for arrogant factory bosses, and the sense finally that the struggle could be merged into a single wave. The thrust of this movement was liberating, prepolitical, almost precultural, and its unleashed energies made for a bumpy ride.

"I realized that Feltrinelli was going off the rails, that he had fallen in love with an analogy," wrote Enrico Filippini, "that he no longer understood the value of cultural mediation, that he had exceeded his own role, that his impatience had won. He became hasty, slapdash, headstrong." This is what happens when history becomes religion.

When 1968 came, Feltrinelli was ready for it. In fact he was a precursor whose ideas were shared by many. He knew the world and had traveled extensively; he was not insular, he had a global strategy. He had become convinced that taking up arms against the enemy was inevitable. Some people were amazed by this. The most generous interpreters maintained that his decision was "tactically" mistaken. His guerrilla strategy was understandable: if the Revolution was in danger, how else could it be rescued?

On his return from Bolivia in August 1967 he found numerous messages of solidarity (there was even a Marxist movement in the Valle d'Aosta), and he received invitations to speak in public from all over: Florence, Lugano, Livorno, Novara, Palermo, Catania, Rome.... In Modica, in the province of Ragusa, he was denied the use of the assembly rooms in the city hall, so the conference was held in a seedy motel.

Plainclothes police attended every meeting, and their reports were transmitted to the Ministry of the Interior.

In Genoa, Feltrinelli was approached by Giovanbattista Lazagna, who had been awarded a silver medal for his work with
the wartime underground movement. Lazagna was a member of
the PCI who felt frustrated by the party's soft line, or perhaps he
was just frustrated by life. He was a sanguine, slightly bitter fifty-
year-old. He had written to Feltrinelli to tell him about a series of
meetings to be held in the Anpi (National Association of Italian
Partisans) Club of Novi Ligure. The idea was to invite Feltrinelli to
talk about Latin America. They met in Genoa, where Feltrinelli
was scheduled to speak. Lazagna gave Feltrinelli a book of memoirs of his experience with the Resistance and invited him to a
meeting in a farmhouse complete with a meal of spit-roasted goat.
Around the fire sat about thirty comrades with long memories.

The meetings in Novi Ligure soon became important not only
for ex-partisans or young radicals from the area. The topic
changed from time to time, but in the debates that followed the
same questions kept surfacing. How to give the Italian left a revolutionary strategy once more? What was the lesson of the struggles
in the Third World? Before every meeting, cars with a variety of
out-of-town license plates arrived. Some faces were well known.
There was the Sienese Viro Avanzati, the commandant of the Spar-
taco Lavagnini partisan division; there were the Cattaneos, father
and son, from the Piacenza area. Then it was Pietro Secchia's turn.
Although the debate had been fixed for nine in the evening, at ten
in the morning he was already on the platform of the Alessandria
railway station. Lazagna, who went to pick Secchia up, gave him a
military salute and said he wanted to show him what activities
were going on locally. "There's no need, I know all about you," said
Secchia, cutting him off. According to Lazagna, Feltrinelli had told
Secchia all he needed to know.

Before his death, the PCI member and shadow Minister of the
Interior Ugo Pecchioli mentioned the Ligurian affair in a book: "I
talk of some of these people with respect, because they believed in

what they were doing and stuck their necks out in full awareness
of the serious risks they were running. [...] Lazagna and Feltrinelli
were neither provocateurs nor adventurers in anyone's service,
they were comrades who felt that the time had come to take up
arms once more. There was not merely dissent between them and
us [the Communists] but complete and outright opposition."

Feltrinelli accepted many invitations in the fall of 1967 as he
shuttled to and fro, talking to groups of one to three hundred
people. I can see him, both impassioned and fatigued. "I haven't
come here to talk in geographical or historical or ethnic terms,
which is perhaps what many people expected of me." The subjects
were the death of Che and the Debray affair, but above all, "political action." When "the Italian road to socialism no longer exists,
peaceful solutions no longer exist, and the space for mediation no
longer exists." The only way to combat Fascism and imperialism is
a clash head-on with them.

On 13 November 1967, Feltrinelli gave a talk on South America at
the San Saba Club on the Aventine, Rome. "He attracted a large audience composed mostly of 'left-wing groups' in the capital," says a
police report* dated 25 November. An informer said that in the
course of the evening Feltrinelli announced to the audience the
fundamental planks of the revolutionary platform sanctioned by
the Tricontinental Conference in Havana. The death of Che was
described by him as a grave loss that would not slow down the
struggle, but lend it new vigor. It had become important to take an
active part rather than indulge in Marxist-Leninist debates. Cuban
empiricism had achieved more than all the doctrines elaborated by
the various Communist parties faithful to Moscow. The PCI too
had become a tool of conservatism. The concept of political guerrilla warfare held good not only for Latin America but for the en-

*This document and the police reports that follow all come from the Confiden-
tial Affairs office of the Ministry of the Interior.

tire Third World and even for many advanced capitalist countries–
especially where the shadow of an authoritarian regime loomed.

According to the report made by the political police, Feltrinelli's
public activism was a disappointment to the PCI; the use of PCI-
owned premises and associations for such conferences was not
appreciated. The Rome Federation opened an inquiry into Feltrinelli's presence in the area.

"There is a great ferment in the circles of the so-called Roman
left concerning Giangiacomo Feltrinelli," stated the latest report to
end up on Minister Taviani's desk. At the San Saba conference, Feltrinelli apparently contacted some representatives of the local radical left to inform them of his plans and ask for their support. He
spoke of *La Sinistra,* the revolutionary Trotskyite magazine that he
was trying to relaunch with the aid of its founders. Transformed
into a weekly, *La Sinistra* could serve as a forum for those to the
left of the PCI. Feltrinelli asked the Romans to get their forces into
the streets and to take part in the nationwide coordination of the
"revolutionary fragments." As he wrote at the time to Toni Negri*
of Padua University, the point was not unification: what was
needed was to link up in the interests of common action.

In Rome, the police reports tell us, the various extra-
parliamentarian political groups in the city found themselves
obliged to decide whether or not to meet with Feltrinelli. Informers
were always present at the meetings. On 15 December, seven or
eight people met in the home of a member of a group known as the
Revolutionary Tendency of the Fourth International. Some spoke
for the Maoist faction, others for the League of Marxist–Leninists.
There was a Trotskyite, another person representing the magazine
Classe e stato, and a pro-Castro journalist formerly with *L'Unità.*
The Maoist faction said they would not talk to anyone who did not
support the leadership of the Chinese Communist Party. Others

---

*(1933–). One of the founders of Potere Operaio. He fled Italy for Paris, where he
taught at the Ecole Normale. Now in prison in Rome.

said that each faction had to preserve ideological autonomy. In the end, however, they decided that something could be done, that some trust was necessary. Some had doubts about Feltrinelli, but at least he had the means: they decided to go along with him and see what happened.

Five days later, they met with him in the backroom of his bookstore on Via del Babbuino. As well as those already mentioned, the meeting was attended by people from *La Sinistra* and another two magazines that came out irregularly, *Quaderni rossi* and *Classe operaia*. And of course there was an informer. Feltrinelli chaired the meeting and explained his ideas, talking of the role the new weekly could play, avoiding ideological polemics between the different factions, and saying that "liaison committees" were taking shape in Milan, Naples, and Palermo. He told them it was time to make a move.

The Roman "liaison committee" soon went up in smoke. As did the idea of relaunching *La Sinistra*. The willingness to work with Feltrinelli became an attempt to isolate him: he was seen as useful to the movement but at the same time too distant from it. Feltrinelli meanwhile began to see the "mechanical" nature of the radicals' internationalism, the "rhetorical" quality of their anti-imperialism, and, when it came to their concept of the class struggle, he thought they were much too traditionalist.

In late 1967, his attention turned to Sicily (where he sent the journalist Saverio Tutino to make a reconnaissance) and to Sardinia (where he went in person). On 8 December, a local newspaper ran a small article about this:

Feltrinelli Booed in Cagliari

After receiving a warm and enthusiastic welcome from the large audience that had come to the Winter Garden rooms in Cagliari to hear his talk on Latin America, the publisher Giangiacomo Feltrinelli was later the target of a show of hostility near his hotel from groups of youths. The protest ended with the well-known publisher,

at the center of a heated debate over his visit to Bolivia, being subjected to a barrage of booing and whistling. It seems that this protest
was organized by extreme right-wing youth groups. But everything
went off without further incident, and as Feltrinelli left Cagliari, he
made a good-natured comment on the episode, stating that he had
become a political figure and as such expected to receive not only
applause but also the insults of his opponents.

Carla Frontini remembers Feltrinelli, in an article published in
a Sardinian magazine:

Despite certain incongruities in his talk, we were captivated by his
charm. He was a strange man, so different from us ordinary folks!
He came across as brilliant and powerful, with a touch of folly. On
that occasion, a deep and strong friendship grew up between us. He
came to our house and slept on the settee in the study. And so our
little house at the foot of Monte Urpinu became his pied-à-terre for
the whole time he frequented Sardinia: 1967–68 and a part of 1969. He
was a good, kind, and very generous man.

There were good reasons for Feltrinelli's interest in Sardinia.
The island bred that stubborn spirit of resistance and courage,
known locally as *balentia,* that lives on today in the rugged folk of
Sardinia's equally rugged Barbagia district. In Sardinia at the end
of 1967, it was not a matter of a handful of intellectuals goaded into
action by the inequality of relations with the metropolis but whole
towns like Orgosolo that revolted against everything, students who
rejected a future as specialized migrants, militants repressed by
the police, bandits who fled and never got caught. Is there a connection between banditry and politics? The first to ponder this
were the Rome-based offices of the underground political movements. Armed shepherds and guerrillas are not the same thing.
But both inhabit the same impassable terrain, where bandits flour-
ish, and a rebel enjoys popular respect and support.

Feltrinelli's trips to Sardinia produced six pamphlets for the
Edizioni della Libreria series. Youth clubs protesting against the
national park in Gennargentu, the agropastoral economy, an emi-
grants' "charter," the grounds for separatism, and notes on the

police state and military exercises were the topics of these small
best-sellers. Feltrinelli even went so far as to contact the bandit
Graziano Mesina, a legendary figure at the time. Did he really offer
Mesina "rehabilitation" in exchange for "insurrection"? The bandit
did not need money or weapons, which he took whenever he
wanted. But the notion of Sardinia as "the Cuba of the Mediterranean" appealed to many people. Feltrinelli realized this during
his first visit to the Supramonte area. After having gone through a
normal police roadblock, a young national serviceman ran after
him and said: You're Feltrinelli, aren't you? Don't be surprised if
one day you find that many people see things the way you do."

Sardinia and the south of Italy in a Third World light: like Vietnam and Korea, Guatemala and Venezuela, Laos and the Philip-
pines, Mozambique and Guinea. Guerrilla warfare waged in Italy
was seen as the synthesis of political struggle and military conflict,
a struggle against imperialism fought from trenches of a new kind
dug in the cities and the countryside, in the schools and neighbor-
hoods. Feltrinelli remodeled the idea of partisan war in order to
tackle what he believed was the imminent danger: an Italian-style
coup d'état.

If you make a diagonal across Italy, north of Sardinia, you come
to the area known as the Trentino. Feltrinelli went there to talk,
still on the subject of Latin America. "The problem of the South
Tyrol," he maintained, "is exactly the same as that of Sardinia." He
met Sandro Canestrini, a lawyer and local celebrity. Canestrini had
defended many left-wing extremists during the hard years, not to
mention the Schützen (a South Tyrolean separatist terrorist group
inspired by memories of the peasants' resistance against Napoleon),
Jehovah's Witnesses, and an assortment of poachers.

Canestrini and Feltrinelli were friends: "Feltrinelli would often
arrive without warning. If my wife and I were out, he would climb
over the fence and stretch out in the garden, smoking and gazing at
the moon. When we came back, if there was a shadowy figure lurk-

ing somewhere, it was Giangiacomo." The South Tyrol had a special significance for Feltrinelli: his family came from there, the Valle dei Cervi was not far away, and Sibilla, his newest girlfriend, was from nearby Merano. But Feltrinelli was also struck by the pride of these frontier folk, and by the particular social relations and rules of the peasant communities: if the values that traditionally underpinned the defense of local independence continued to be upheld, then it might be possible to link up with a new socialist ethic that would serve to weld the ideals of the new world onto a preproletarian culture. In other words, the bells of the country churches might ring out one day in the name of an anti-Fascist independence movement inspired not so much by Lenin as by the "peasants' war," by the battles against Napoleon, or by the Anabaptist traditions.

Was coup d'état the nightmare only of madman Giangiacomo?

The end of 1967 witnessed a sensational political scandal. In the course of a libel suit against *Espresso* brought by General Giovanni de Lorenzo, top-ranking carabinieri and army officers confirmed that in July 1964 Lorenzo was plotting to lead a coup in Italy: one night carabinieri units were to have arrested labor union and left-wing political leaders. The general's armored brigade and the Folgore regiment of paratroopers were standing by. Perhaps it was only a plan to respond to street agitators in the event of a new authoritarian centrist coalition government, in order to prevent another July 1960, when unrest in Genoa forced Minister of the Interior Tambroni to resign.

In a 1964 series of articles written for *Avanti!,* Nenni* maintained that the socialists had to accept the mediocre compromise that was

---

*(1891–1979). A great tribune of the people, he played a key role in the socialist movement during the Spanish Civil War. Nenni was the architect of the rapprochement with the Catholic right that took concrete form when the Socialists were invited to become a part of a right-wing government in which he was deputy prime minister.

the reconstitution of the Moro government in order to prevent a
shift to the right of such dimensions that "the memory of July 1960
would pale by comparison." Basically, the rest of the left interpreted these events as the yielding, the weakness, and the capitu-
lation of the socialists, who were internally divided and saw the
possibility of an authoritarian threat as an excuse for them to join
the government.

Now, in 1967, the world was in the grip of political fever, and the
fear of coups was more plausible. The squares and the streets of
Italy were embellished with new slogans: on the left, "The University Is Our Vietnam" and "The Shop Floor Is Our Indochina!" on
the right, "Let's Cut the Crap, Bring in the Colonels." There were
creeping symptoms of an authoritarian "silent majority," and you
never knew what the Christian Democrats might do. Fear of a
coup was widespread. Militants of the PCI and PSI were advised to
act with circumspection, party branch offices were kept on an
emergency footing, and activists were advised to sleep away from
home and have a "safe" address.

Less and less a publisher, more and more a political figure, Feltrinelli split Italian society in two. He became a kind of lodestone.
As far as the (die-hard Fascist) right was concerned, he was a symbol of the corruption of the reds, the "eau de cologne revolutionary" who printed subversive pamphlets. If he so much as stuck his
hands in his pockets and strolled out to the theater of an evening,
the matter did not pass unobserved. An indignant letter to the
right-wing weekly magazine *Borghese* was inevitable:

2 Nov. 1967

Sir,
Some weeks ago, I went to a well-known theater in Milan to see a
show called *My Name Is Abel*, a collection of popular songs. Four
young Communists sang songs protesting against the military, the
capitalist Agnelli, the monarchists, and the war in Vietnam: in
short, against everyone except the Communists, of course. [...] Pic-

tures of Johnson and other personalities were projected as the four youngsters sang "The Red Flag" and "Bella Ciao." After the show, a public debate was proposed. Among the persons present were a mustached long-hair and a young woman in an audacious mini-skirt: Giangiacomo Feltrinelli in the company of a girlfriend. Having drawn attention to himself, our Giangiacomo held forth. He talked of the wartime Resistance movement, of world revolution, and of the "profound emotion" that he and the audience had felt on listening to these songs, but he was disappointed because people are content to be moved emotionally and do not come together to demand "freedom." This was the speech made by Giangiacomo Feltrinelli, carried away, with his miniskirted friend, who was carried away even more. Yours sincerely,

[signature]

The more Feltrinelli's antics were ridiculed, the more he enjoyed them. He posed for two photographs for *Vogue uomo,* wearing an otterskin cape and a busby. "From the heights of his bristling mustache, the publisher, turned male model, invites us to throw caution to the winds, to claim our rights, to face up to the need for the last consumer good that we men have neglected: male fashion." This was the benevolent comment of a centrist newspaper.

After this issue of *Vogue,* Alba Morino Laricchiuta, the spokeswoman of the "Feltrinelli collective," withdrew into that silence typical of southern Italian women. "We all tried to cover his back, we were really in the trenches, but Feltrinelli permitted the publication of those photos.... Only later was I led to think that the photo feature was merely a way of throwing people off the scent, he had other things in mind."

1968. Family chronology.
4 January. At Omi's place in Gottingen. Omi was my maternal grandmother. Christmas 1945 seemed eons ago. Inge, who was agitated, seemed to be thinking of that time. On that occasion a feast was half a chicken and two potatoes bartered for a couple of pieces of cutlery. Her recollections of girlhood: "we were always hungry."

This time, Omi had to cater to other appetites (and my bronchitis too). Gg must have been in Oberhof with S.

Early in the New Year, Giangiacomo left for Cuba.

20 January. Gaia's [Servadio] book was launched in Turin. Inge introduced Italo Calvino to Gianni Agnelli. The same launch featured Ernest Nagel's *The Structure of Science.*

23 January. A letter arrived from Venezuela: but wasn't he supposed to be in Cuba? "How far gone is he?" noted Inge in her diary.

1 February. Back in the office. Calm. Feltrinelli had not seen Fidel. During the journey he wrote the rough draft of an essay. The intelligence services mention this.

2 February. He was in Via Andegari, lunch in Gaia's honor.

He told someone to note that the new book by Max Frisch was on the way, and advised someone else to read the first biography of Kim Philby. Then he headed off to Via del Carmine. By then, he was living with S on a regular basis.

3 February was a Saturday, with my parents at Villadeati.

6 February was my sixth birthday. Family lunch. Gg took a nap. In the afternoon a little party with my friends. He bought a cake, *Mama's in the fact'ry (she ain't got no shoes).*

7 February. Gg wasn't around, no one knew where he was. Not even Tina. Chaos in the office.

9 February. Gg dropped in briefly.

14 February. He asked Inge if she would like to take over the foreign literature series from Riva, who might be leaving. She turned the offer down.

16 February. Gg in Berlin, where he gave a speech at the Technische Universität during the Vietnam Congress (a key moment for the local movement). He spoke, in German, as a representative of the foreign delegations, and on the subject of Vietnam he found a way to mention the chemical workers' strike in Hesse. "We were all amazed that he knew something about the strike in Hesse," recalls Günter Amendt, one of the strike leaders.

16 February. Feltrinelli published a paperback edition of the writings of Ho Chi Minh. Inge went to the cinema: *Blow Up*. Alberto Arbasino and Mario Schifano went with her. Gg called: he asked her to send greetings to the Berlin Congress from Moravia, Monica Vitti, the mayor of Reggio Emilia, the usual cast of characters.

21 February. Gg back in Milan. Rather cantankerous in the office, nice at home. He told Inge about the situation in Berlin.

22 February. I heard Brega saying: "He is convinced that he wants to go all the way. It's not the best idea, but I understand."

26 February. Editorial staff meeting. On the way out, my parents linked arms: "I have become what I am thanks to you, but as far as politics goes, I have to go it alone."

29 February. Bad dreams. I talked about them with I. The editor of the *Corriere* to lunch on Via Andegari. Giorgio Bocca called the writer Alfredo Todisco a Fascist to his face. No one left the room.

1 March. Gg was ill, according to Tina.

On 4 March he showed up again in a good mood; he turned down an offer from Rowohlt to produce a series together.

7 March. Gg in a bad mood. Misunderstandings with the *La Sinistra* people; he had trusted them, now he felt he had been ripped off. That evening Inge and Montale were invited to Vittorini's place. Vittorini had always been nice to her, with or without Gg.

Mid–March. An informal meeting at the Institute with four or five young people from the Milanese movement, a couple of Germans, two members of Gauche prolétarienne, a Portuguese, and a student from Trent. Half of Italy's universities "occupied" at least once a year. Trent was in the vanguard of the movement.

8 March. Everybody in Villadeati. Gg and I cleared the Bermuda grass from the English lawn. That same day, the intelligence service of the Interior Ministry sent out a circular in which they showed they were doing their duty. They knew all about the "liaison committees" promoted in Milan, Rome, Perugia, and Palermo. They had read in secret what the publisher Feltrinelli had written

during his trip to Cuba. They knew about his theories of guerrilla politics and his desire to pull Italy out of NATO.

20 March. Inge suggested that Gg use a pseudonym for the new pamphlet he wanted to publish. He talked about this with the editorial staff. He made up his own mind: no pseudonym.

The next weekend, Villadeati again. On Sunday a party for Iris Murdoch, visiting with her husband. Lots of guests. Gg arrived on Saturday night.

27 March. Pasolini to lunch on Via Andegari.

28 March. Carlos Fuentes's turn. Gg never shows up any more.

4 April. Memphis. Martin Luther King killed.

5 April. Friday: Gg went to Bologna in the evening.

6 April. Toward midday, he dropped in on the bookstore on Piazza Ravegnana, tried to call mayor Fanti, ate a sandwich in Toby's bar on Via dei Giudei (with Romano Montroni), had a nap in his hotel. At 6 p.m. he met some young people from the Marxist Center, a Maoist association. That evening, a brief visit to the Arci club and dinner in company at the San Donato restaurant on Via Zamboni.

7 April. Back to Milan on the 6.45 express. The police did not miss a second of his Bologna visit. Telephone calls, photos of all the people he met, his movements, all was noted. They filmed him on his way to Toby's with the bookseller Montroni.

11 April, toward evening. Inge was in the garden at Villadeati when the housekeeper Piera arrived, out of breath. She said they had called from Germany and that she had understood that Mr. Huffzky was dead. Three bullet wounds. Hans Huffzky was from Hamburg, fifty-four, a self-made man and a journalist since he was eighteen (with the *Frankfurter Allgemeine*); a friend of both my parents and my friend too. Inge met him when Hans was creating the first women's magazines in Germany and she was a photo reporter. He was a cheeky Saxon who had always loved us. In fact, on

11 April 1968 they had not shot him (Piera was a little confused) but Rudi Dutschke, who was cycling through the streets of Berlin. His attacker was Josef Bachmann, a house painter and a fanatical devotee of Hitler. Months and months of campaigning in the "bourgeois" press had borne fruit. Militant students launched a furious campaign against the Springer newspaper group. Clashes with the police.

12 April. Milan. Filippini recalls Gg taking an Einaudi publicity poster, turning it over, and writing in felt tip on the back: "Berlin, 11 April, Rudi Dutschke has been shot, Fascism will not overcome!" He hung it up outside the bookstore on Via Manzoni. In Milan, too, meetings were held to decide on what to do.

13 April. A group of extra-parliamentarian student activists, most of them Maoists, assembled in front of the German consulate on Via Solferino and headed for the offices of the *Corriere*. Stones were thrown at the windows. Feltrinelli, who had gone to see what was happening, was charged with having organized the demonstration, but was cleared of all charges. Dutschke did not die.

16 April. Gg regularly in the office, very affectionate.

17 April. Roberto Olivetti to lunch. He had the knack of talking about intimate matters without embarrassing people: "How goes your ménage?" he asked my parents. "Very well," replied my father, "we even flirt."

In April, all the most important Italian universities were in turmoil. After the riots at Valle Giulia (1 March) at the University of Rome, in which 146 police officers were injured, as well as an unspecified number of students, it was clear that the students were not running away any more. The character of the movement changed. The PCI's newspapers backed the struggle.

1 May. Gg took part in the Berlin demonstration. The Italian intelligence services warned the Germans that Feltrinelli was a dangerous individual with a "frenetically subversive personality."

4 May. Weekend at Villadeati. The guests were one of Inge's schoolmates and her husband, who was an astrophysicist with NASA. They lived near Berne. Gg made a surprise visit. Everything OK, it seemed as if nothing had ever happened.

7 May. Gg asked I to send money to Venezuela through a well-known German industrialist who was to be kept in the dark.

8 May. A book party for the writer Antonio Barolini. Gg came from Brescia. Guests included the banker Cingano and Roberto Olivetti.

12 May. Gg asked if he could sleep for a few nights in the guest apartment (problems with S. too?). Inge told him that he didn't have to ask: "You own the whole building." That same evening, Gg bumped into a group of students in front of La Scala. They attacked him verbally; he was not one of them.

13 May. He read me a book before taking the night train to Paris.

18 May: the *aula magna* of the University of Rome, an assembly of the student movement. Gg was present. The students asked him for support of their cause. Very much on edge, Gg stepped up to the microphone to be met with shouts and wisecracks. *The cash, give us the cash...* "I don't think that indulging in public tomfoolery, like signing a check here and now, would be dignified either for me or for you." Howls, whistles, catcalls, and the publisher left, vastly disappointed. Rome was already basking in summery heat, but the tourists hadn't arrived yet.

20 May. Fidel called about the *Bolivian Diary;* Gg was probably in Madrid.

26 May. Brega and Del Bo conferred in the presence of I: "As a friend, he no longer gives anything. He is going downhill with no way up."

End of May. At the Warsaw fair, the books on the Feltrinelli stand were confiscated. In France, Gg was on the *persona non grata* list. The French maintained that he had financed half of the extra-parliamentary left-wing groups of Paris. President Pompidou was to say more or less the same thing at a state dinner attended by Marella Agnelli and Lord Weidenfeld.

1 June. Inge attended a soirée in Milan in honor of Arthur Schlesinger, Jr., formerly adviser to John Kennedy.

3 June. Gg sent a telegram to Tina from Havana.

5 June. Robert Kennedy was assassinated. Andy Warhol was shot and wounded.

6 June. Gg returned. Inge was in Holland for an international publishers' conference.

12 June. Gg sent an unsigned telegram to I. Two days later, they were both in the office and in Villadeati for the weekend. One talked of Cuba, the other of Amsterdam.

20 June. Inge left for the Venice Biennial. Gg said he was in Rome, Paris, Sardinia, no one knew for sure.

24 June. Family lunch on Via Andegari with Morino of the press office. The person in charge of the science series had resigned. Gg reacted badly when Inge told him that his publishing house was falling apart.

26 June. Fritz Raddatz, who was with Rowohlt, phoned to propose that he publish Daniel Cohn-Bendit, the leader of the French student movement. His book would certainly be a success, but Gg's response was cool. "I don't publish books by anarchists." The following day, he left for Hamburg.

28 June. Inge got a good report on my behavior in kindergarten. Gabriel García Márquez to dinner on Via Andegari.

Surprisingly, someone recalled having seen Gg on 29 June in Val di Chiana, in Cortona, decidedly very far from Hamburg. According to the witness, Feltrinelli's Citroën DS picked up a Florentine youth who was wanted after striking a policeman with a shovel during the election campaign. Gg parked him in Switzerland for a while.

2 July. Letter to Olga Ivinskaya. Talks with the Soviet State legal advisory office were dragging on: "I assure you, dear Olga, that it

almost drives me crazy when I think of the lack of understanding I have to deal with: I find it incredible that people try to prevent me from fulfilling what I consider to be a moral obligation toward the persons dear to the Poet and thereby obtaining, at the same time, the full and very well deserved rehabilitation of his noble memory." Gg sent her five thousand dollars.

3 July. Cohn-Bendit phoned five times: "Why don't you want my book?"

A number of books on sex in the works: *Love and Orgasm* by Alexander Lowen, a reprint of the Masters and Johnson report; Malinowski's *The Sex Life of Savages in North-West Melanesia*; and Lely's biography of the Marquis De Sade (in paperback).

6 July. Everybody off to Gargnano, Gg included. There was Hans Huffzky, the writer William Samson, and Anna and Roberto (whose marriage was heading for the rocks). I could hear them talking late into the night on the veranda. There was talk of my first school (not private); I was to go after the summer. My father would have gladly sent me to a kibbutz.

7 July. A present. A real bicycle. Pea-green, beautiful, with a high saddle. Gg had to put blocks on the pedals so I could reach them. First attempts on the avenue lined with linden trees. We stayed on Lake Garda all week, without my father. Brega called Inge and told her: "Save your energy, you'll need it."

13 July. Gg arrived unexpectedly. He spent the night playing chess with Hans. In the morning he's wearing orange-colored pants. He was nice to everyone.

16 July. Valerio Riva left the publishing house.

6 August. According to Cuccia's diary, Feltrinelli saw him at his Milan office early in the morning.

7 August. Gg sent a telegram saying something like 'I'm deeply in love with Bo. "Bo" was the code name for his son.

19 August. Inge and Gg meet in Rome for lunch.

27 August. Gg, expected, failed to arrive.

7 September. Inge: "This is really the end."

9 September. Gg sent a telegram, a disagreement with Balestrini.

10 September. Parise felt misunderstood and neglected, all the authors were complaining.

11 September. Much aloofness. Del Bo said: "The Giangiacomo we knew no longer exists." Inge was worried about me.

16 September. Gg was in Milan but did not go to the office.

18 September. An evening for Saul Bellow. Gg behaved badly and left early.

End of September. The book fair was unlike all the others, Frankfurt was completely militarized. Gg serene with I. During the 1967 book fair, Gg was seen protesting outside the Greek consulate wearing a shocking pink jacket (so the papers say). That year, at the head of a tiny delegation of publishers, he descended on the mayor's home to protest police repression. Inge was thrown out of the best hotel in town because she had met a student leader in the hall. A new generation of European publishers: friendship with Klaus Wagenbach, and with Dominique and Christian Bourgois.

2 October. Gg came home to find out about my first day at school. We played chess. The bell rang: it was Giannalisa. Gg did not let her in.

3 October. Gg visited his mother. He told her not to torment Inge. When she was in Italy, Giannalisa spent a good deal of time seeking information on him, on I, and on S. I have her notes.

4 October and following days. A new clash between Giannalisa and Gg. Hans arrived. Weekend at Villadeati.

8 October. First real day of school.

10 October. Chess match. Advance copy of *Bacacay*, the new Gombrowicz.

13 October. Gg with me at judo lessons.

16 October. Even Arbasino was fed up, all the authors were fed up.

22 October. Calm lunch, all the family together. Inge had been to London and talked about her trip.

24 October. They forgot me at school. I watched the janitors eating.

29 October. Afternoon and evening with Gg. We played.

7 November. He was in the office. Frigid with Inge, then affable again.

Evening of 11 November. Ruckus at Milan Central Station. "Red Rudi" had arrived with his family. He was met by Gg. Too many photographers, some shoving, police intervention required. Rudi was *persona non grata* in half of Europe, and at home in Germany the climate was intolerable. At first, he stayed in our house.

14 November. Strike at Feltrinelli.

19 November. Rudi was very agitated. He got angry because lunch was served ten minutes late. Gg in a foul mood. The German writer Peter Schneider arrived.

27 November. Our guest was still rather ill, afraid, anxious, hypersensitive to noise, but he changed and became more likable. His visitors included Fritz Raddatz (who wanted to write a book with him), Bahman Nirumand (who had written a book on Persia for us), the German playwright Rolf Hochhuth and Günter Amendt.

28 November. Gg was in the office. He seemed kind but totally uninterested.

29 November. Tax inspectors visited the publishing house.

2 December. Gg was in Sardinia. The responsibility for everything was on Inge's shoulders.

5 December. St. Nicholas Day party with thirty children. Rudi played with me, taking off his shirt to show the holes made by Bachmann's bullets: "So now you go back to Germany, you get yourself a submachine-gun, and you knock him off. Ta-ta-ta." This is what I apparently said to him.

6 December. Lunch with Gg and Inge. He talked a lot about politics and I didn't understand much.

9 December. Row between Gg and I. She threatened to take me

to live in New York. He said that within six months I would have to know the truth. What truth? That evening, a party in town for Eco. Inge went with Bocca, Arbasino, and Camilla Cederna. Milan was still a beautiful city.

14 December. Inge in Paris. On 17 December, Gg arrived and took a room in the hotel.

18 December. Giannalisa gave Inge a silly spoon as a present. Christmas gifts in the publishing house. Tina refused hers because it was not a politically correct gesture.

21 December. Pre-Christmas lunch with Benedetta, Giannalisa, and the director Franco Parenti. Grandmother talked only with him. She did not know he was her daughter's fiancé.

23 December. With Inge first to Frankfurt and then to Göttingen. Mamma had a fever, but we went just the same to the Schiller-wiese, to Cron und Lanz for cheesecake, and to the theater for the Christmas show. Gg did not call. I asked only once where he was. We checked out our horoscopes with *Fatevi il vostro oroscopo!*, which had just come out in the "Universale Economica" series. Düstere Eichenweg 27 was still a great place to stay.

In 1969, taking a train in Italy was becoming risky, and it was not the fault of the state railroads. On the night of 8 August explosions rocked about ten trains and stations. And unexploded bombs were found. Was this the dress rehearsal? Police first looked for South Tyrolean separatists, then for the anarchists. Some years later, the courts indicted the extremist right-wing group Ordine Nuovo (New Order), headed by Franco Freda and Giovanni Ventura.

In the early days of that month, Feltrinelli was preparing to face the coup. In the Apennines above Genoa, he rented a farmhouse procured for him by Lazagna through a butcher living in Roc-chetta Ligure. The ex-partisan functioned as an adviser and secre-tary, especially in the disbursement of cash. For about twenty days the farmhouse was occupied by Giuseppe Saba, the Sardinian,

with a couple of his compatriots who had been recruited during
the meeting in Ulm. One evening "Fabrizio" swept in and unloaded
two radio transmitters from his gray Citroën. He had a good relationship with Saba but spoke little with the other two. The message
was to stand ready for guerrilla action in the event of a coup d'état.
Three sealed crates made their appearance, a Winchester carbine
and a Colt Cobra revolver.

At the end of the month, the second Rumor administration having been installed (without a coup), Giangiacomo left for Cuba with
Sibilla. By that time, his relationship with the Cubans was close—he
was said to have delivered to them a cargo of seeds, powdered milk,
medicines, and turkeys and breeding hens from Arkansas.

The welcome he received was as friendly as ever, with a couple
of one-on-one meetings with Fidel, all amid the usual feverish
atmosphere. One evening, he noticed that the black elevator oper-
ator in the Habana Libre was weeping: "*Que pasa?*" "Ho Chi Minh
died."

After Havana, a meeting was scheduled in Caracas with the
bookseller Valerio Bertini. Bertini had been sent for a three-month
trip to Uruguay, Brazil, and Argentina. The official purpose: a reconnaissance of the (legal and otherwise) left-wing organizations
there. But the Venezuelan appointment fell through and, on his return to Milan, Feltrinelli conducted a tape-recorded interview with
Bertini: he had done a good job. But was it not strange for a sophisticated Florentine bookseller, accustomed to meditating with
Henry Miller in the squares of San Gimignano and politically a
right-wing social democrat, to end up in South America playing a
secret agent?

The Hot Autumn began in Turin at the end of the summer, when
Fiat suspended 35,000 workers after a long series of strikes. At the
Mirafiori plant, they were protesting the company's noncompliance
with agreements on compensation. But there was more than that in

the air. Preparations were being made for a hundred days of agitation, 520 million hours of strike action, and huge demonstrations.

On 19 November, ten million Italians joined the housing strike called for by the labor unions. In Milan, the streets were full of families with children. Outside the Teatro Lirico, there was an encounter between supporters of the same strike, "proud adversaries" in dialectical opposition to one another. The inevitable scuffles followed. The police supervising the situation were jittery. Then someone ordered them to move in, the nightsticks came out, and jeeps gave chase to the demonstrators. The circumstance surrounding the death of officer Antonio Annarumma are not clear: the police maintained he died from a blow with a metal bar; maybe he struck his head as the jeeps were bouncing up at high speed on to the sidewalk. It was the first of a long series of funerals that rainy autumn in Milan.

The Annarumma killing caused an uproar: one of the leading members of the DC, Giulio Andreotti, stated that any weakness on the part of the state toward violent minorities could lead to an uncontrollable situation. President Saragat let it be understood that the moral authors of such crimes lurked in certain newspapers, and called for "criminals, whose purpose is to destroy life, to be put where they can do no harm." His spokesman stated that no progress could be made if matters continued like this: there were rumors of immediate elections, of a strong executive, of a revision of the constitution.... The atmosphere was that of a last stand, of imminent cataclysm.

On 4 December, at 11 a.m., the accused replied: "I am Giangiacomo Feltrinelli." He arrived at the court in Milan wearing a polka-dot tie, a dark jacket, and an even darker expression. Judge Amati questioned him about his giving "false witness" in the April episode, but it was a pretext: the views of the publisher, "known for his revolutionary oddities," had been subjected to extremely thorough investigation. They wanted to link him with some embarrassing

acquaintance, some compromising pamphlet. Inspector Calabresi
had done his damnedest, and had not always played fair. Today, the
attorney Canestrini recalls that Feltrinelli was aware of this escala-
tion, of a larger scheme involving him. He seemed shaken. Then
came Piazza Fontana.

Milan, 12 December: sixteen dead and eighty-four injured in an
explosion at the Banca Nazionale dell'Agricultura. A second bomb
failed to detonate in the premises of the Banca Commerciale, in
nearby Piazza della Scala. In Rome, three synchronized explosions
caused slight injuries. It was a coordinated operation. Antonino Allegra, the chief of the police political squad, had a name in mind.
That night, a hail of dispatches arrived in Milan from the Ministry
of the Interior and from counterespionage centers in Cagliari,
Genoa, and Livorno. The name cropped up every time.

On the morning of 13 December, the name rang out for the first
time during the packed press conference at Milan police headquarters. Some journalists asked police chief Guida if it was true
that the publisher Feltrinelli had been arrested. Guida paused before replying. "For the present, the publisher has not been arrested." "Is he wanted?" pressed the journalist. "I cannot answer
that," said the police chief.

Feltrinelli could not be arrested because he wasn't around.
Anonymous phone calls came in: "Where is the rat?" Well-known
journalists like Zicari, Spadolini, Ronchey, Pansa, and Tortora
called at all hours. Newspapermen in search of a scoop rushed to
Villadeati. The police wondered: Is he in Cuba? The south of Italy?
Algiers? The Far East?

The last time we saw him at home was in early December. Inge
couldn't rest. "I hope he isn't framed" was all she could say. At a
party, the famous literary agent Erich Linder gave the impression
he knew a lot about things: "Inge will desert the sinking ship."

On 14 December, Inspector Allegra requested a warrant to search
the offices and home of Giangiacomo Feltrinelli: "We believe that in

his domicile and in the offices of the publishing house there may be evidence pertinent to the bombing." The judge, Ugo Paolillo, denied the warrant. For want of anything better, tax inspectors checked out the publishing house. Judge Amati signed a warrant permitting the carabinieri to inspect the Feltrinelli Library, ordered the withdrawal of the publisher's passport, and signed a prevention order forbidding him to leave the country. Judge Amati's initiative was occasioned not by the events of 12 December but by an extremely convoluted affair in connection with an anarchist pamphlet dated February 1969. The forty-something mistress of a young anarchist confessed to having sent a flyer to the Feltrinelli Library after a minor terrorist episode in the city. The witness, primed by Inspector Calabresi, was later declared unreliable by the judges. It is not clear whether any flyer arrived: sending communiqués to the "library of the workers' movement" was common practice in ultra-left-wing circles.

The hunt for Feltrinelli was an ideal way to drag the PCI into the kind of 1948-style, under-the-threat-of-terrorism election campaign that Saragat wanted. By implicating Feltrinelli, whose political career had begun in the Duomo branch office of the PCI, who visited Castro, financed Potere Operaio, and did not finance the anarchists but had friends among them, it would be possible to show that the PCI was fomenting "red thuggery."

On 15 December, around midnight, the railway worker and anarchist Giuseppe Pinelli, illegally held in custody since the evening of 12 December, fell from the fourth floor of police headquarters in Milan. Chief Guida made a statement: "His alibi had fallen apart. He thought all was lost. It was a desperate gesture, a kind of confession." That same day, Pietro Valpreda, also an anarchist, was greeted by a question from Judge Amati that resounded throughout the entire courthouse: "Who are you anarchists? What do you want? Why are you so fond of blood?" They arrested him for the bombing. Outside, in Piazza Duomo, they were holding the funeral service for the victims.

9

In 1969, some of Feltrinelli's analyses no longer seemed to make sense. Perhaps he had been misled by impatience (political, personal), adventure, fanaticism, the allure of arms, an exaggerated desire for justice, vanity (is there audacity without vanity?), a sense of order and not disorder. There is no need to make posthumous excuses (moral, historical, or political); the words of Leo Valiani, one of the founding fathers of the republic, should suffice: "Feltrinelli acted in perfectly good faith and in a spirit of total disinterest, which deserve the maximum respect, in the course of his political and conspiratorial development, which led to the personal sacrifice of a man who believed in the imminence of a Fascist reaction in Italy." So, it's all clear. But why doesn't it add up to me?

Forty-three years old, an internationally successful publisher, having a diary filled with internationally known names, fluent in four languages, with a son to raise, with a twenty-year-old fiancée and a life partner hoping for a return match, enjoying a financial position of the first order—and then complete abdication. No one has done what he did. "Because we had nothing to lose, he had

everything to lose," said Augusto Viel, who before following Feltrinelli's lead (because others made the same choice) was a part-
time painter and decorator.

My father heard about Piazza Fontana from a radio news broadcast. It was in the chalet in Oberhof, which Sibilla (officially his
fourth wife since early 1969, with a wedding in Lugano) was trans-
forming into a real home. They would have liked to stay there until
Christmas ("He wanted to write an essay"). His reaction, as he
listened to the news was immediate: "It's like the burning of the
Reichstag, I must go back to Milan and call a press conference at
the publishing house!"

The Citroën shot across the Brenner Pass on 13 or 14 December,
heading for Milan. But in those hours, something changed. Perhaps they warned him: "The papers have mentioned your name."
He came to know that Via Andegari was staked out by plainclothes
policemen. He could not know, but perhaps imagined, that they
were building a case against him (the scheming of the carabinieri
and their stool pigeons emerges from the records of the Milan
courts).

He had to make up his mind. Go back to Milan, place himself at
the disposal of the police, and defend himself against the accusations that he saw (and he wrote this without thinking of himself)
as inspired and directed by one great repressive design? Or go the
other way, into hiding, for which he was already prepared (and the
events of 12 December merely confirmed his theory)?

The Citroën ate up the foggy miles, and he turned off toward
Borgosesia. It was late when he knocked at the door of "Cino"
Moscatelli, perhaps Italy's most celebrated partisan commander.
Cino listened to him, but he was in a quandary over what the party
might think. A couple of hours later, the sharklike snout of Feltrinelli's car slipped into the first of the tunnels, and Genoa spread
out before him in the tenuous wintry dawn. It wasn't a random decision; Genoa is the "red" city by definition, home to many people

who fought in the Resistance. He hid in Giovanbattista Lazagna's house. Here, he collected his thoughts and sent off a letter to the staff of the publishing house, to the bookstores, and to the institute. He said he had opted for "untraceability":

> It is the only condition that allows me to serve the cause of socialism, the cause I chose 28 years ago, when in 1942, at sixteen years of age, I wrote "Death to Fascism" on the walls of Milan; when in February 1945 I joined the Communist Party; when I created the Feltrinelli Institute and the publishing house in 1948 and 1954; and finally when we used that organization to develop political and cultural themes that were ever more bound up with, and ever more the direct expression of, the working classes in Italy and in the world.
>
> My predictions were not unfounded. At the first opportunity, taking its cue from the criminal attacks of the Fascists, the campaign of hatred, denigration, slander, and persecution launched by the right against the publishing house, the bookstores, and myself has exploded with the fury and violence of a hatred bottled up for over twenty years. Hired journalists, police, and judges are now hand in glove and resorting to all kinds of iniquity to involve me in events and situations that not only have nothing to do with me but also are a far cry from the revolutionary strategy that some, for reasons that are not clear, have honored me with championing.

This letter was followed a few months later by an interview of Feltrinelli for the new magazine *Compagni* ("Comrades") edited by Nanni Balestrini after *Quindici*. It was in much the same vein.

What do you think of the recent terrorist attacks and the Milan bomb outrage?

They are the work of right-wing extremists, people under the control of a right-wing command organization that has a specific political plan, which is implementing a specific conspiracy against the institutions of parliamentary democracy and especially against the Italian working classes. The plan underpinning this conspiracy, the intermediate objective, is that of providing a pretext that will enable the forces of repression of the Italian state apparatus to unleash a violent attack, to create a political climate that justifies suffocation of the claims of industrial and agricultural workers. These attacks are not the result of an offensive launched by the political vanguard of the Italian proletariat.

And the Italian situation?

It is grave. The coalition of the Italian and foreign right is far from being beaten; on the contrary, it is stronger and more united than ever. […] The center-left has shown itself incapable of implementing decisions suited to the needs of the country. It cannot opt for the left, because of the strongly right-wing leanings of both the social democratic movement and broad strata of the DC, and out of a cold calculation of their own strength: Rumor recently stated that the government no longer controls either the army or the police, both of which are forces of determinant political importance in the current situation. There is consequently nothing surprising about the fact that the government is incapable of defending institutions and citizens against the threat of the right, and that the perpetrators and instigators of the carnage in Milan and the terrorist attacks in Rome go unpunished.

What can the traditional left do in a pitched battle against the right?

I very much doubt that the traditional political organizations, the ones that would have the strength [to fight] today, are contemplating such a strategy. For twenty years now, they have been working on the basis of a different, Laborite standpoint; cells were selected with prospects of a parliamentary, electoral path to socialism in mind. Let's not forget that the strife of last autumn was forced on the labor unions by the working class, which would otherwise have ousted them, and so, today, faced with a dimension of the struggle that was neither foreseen nor desired, perhaps the political organization, in many places at least, would be unfit to play the kind of role in the struggle that such a strategy involves.

Why would anyone want to frame Feltrinelli, harm him, or have him liquidated?

In my capacity as publisher, I have been found guilty of defending liberty, of having denounced the plotting of the right-wing coalition and its plans for a coup d'état, of having conspired to further the political and economic freedoms of our country. I published pamphlets advocating the independence of the Sardinian people, and I supported the Italian proletariat, the population of the underdeveloped regions, the migrant workers forced by the violence of hunger and poverty to leave their homes and their lands. In the eyes of the Italian and the international right, I am guilty of having sustained the struggles for independence and socialism of the peoples who, arms in hand, are struggling against imperialism. [...] I take full responsibility for these things that the right sees as crimes: if they are crimes, then I am proud of having committed them. [...]

If I don't show up in my office, it is because, faced as I am with the ongoing conspiracy of the coalition of the Italian and the foreign right, I have no confidence that the truth will triumph. Against a press that systematically carries out terrorists acts, I feel, as all citizens do, defenseless. Against the intrigues and the provocation of the right and of certain forces in the executive, I feel defenseless in a country where, at the end of a "normal" interrogation, you can fall to your death from the fourth-floor window of police headquarters. [...] But democracy, justice, and liberty cannot be measured by the "Feltrinelli case." They cannot be measured by safeguarding the political and civil rights of a Feltrinelli. [...] Until the rights of the working classes are recognized and safeguarded, I refuse both the convictions and the acquittals of a system that discriminates between citizens, dividing them into those who have friends, money, and lawyers, and therefore rights and power, and those who have no money and are therefore exposed daily to the ugliest forms of harassment and the most atrocious abuses.

The publishing house, in the days following 12 December, was under siege. There was still no news of the publisher but plenty of insinuations in the press. From Via Andegari, appeals went out for statements of solidarity from the intellectual world. Some sent generic telegrams ("I share in the contempt for neo-Fascist speculation. Lalla Roman"); others spoke of the publishing house ("I affirm that the Feltrinelli house has published morally praiseworthy books. Giuseppe Ungaretti"); others made distinctions ("Despite ideological differences I express full solidarity against continued defamation of the institute and publishing house. Davide Lajolo"); others offered wholehearted support ("Outraged by the shocking libel campaign against your person and publishing activities. Ludovico Geymonat"). From the philosopher Norberto Bobbio: "I add my voice, weak as it may be, to the chorus of protest against the gradual—but not imperceptible—transformation of a vaunted constitutional state into a police state."

A guest in the Lazagna home for two weeks around Christmas time, Feltrinelli contacted the Roman group Potere Operaio. They fixed a meeting.

A few days later, a second meeting was set up, again in Genoa, again with the ex-partisan Lazagna guarding the door, and thanks again to the good offices of the inscrutable Balestrini in his corduroy jacket. This meeting was also attended by Franco Piperno, the national leader of Potere Operaio, and Professor Toni Negri. The embryonic organization that Feltrinelli had conceived emerged clearly. He accepted that he would have to live in hiding. They decided to use pseudonyms for greater security. Lazagna's apartment overlooked a small factory with the sign "Fratelli Ivaldi" ("Ivaldi Brothers"). Feltrinelli said: "I'll call myself Osvaldo." Scalzone recalls that he later realized that "Osvaldo Ivaldi" was the false name used by Giovanni Pesce during the Resistance. He never asked Feltrinelli if "Osvaldo" had come to him by chance or whether it had been a deliberate choice.

Cocco Bill, a comrade with the network in the Como area, was told to be ready for the evening of 30 December: "We need to cross [the border] at the safest point." It was a bad time because of strict antismuggling surveillance. Cocco Bill did not know who he was to take out of the country: "I thought it was a comrade with Potere Operaio. There had been a few dragnets at the time, and there were a lot of wanted people about." But so much snow fell that night that the crossing was postponed for forty-eight hours. On 1 January 1970, Cocco Bill met with Cinto. They waited. Three men got out of the car on the valley floor: two were leaders of Potere Operaio, and the third was a stranger to Cocco Bill. The crossing into Switzerland, through snow over a meter deep, took little more than an hour. On the other side they were supposed to meet up again with the two Potere Operaio men after passing through customs. But the men did not show, they were lost in the maze of small local roads. So Cocco Bill left the stranger at the railroad station. The stranger asked the smuggler what he could do for him in exchange for his help. It turned out that Cinto had a son who wanted an encyclopedia. Only after the train left did the two comrades from Potere Operaio arrive with a screech of tires. "They came up to me, excited, saying, Do you know who he is?" Until then, all Feltrinelli had meant to Cocco Bill was a publishing company that produced books he was interested in.

In an article run by *Espresso* (January 1979):

> We have to express strong disapproval of Feltrinelli's recent behavior. The police have been searching for him for twenty-six days. His duty is to present himself before a magistrate or the chief of police in Milan, thus clarifying his position. There are some who say that Feltrinelli is refusing to do this out of an overwhelming desire to play the revolutionary.

A reply in a letter to the editor:

> I believe that these events mark—with or without a coup d'état in the short term or in the distant future—the end of the delusions and hopes that go by the name of the Italian road to socialism [...]. From now on, everyone has been invested with new responsibilities, foremost among which is grasping and judging with clarity the real terms of the question and of not deceiving themselves or others.

When Feltrinelli decided to disappear, he was ruling out any possibility of return. He wrote to the companies that he ran, telling them that since his "publishing commitments" were in conflict with those of the companies, he was resigning. His representatives were given spoken and written instructions to keep the assets liquid, to safeguard some positions, to realize others, but, above all, to make no more investments.

On 1 February 1970, Feltrinelli expressed the wish to transform the institute and library into a foundation bearing his name ("Forgive my impudence or my vanity").

The situation was less clear regarding the publishing house and the bookstores. "You'll have to shift for yourselves!" was his most frequent message. But financing had to be guaranteed as long as there were assets to cover the operations. The publishing house's continued existence was in jeopardy. "I know that the DC and the government have plans to close it down," Feltrinelli wrote to Tesone. In the event it was closed down, the idea was to honor all commitments to employees, suppliers, and authors, but the claims of the banks were to be resisted at all costs. Inge became vice president of the company, Del Bo was made managing director, and Giampiero Brega became the editorial manager. All were given power to make decisions. Those running the other companies in the group were also given carte blanche. They did not agree with Feltrinelli, and in fact they all tried to stop him (but who could stop him?), except perhaps for Filippo Carpi, the lawyer. Carpi lived in Rome, in contact with the circus that was the capital city, but he was an anti-Fascist who had marched side by side with Pertini* in 1945. In February 1970 he wrote to my father:

> The alternative seems simple to me: either you come back and personally accept your responsibilities, or you keep faith with those in whom you have placed your trust, those who have been put to the test and proved themselves. As for coming back, my (fraternal) advice is to stay out of circulation for a while. Over these last few days leaks from reliable sources suggest that your recent activities in the country have been subject to close surveillance (what kind of people are close to you?). So don't add any fuel to the fire.

My father replied to everyone with a metaphor: "When the weather turns foul, strike the sails, head into the wind, and wait for

---

*(1896–1990). Resistance leader and highly popular president of the republic from 1978 to 1985.

the storm to blow over. It's an old rule of the sea that holds for the land too."

At this difficult point in his life, he wrote me a letter for my eighth birthday.

29 January 1970

Dear Carlino, first of all, may you have a very, very happy birthday. I hope that Mama has organized a nice party for you. I'm sorry and I'm sad about not being able to be there too. Unfortunately I am far away and, in all probability, I shall have to stay far away for some time. I tried to explain to you once how the world, and Italy too, is divided into two kinds of people, into two classes: those who have money, lands, factories, and houses and those who have no money and have to work like dogs to earn a little, often so little that it's not enough for them to live on. Those who have money become richer and richer by making others work and by profiting from their labor. Between bosses and workers there has always been a struggle that sometimes becomes violent. Then the bosses recruit the Fascists, common thugs, and they call in the police and the carabinieri. This is exactly what is happening today. As you know, your dad is on the workers' side. Even though he has money, he used it to publish books that defend the cause of the workers. The bosses, the wealthy people, have organized a campaign against him. All this is part of a bigger battle between the bosses and the rich people on the one side and the workers and farm laborers on the other. In Italy today, this battle has become particularly sharp. And your dad is in this battle up to his neck. It is a battle for freedom and against the injustices of the bosses, so that the poor people, the workers, may finally have a decent life, so that they may send their children to school. How long will this battle last? I don't know, Carlino. Let's hope it doesn't last long, let's hope that tomorrow you may live in a society, in a country where all these injustices do not exist. [...] Have a happy birthday, Carlino. It's not going to be an easy year for you. Mama wrote me to say that you got really excellent marks at school: I am very happy and proud of you. I know you like the school where you are now, your friends, and your teacher. It is right that you study and learn many things. That way, you will always be able to think using your own head. If in the coming months I find a little time, I will try to write you a history of Italy. The history they

teach you at school is all wrong and specially made to confuse you.
I am well. Over these recent weeks I have been studying and working very hard: in the evenings I am always dead tired. Well, Carlino:
a big hug and lots and lots of love.

Your daddy

In a pamphlet titled *Against Imperialism and the Right-Wing
Coalition* (published in March 1970), Feltrinelli drew on Gramsci
and Marx to reveal the limitations of parliamentary democracy,
and on Lenin to explain how strikes are immediate instruments in
the class struggle and a useful phase in the dynamics of revolution.
He went on to present a complete political platform: demands for
economic rights for factory and office workers (working hours,
good salary policies, decent free housing for all, the development
of workers' committees), economic rights for poor agricultural
workers and shepherds (guaranteed salaries and free seed, the
suppression of landed income, the assignment of expropriated
lands), the reform of the education system (free schooling until
eighteen years of age, real student grants for adolescent students,
the elimination of report cards, free housing for those living more
than fifty kilometers from the university, a teacher assessment system done by family members and students), and important changes
in the criminal code (no preventive custody, a general reduction of
sentences, and the abolition of life imprisonment). Naturally, Italy
would have to leave NATO and cease producing arms. The workers' committees would disarm the military forces (whose budget
ought consequently to be reduced by 80 percent). As far as the
question of the recovery of economic independence was concerned, it was easy to imagine the fate reserved for RAI-TV or for
foreign companies, but this was only part of a long list that for all
its words was a crude and unrealizable representation of socialism. It seems as useful as an old phone book found in the cellar.
Nor is there any point in taking a scalpel to separate the words,

because too much time, more time than the calendar would indi-
cate, separates us from them.

                                                            28.2.70
> Dear Carlino, I am sending you, a bit late, a present for your birth-
> day: a small collection of stamps from various countries. Each stamp
> has a drawing of a typical fruit from that country. With Mama and
> a big atlas, you can find the countries whose stamps I am sending
> you. Dear Carlino, thank you for your letters, which always make
> me so very happy. I am glad that you're doing well at school and
> that you have taken up judo again (are you already a champion?). A
> big, big hug. Your dad

Radios came from West Germany. They were one of Feltrinelli's tools of subversion. He had always been attracted to tech-
nology. I remember the bulky electrical apparatus he bought
before leaving Milan. It transformed a sheet of paper into thousands of tiny little strips. He advised me never to trust to fire when
destroying documents: you have to reduce the ashes to dust after
the flames are extinguished, otherwise the material can still be
read.

The radios were big, fairly sophisticated for the period, and
came in handy when it was announced that the neo-Fascist leader
Giorgio Almirante was to visit Genoa. A public meeting was scheduled for mid-April. This was unheard of; these people did not,
could not, speak in Genoa. On the national political scene, a government crisis had just been resolved, and sensitive regional elections were coming up. The only really unusual thing was the rising
temperature of the conflict. Even the pope was afraid when the anarchists from Cagliari took to the streets.

At television news time, while the talking head Tito Stagno was
commenting on the third manned moon mission, a small compact
car was wandering through the outskirts of Genoa. The prere-
corded tape was ready, and the antenna was tuned to a nicety: "Attention please, attention please, this is radio GAP, *gruppi di azione*

partigiana, this is radio GAP, *gruppi di azione partigiana,* stay tuned…" In the bars, people's gaze shifted from their playing cards to the television, and I have somewhere a small collection of press cuttings: the typical item read "Mysterious Television Interference in the Genoa Voltri Area."

The mobile radio station was a Morris Mini. The message was recorded on a small tape recorder. The equipment was the car radio antenna, a hook-up to the car battery, and details of the frequencies passed on by some comrades who worked at RAI's headquarters in Genoa.

Feltrinelli did not take an active part in the operation, but the voice talking over Tito Stagno's commentary was his:

Workers of Genoa, stay tuned… MUSIC… Attention please, a Fascist demonstration is to be held in Genoa Saturday afternoon. Fascist action squads from all over Italy will be massing in Genoa to hear a speech by Almirante. As in Milan and Rome, the Fascist action squads will employ all forms of violence. Workers, comrades, young people, citizens, let us all rally in order to strike at and destroy these squads, to drive the Fascists out of Genoa… Let us get ready for a great day of struggle, against the bosses, against the Fascists, let us strengthen the unity of the working class.

More cases of television interference occurred in the Genoa area, then in the Trent area, and also in Milan. A young Milanese militant with the GAP recalls an attempt to make an illegal broadcast in the city's historic Porta Ticinese area. Years later, he recalled that trip over the cobblestones in the little runabout, with Feltrinelli at the wheel and the radio in the trunk behind them.

On 12 March 1970, my parents met in Nice. Inge was a wreck. She had come by car and felt she was being tailed the whole way. My father had another face: no mustache and new metal frames for his glasses. He told her to follow him. They went into a beachfront restaurant, where they sat without eating. The conversation was harrowing. From my mother's diary: "No one can understand him, neither Brega nor Del Bo. He's lost."

Although he had been hiding since December 1969, he kept in periodic touch with the "old guard," mainly Del Bo and Brega.

"Uncle Sergio" was not made for adventure. He looked like some reserved monsignor. "Giangiacomo, don't take risks," he would say every time he saw my father. As from a big brother. One evening, near Cormano, on the outskirts of Milan, they met to talk over some publishing business. The meeting was also attended by the accountant Pozzi, the former dispatch rider with the partisans. The three men came across a roadblock. Feltrinelli had false papers, and everything went smoothly. "The next time he'll be arrested," murmured a desperate Del Bo to Pozzi. The tension led to his first heart attack: I saw him collapse over the table at dinner at Via Andegari.

With Brega, it was different: Feltrinelli and he were the same age and on more intimate terms. Brega, a pragmatist, saw that there were few ways out of the situation. He tried to make his case to Feltrinelli on a logical level, but the boss is the boss, and above all there was a publishing house to be run. One night, while he was waiting for Feltrinelli near a park in Milan, a car sped by and a pistol shot rang out. A bullet buried itself in the door of his old Volkswagen. An underworld feud or a warning?

Sergio and Giampiero usually met with Feltrinelli in Milan, in Switzerland, or in Oberhof, in Carinthia. Whenever he called, they would show up. The meetings were arranged in writing: "We'll meet in front of your house at 5:30 p.m., that way you can accompany me out of Milan to chat a little." Or: "I propose that we meet in Zurich at the usual railway station restaurant." If Feltrinelli did not show, they automatically came together the following week, same time, same place. Otherwise they kept in touch through letters addressed to the house of a friend of a friend.

The most important topic discussed at their meetings and dealt with in their correspondence was the publishing house. At Via Andegari they were trying to maintain a delicate balance in the way things were planned and managed, but for Feltrinelli the party was over: it was no longer possible to develop the house in a conventional way, everything had to be subordinated to political ends. Basically, the house's offerings had to be "very aggressive," bypassing even copyright laws. Feltrinelli came to attach more importance to a text on the costs of motorization than to an essay on literary criticism; a report establishing the responsibility for pollution, province by province, was preferred over any poetic work; and an atlas on accident prevention in Italy or a pamphlet on the phenomenon of commuting was more desirable than any essay on the Risorgimento. Money was spent on publicizing a book on the military machine and not the "rather ugly" prose of a Balestrini. Brega was told to read the articles in *Punto final* for the pamphlets on Latin America; told that he "absolutely must" publish the speech made by Fidel on the centenary of Lenin's birth; and as for the rights to Arghiri Emmanuel (*Unequal Exchange*), even though Einaudi had bought them, "it may be that they are not that much interested in publishing this fundamental text for the understanding of modern mechanisms of colonial exploitation. Try to persuade them to sell you the rights and speed up publication as much as possible. I don't give a damn whether it comes out with Feltrinelli or Einaudi: as long as it comes out fast."

I have reason to believe that on the night of 29 March 1970 my father visited Villadeati. Perhaps he made the detour as he was traveling between Milan and Genoa. No one saw him as he emerged from the shadow of the great cedar of Lebanon. Behind the house, on the lawn, gleamed clumps of primulas, narcissi, and snowdrops, even the first tulips. I imagine him lingering for a few minutes before going back down through the woods and disappearing. New roads, new journeys awaited him

Two weeks later, on 11 or 12 April, he was in Rome. He gave Secchia advance notice in writing. "I would be very glad to see you again and to have a chat with you. Let me know, through the comrade that will bring you this letter, where and when. You choose the time and the place while taking the appropriate precautions. Yours, Giangiacomo." The subject of the chat was not mentioned.

There has been much conjecture about the relations between Feltrinelli and Secchia (who was by that time isolated from the bureaucracy of the PCI). Even the former Israeli prime minister Benjamin Netanyahu has offered a wild theory in a book called *Fighting Terrorism*. Secchia is represented as the head of a terrorist structure connected to Soviet military intelligence, and Feltrinelli was one of his associates.

I would put things differently: Secchia was a natural reference point for the strategy of the new GAP movement in Italy, and he was one hundred percent in agreement with their fear of a coup. He had written about this in *Colpo di stato e legge di pubblica sicurezza* (Edizioni della Libreria, 1967). But Secchia was getting old, and he was a bit out of touch, even though he was very much in the public eye (as vice president of the senate of the Italian republic). He might have offered suggestions, analyses, even a few trusted addresses, but the world was changing and he could no longer change. All this is well expressed in his letter to Del Bo in the spring of 1970, in which he comments on the monthly *Compagni*. He did not understand those youngsters that wrote for the magazine; they spoke an incomprehensible language, full of empty, maximalist expressions; they were inconsistent; and they attacked (instead of criticizing) the PCI and the Soviets. But the interview with Feltrinelli, in the first issue, was "the most thoughtful piece, clear and intelligent." Some of Feltrinelli's statements were debatable, but he was "a diamond among potsherds." Secchia was not sure what to make of some of Feltrinelli's decisions. "I don't know, I don't criticize, and I don't judge," he wrote to Del Bo.

On 15 April, Giangiacomo was expected in Chiasso by Inge, Brega, and Roberto Olivetti. It was Inge's idea that Roberto come:

perhaps he could talk to Feltrinelli or make him talk. My father did not appear.

Twenty-four hours later, my mother and I were waiting on a platform at the Innsbruck station. Inge nearly failed to recognize him when he came up to us. They had taken their first train from here, twelve years before, and now he looked like a tramp. We went to eat something at the Gasthaus. I was all over my father, playing with him. I was, after all, responding to an invitation he had made.

1.4.70

Dear Carlino, I'm sorry I didn't manage to send my Easter greetings in time. I hope you had a good time in Villadeati. I know the weather was good, and the flowers behind the house must have been in bloom. I'd like it if you were in Innsbruck on 18 April. If you take the Trans-European Express from Milan, I'll wait for you at the station, and we can spend a week together in Austria. Would you like that? You can't imagine how much I want to see you again. I know I'll be making you miss school for a week, but maybe that's not so serious. What do you say? give Mama a hug and tell her to be happy and not to worry.

Ciao Carlino, your dad.

For those days in Oberhof, Nanni Balestrini and Cesare Milanese were also there, as well as Sibilla of course. Milanese had worked for *Quindici* and was writing a book on Clausewitz for the publishing house. He had been the one who took the letter to Secchia, and it was he whom Giangiacomo asked to keep in touch with some of the old guard of the partisan movement. Milanese refused and couldn't be persuaded. "Better men than you have tried to tell me that," replied Feltrinelli, annoyed when Milanese said that guerrillas didn't usually win wars.

For a couple of months now, the press had been talking less of Feltrinelli. Investigators inquiring into the Piazza Fontana bomb outrage were convinced that it had been the work of the anarchists, but his name no longer came up. Nothing was known about the GAP groups, nor did anyone know where Feltrinelli was. The odd journalist ventured into Carinthia, but without getting much done. The Italian consulate in Klagenfurt had no information. Feltrinelli made a brief visit to Paris (in January), where he was interviewed by a German journalist. The French police maintained that he had left for Pyongyang, North Korea. The Italian secret police did not rule out the possibility that he was still in Italy, perhaps in Sardinia: "The publisher's hiding place is probably in the open country near the home of a trusted friend." According to Netanyahu, Feltrinelli was in Prague every other week.

He very likely was moving between Austria, Switzerland, and northern Italy. And Paris, because he signed up under a false name to follow a course in forgery held by Joseph, a fifty-year-old of Armenian origin with an Argentinian passport, a black beard, and slippery ways. Joseph had hundreds of forged IDs under his belt, and he dreamed of flooding France with counterfeit francs. He was wanted by the police, but enjoyed certain privileges because he had collaborated with the Maquis against the Nazis. Feltrinelli spent about ten nights in his studio, until the forger said: "You wouldn't be Feltrinelli, by any chance?"

6 June

Dear Carlino, round about now you will be finishing your second year of school: I'm sure you will finish it brilliantly, with excellent marks. Good boy. It has been a hard year for you too, just as, unfortunately, the years to come will be difficult. That's why I am telling you this: enjoy your vacation now, because you have earned it. Where are you going this summer? To Villadeati, of course, but after that? To Porto Ercole? I really hope we shall be able to spend at least a week together, although I still can't tell you what my trips and movements will be for this summer. But I shall try to keep in touch, in some way, with you and Mummy. For now a big hug.

Your dad.

In August, I went to Oberhof for two weeks. I took along my dog, a shaggy-haired basset hound called Enzi. My father and I did simple things: reading the papers, playing records, strolling through the village talking about personal matters. And we ate pineapple Caribbean-style, North African fried bananas, Palat-schinken. I loved playing tricks on him. I invented a new trick every minute: I wouldn't let him sleep, I hid things and I followed him everywhere; all a bit obsessive. I began to understand the life he was leading, I found the drawer with the pistol. I sprayed myself with his self-defense spray. It blinded and hurt.

One afternoon, I went with the dog to a dell I knew in the woods. You follow a dirt trail for a spell, then the trail swings up toward the wood. The objective was a place where bilberries grew. But I also saw golden-yellow mushrooms and specimens of every tree in the world, including the Serbian pine, birch and sycamore. The incident occurred on the way back: we came to a bend and I realized we were no longer alone. I don't recall the type of horns, but I recall a pair of eyes as surprised as ours. The animal ran off and the dog chased after it. When it got dark I had lost the dog I dragged on the train all the way from Milan: dear Lord, dear Lord, let him come back! In a flash, nature had become a cavern, and I ran home to get help. My father didn't believe the story about the animal encountered on the path, or perhaps he was pretending to make the adventure even greater for me. When he came back, it was already night, and the dog was lolloping along behind him.

On 28 August, I stepped off the train in Stuttgart. Inge came to pick me up.

In the autumn of 1970, Italy was rocked by the riots in Reggio Calabria. The first phase of the revolt had already exploded in July, when the city's application to be recognized as the regional capital was turned down. A railway worker and a union member died, the police injured a hundred or so people, and crowds stormed the police headquarters. Reggio, a right-wing city, was in bad shape. In September, the MSI's rabble-rousers urged the people to take to the barricades. The police response to this was brutal. Another death. Four bomb attacks on trains.

In May, the Genoa-based group known as 22 October organized

two (unsuccessful) bomb attacks against the offices of the PSU in Viale Teano and the US consulate in Genoa. They also kidnapped a scion of one of the wealthiest families in Genoa and kept him for five days in exchange for 200 million lire. It was probable that the group had the support of the Milanese GAP, but "we did not want bosses of any kind," one of its former members recalls today. Indeed, a couple of them did not trust any support that came from people "who had no firsthand knowledge of material suffering."

In the meantime, the Milan-based GAP was trying to make its presence felt with a series of operations intended to shift the idea of sabotage to a "mass level." The target was the sector with the highest percentage of fatal accidents and injuries in the workplace. Between 28 August and 17 September, in Lombardy alone, ten construction workers had died.

The requirements were two or three bottles of gasoline, a few cans of tomatoes stuffed with explosives, and some adhesive tape and lime as a sealant. During the night, when no one was around, fuses were lit underneath the cement mixers. On 22 September, explosions occurred in the Fratelli Proverbio and Socogen building yards; on 24 September in the Torno yard; and on the 26th of the same month in the Stefi yard. Who were the bombers?

Comrade "Osvaldo" played a direct part in the nocturnal raids on the building yards. I asked Giuseppe Saba: "What was he like?" "He inspired confidence in everyone." Sardinians know how to keep their mouths shut.

On 1 November 1970, my parents met once more outside Italy. Inge was heartbroken: she hated to see my father in such a sorry state and thought he was completely lost. He said that the publishing house was bringing out inaccurate books on the Tupamaros, and he asked her to take me a letter.

Dear Carlino, I haven't written to you for a long time and I haven't heard how you are doing. In any case, I hope that you are well and

that, in these first days of school, you are among those at the top of
the class. How did the grape harvest go at Villadeati? Did you pick
the grapes before the rain came? Have you been doing your homework? And are you managing to control your outbursts of rage, as
you promised? I had to go to Oberhof for four days and I really
missed you. It had already begun to snow when I left. Sibilla sends
you a big hello. I'd like to know all your news. Write me a long letter.
And be close to Mummy, who is really on the ball. Dear Carlino: I
sent you a big hug and hope to see you again soon,

your dad

For Christmas 1970 I went back to Oberhof to see my father. As
well as the majolica stoves, the stalactites of ice hanging from the
eaves, and the usual dog I had taken with me on the train, there
were a few guests with us. Valerio Morucci of Potere Operaio was
one of the group, and he joined in our snowball fights. My father
built a real igloo in front of the house, perfect, inhabitable. He
equipped it with one of those metalized plastic covers that astro-
nauts use. It weighed twenty grams and protected you from the
cold. As a matter of fact, if you wrapped it around your body you
could survive at any temperature. We also went for long walks. In
the evening I would be staggering with tiredness. The dog, sitting
at the top of the stairs, would bark at anyone who came near the
bedroom. Benevolently, my father tried to quiet him: '*Aber Enzi.*'
On 10 January 1971, I went back to Milan.

My father's "foreign policy." Did he have one or not? Contacts
with Habash, the most intransigent of the Palestinian leaders; with
Algerian circles; with the Germans of the Rote Armée; with the
American black panthers; with the Tupamaros in Uruguay; with
Eastern European intelligence services. Through a group of busi-
nessmen with offices in Geneva, Feltrinelli supposedly plotted on
behalf of Arabs and Palestinians, supported the Bolivian and
Venezuelan guerrillas as well as the Irish irredentists, procured
weapons for the Greek resistance movement and for those fighting

Franco in Spain. CIA documents describe him as "Castro's most important agent in Europe," while the conservative American journalist Claire Sterling did not mince her words: "No matter how you judge him, unbalanced, sexually disturbed, vain, weak, arrogant, fanatical, frustrated, reckless, eager for adulation, and a wild dreamer, Feltrinelli affected the history of a decade."

True or false? The motto of the Tricontinental (1966), "a global strategy to counter the global strategy of imperialism," is unambiguous. But in 1970 this strategy was in poor shape in the countries it had sprung from: some key figures (like Che) had died, and the forces of reaction were in the ascendant. Even so, 1968 in Europe had rekindled the idea of linking up revolutionary vanguards wherever they might be and, in Giangiacomo's mind, of building an organizational bridge between Europe and the Tricontinental.

"He wasn't one of our agents, there was never anything coordinated about his activities in Europe. He kept us informed, and we knew we could count on him. But Europe wasn't a priority for us. With Italy we had only normal relations, and we weren't even that close to the PCI." This is what Manuel Piñeiro had to say from Havana (in December 1992). Markus Wolff, the intelligence boss in East Berlin, could say nothing about Feltrinelli's activities in Europe.

Feltrinelli was said to be shuttling continuously between Italy, Austria, Switzerland, and France, with a network of contacts in which, however, it was not always clear who represented what. Jan Stage, the Danish journalist in the service of the Cubans until the early seventies, was often with him. They had met at the Copacabana in La Paz in August 1967. Now Stage called himself "Camillo." He thought that Feltrinelli's plan to set himself up as the European depository of the world's revolutions was utopian. Very little had been done in concrete terms. As for the Eastern countries, he denied that there were direct contacts of any kind, while Sibilla, who at the time was on standby in the silent valley of Oberhof, dismisses Netanyahu's assertion of the twenty-two trips to Czechoslovakia. And when the circulars of the European intelligence services said Feltrinelli was in Beirut, he was with me, I swear, on an asthmatic old train between Villach and Klagenfurt.

11 January 1971. Feltrinelli met Brega. The two men no longer understood each other. Del Bo, upset about a cold letter he received, no longer wanted to see to the running of the publishing house: "Either he comes to get us out of this mess, or he gives us the cash as promised." But he carried on. The managerial situation was not good. The seven bookstores were breaking even, but everything else was going badly, and the banks were putting on the pressure. The men at Via Andegari proposed downsizing, cutting costs and titles. But for the publisher who was no longer a publisher, downsizing was out of the question. The house had to carry on its political battle against the hostility of the capitalists and of the PCI. At the end of January, Feltrinelli asked his men to make a decision: agree with him or leave. He also had the idea that a collective could control the house's line and that some carefully selected political figures could form a supervisory committee and even become shareholders. In pursuit of this objective, he proposed refinancing with a fund to be used to protect those earning the lowest salaries. Then the publishing house would have to stand on its own two feet.

During the secret meetings with the staff at Via Andegari, Giangiacomo talked tough. But Inge thought he looked awful and that his teeth were going bad.

Dear Carlino, happy birthday! I would be glad if at this time you could feel all the friendship (you're not a baby anymore, but a big boy, and you know what friendship means) and, naturally, all the affection and love I bear you. I have no great present for you: only a seashell. I haven't been able to find anything else, for the time being. But perhaps the best present I can give you is to struggle for a better world, for a fairer world. Now that the Fascists are filling

the newspapers with the stories of their exploits (and, unfortunately, the hospitals with the injured), you will begin to understand
that, outside the tranquillity of your home, of Villadeati, and of
Oberhof, a ruthless life-or-death struggle is going on, a battle for
justice and freedom against the terrorism of the Fascists and the
bosses, against injustice, poverty, and hunger. And the greatest wish
I can make you, Carlino, is that by the time you grow up, all these
struggles and all this suffering will be only a distant memory,
something that you read about in books and study, but not the way
it is today, a reality against which, believe me, every honest man
must fight. Dear Carlino, I haven't heard from you for a long time.
But I am sure you are well (even though this January Villadeati
must have been submerged by snow and rain). How's school going?
Write to me some time. A big hug and loads of birthday wishes,

                                                          Your dad.

In the first half of February 1971, the Genoa-based column of the
GAP struck at the factories owned by industrialists believed to be
financing the MSI: the Borghi family's Ignis plant in Sestri Levante
and the Garrone refinery in Arquata Scrivia. The group later interrupted television broadcasts to claim responsibility for the bomb-
ings. In Milan, Trent and surrounding areas, attempts were made
to take the initiative once more. "More than anything else, these
were demonstrative actions, made to gain experience. We had
no military training, apart from some lessons given by a few ex-
partisans." These ranged from the diffusion of propaganda to the
placing of incendiary devices that could not explode to rudimen-
tary bombs that could. This is Giuseppe Saba's recollection. The
GAP's raids caught the newspapers unprepared. Was this political
terrorism or what?

The organization was strictly divided into watertight compart-
ments, and if one thing was indispensable it was, discretion. At that
time a handbook for subversives was circulating among the most
extreme elements of the left. Things like: Be sure no one is tailing
you, write down as little as possible, and use public telephones
only. There was a paragraph on improvised explosive devices. Rec-

ommended was a blend of potassium chlorate tablets (available in pharmacies) and confectioner's sugar. Or: mix paraffin or tar with sawdust, adding thin flakes of Marseilles soap and kerosene. Valerio Morucci* reports; "One time, at a house in Rome, Feltrinelli made a demonstration. He mixed up two really improbable ingredients and managed to make them explode." Morucci saw the flames reflected in the lenses of Feltrinelli's glasses. The publisher's face was thin, bony, ascetic, with a short beard streaked with white. The face of an Italian anarchist or a Cuban Communist, but it also reminded Morucci of the face of a man "committed to the study of the Talmud."

The handbook, around thirty pages in all, was later adopted by the Red Brigades, who were about to make their debut.

March 1971 witnessed the issuing of the first arrest warrant for the Red Brigades. It was in the name of Enrico Castellani. In his house, on Via Castelfidardo, fuses and explosives were found.

---

*(1949–). One of the leaders of the BR at the time of the Moro kidnapping, he conducted the interrogation of the prisoner.

10

On 1 April 1971 the new Bolivian consul in Hamburg agreed to see a young Australian woman, Monika, who needed a visa for a folk group. When he went to greet her, the last thing he saw was a pistol. So ended Colonel Quintanilla, torturer, murderer, CIA man. In her flight, the girl dropped her wig, her handbag, her Colt Cobra .38 Special, and a slip of paper with the words "Victory or death. ELN." ELN was the National Liberation Army. Australia had nothing to do with it, and Monika was identified almost immediately as a Bolivian born in Germany.

Chato Peredo never had particularly close relations with the Cubans. Today he maintains that the Hamburg operation was decided autonomously. "It was our idea, I had no relations with Havana. The decision to send Monika was inevitable, she was German, and she knew the language. We claimed responsibility for the operation right away." The killing was the only operation of its kind carried out by Latin Americans in Europe.

It is not clear how the ELN came into contact with Feltrinelli, but Stage had given Peredo a Kleenex box stuffed full of dollars in a park near the University of Santiago. The cash was needed for

Monika's trip to Europe, because the ELN was broke. Before Monika, in January 1971, a couple of Venezuelans (brother and sister) had gone to Europe to kill Quintanilla. On their way through Carinthia, they decided that the enterprise was too risky.

The Cubans probably knew all about the trip planned by Monika, who landed in France in the early spring of 1971. In a harbor on the Côte d'Azur, aboard a secondhand motor yacht, Feltrinelli handed the pistol over to her and an accomplice. "It may come in handy as a reserve," he said to them. At the last moment, before the shooting, the decision was made that the Colt was more reliable than the Browning she had originally intended to use.

According to one important source, Monika and Feltrinelli barely knew each other. According to others, they were well acquainted. Monika fled Hamburg for Chile, via Switzerland and Italy. In Santiago she gave Chato a Dunlop cigarette lighter, a present for him from Feltrinelli.

On 17 April 1971, the information on the pistol used to kill Quintanilla had still not been made public. Inge, Del Bo, and Brega met with Feltrinelli in Paris. After the quarrel of the previous winter over the publishing house, they were ready for anything. But Feltrinelli was calm and thoughtful; he listened, asked questions, and gave advice. "He's still the boss..." Brega and Del Bo took notes. The day before, my father had written me a message about the seven young fir trees he sent me.

> Dear Carlino, for the firs you have planted: remember to buy some peat and put plenty of it around the roots. Then, especially in summer, you have to see that the trees are watered: not too much, but enough. Bye, a big hug, and see you soon, dad.

In a few days the news began to leak out: the pistol had been bought in the armory near the Capitol Cinema on Via Croce Rossa, Milan. The national and foreign press speculated about the involvement of Feltrinelli, the legal purchaser. He had not appeared in public for almost a year and a half. The evening papers ran a headline: "Feltrinelli Arrested in Paris?" (26 April). Interpol was in-vestigating, but no request was made for an international arrest warrant. Feltrinelli was not directly involved with the Hamburg operation. But the Colt was the one Valerio Morucci had seen in Feltrinelli's shoulder holster a few months before. He recalled it decades later with pathos: "Sewn onto the strip of leather that ran up from the holster to the shoulder there was a cartridge belt with six extra bullets. I had never seen bullets like them before. They had shiny, chrome-plated cases and noses of a bright color. I begged him to make me a present of one."

When the hue and cry over the Colt became insistent, Feltrinelli disappeared completely. Inge shut herself up at home and would not answer the telephone. One evening she told me everything, even about the consul and the pistol. The publishing house was plowing ahead blindly, and somehow life went on. New books in-cluded *Silence* by John Cage and Nigel Calder's *Violent Universe*. One day, Eco would drop in; the next day, the editor of the mathe-matics series. Should we ask Salvador Allende for an exclusive in-terview about Chile? He had just been elected head of a democratic government. Debray, back in Paris after a long prison term in Bo-livia, was the right person to do it. We could ask for world rights, and so the absent publisher would be proud of us (a good way of showing him, too, that it was still possible to make books).

At the end of April, Inge received an invitation to Madrid to meet someone who would tell her something about Feltrinelli. She went, but no one showed up. A leader of the Milan Federation of the PCI looked up Tina at the office of the publishing house. He informed her that he had heard from Rome that someone was planning to kill Feltrinelli. Many years later, Armando Cossutta admitted: "Longo called me and said, 'It has come to our attention that some-one wants to kill Feltrinelli. Contact him and put him on his guard.'" I asked Cossutta if he could remember who had given him the word: "Maybe it was the Soviets, or maybe our channels inside Italian intelligence…"

Not even the functionary of the Cuban embassy, Andrés Del Río, knows for sure when his government told him to contact Feltrinelli. They met in the vicinity of the Stazione Termini railway station in Rome. It was their last meeting. The message that Del Río had to give Feltrinelli was exactly the same as the message forwarded by Longo and Cossutta. Perhaps even the dates coincided.

On 17 May, Debray arrived in Milan to talk about a book–length interview with Salvador Allende. He was courteous, liked the idea, and asked for a lot of money. Outside, it was raining heavily. Inge asked Debray if he had any news of Giangiacomo, and if he saw any way out for him." It's too late now," Debray replied. They both left for Villadeati, where they were to pass a weekend that neither would forget. The first guest to arrive was Alberto Moravia. The writer had just come back from a long visit to Latin America, where he had written a series of reports. He put his things in his room, installed himself in the lounge, and started talking. The sole topic of conversation was incest.

The rain was pelting down, it was thundering, and the gravel of the drive ran with rivulets of water. Around nine o'clock, someone rang at the door to say that Feltrinelli was at the foot of the hill. Inge had let him know that Debray was coming. When he appeared in the living room, Moravia did not recognize him. Feltrinelli was not sporting the famous mustache. Moravia was suddenly fearful that he had been lured into a trap. He asked my father if he was living in Paris and went back to his conversation with Debray, as if nothing had happened. They were still on the subject of incest. That was when Giangiacomo got impatient. Moravia noticed, slowed down, and turned toward him. The alcohol slowly helped create a more relaxed atmosphere.

When everyone retired, I was supposed to have been in bed
some time before. I hadn't seen my father arrive, and in fact I
wasn't even supposed to know he was coming. But I knew, because
Inge had not concealed her anxiety very well. So when he came in
silently without switching on the light, I was already on my feet for
a surprise hug.

In the late morning, from the stairs, Moravia's snoring was au-
dible. The weather was slightly better, but my mother was upset,
realizing that we had not been all together here for three years.

In June, the Red Brigades had caught up with the GAP. In terms
of attacks, sabotage, or demonstrations, their tactics seemed equivalent; both counted on an organized underground structure. The
Red Brigades were making converts, the first factory-based cells
were being created, above all in the Pirelli and Siemens plants. The
PCI had already entered that phase in which it did not see, or did
now want to see, what was going on. After the arson attack at
Lainate, *L'Unità* wrote: "Those who carried out the attack, while
using anonymous pamphlets containing revolutionary expressions, are acting on behalf of those [...] who have an interest in
making the workers' responsible struggle for contract renewal look
like a series of acts of vandalism in the eyes of public opinion."

While the papers were still talking about Quintanilla, Feltrinelli
was in hiding somewhere, writing a long letter to the Red Brigades
(20 May 1971). He congratulated them on their initiative and expressed a hope for collaboration and political cooperation in the
broadest sense of the term. He proposed that they work together on
a political, strategic, and tactical platform, with the aim of specify-
ing what they were fighting for and how it was to be done. He sent
off a rough draft for discussion. His objective was the creation of a
People's Liberation Army, which would be the fighting arm of a
Popular Liberation Front. Also needed was a legal aid structure,
and a Red Help lifeline for comrades who might find themselves in

trouble. Feltrinelli financed the idea with a lot of money, which was diverted elsewhere. He would have liked to involve people like Umberto Terracini* and Lelio Basso, who had led many legal battles on behalf of the workers over the last few decades.

In the spring of 1971 the first meetings with the leaders of the Red Brigades, in particular with Renato Curcio and Alberto Franceschini, took place. The latter, a twenty-year-old Young Communist from Emilia and a newcomer to subversion, usually met Feltrinelli in the gardens of the Castle in Milan. "I was well aware that Feltrinelli was much more than the GAP, because he traveled, because of the people he knew, and because of the publishing house. I always had the feeling that he knew more than we did. He was not the kind to react spontaneously, he had a plan, a global project."

According to the Italian secret service, Feltrinelli was in Prague from 30 May to 1 June and from 30 July to 4 August of 1971. Aided and abetted by the Czech authorities, he allegedly entered the country with a passport in the name of Giancarlo Scotti, a resident of Florence. On the first trip (again according to Italian intelligence) he accompanied Mario Rossi's former partner Augusto Viel. Evidence of all this is a postcard of Wenceslas Square received by Viel's mother.

I traced Viel to a bar in the harbor of Genoa. More than twenty-five years had gone by since his presumed journey to Prague, two-thirds of them spent in Italian prisons, very far from the pages of the newspapers. He was getting by on the strength of odd jobs and alcohol. He still had the look of an old-style conspirator. He told me he had never been to Prague, that he had signed the postcard to his mother while he was in Milan. Someone else posted it from the Czech capital to trick investigators into calling off the search for him in Italy.

*(1895–1983). President of the Constituent Assembly, one of the most intransigent fathers of the constitution, and a senator (PCI) from 1948 until his death, he was a dissident who nonetheless remained a party member.

Feltrinelli did in fact go to Prague at least three times in 1971. Prague has a Cuban embassy and an international airport. One trip there may have coincided with a journey to Latin America. This was the expedition to the Tupamaros of Montevideo that everybody has talked about, but no one–not even Sibilla–remembers exactly when it took place. It could have been July or September, and on one leg of the journey there was a stopover in Cuba. According to Debray's recollections, Feltrinelli was with him when they were training at Punto Cero.

I met my father again on 9 August. From the pier in Nice harbor, I saw him bustling about the *Sharopp*, a big Scottish boat that was hard to control. He was nervous. In the course of a maneuver, he collided with the yacht owned by David Niven as the actor looked on from the deck, one eyebrow raised in disapproval. The *Sharopp* was a seagoing craft that could carry crates of arms across the Mediterranean (I don't know if this really happened).

My father put me to bed in a corner of the prow. The swash of the water made me nauseous, and in the bistro facing the *Sharopp* they served salad niçoise with old eggs and old anchovies: on the second night, I vomited. I vomited for the past and the future, for all the anticipation of our far too condensed meetings, from the porthole on the beautiful people I didn't give a damn about. The next day we shut everything up and left for Austria. I traveled with Sibilla, who understood less than I did but was nice. On the plane, a pockmarked American wearing a Stetson sent her a love note from the row behind us.

At the end of September, Rome was the venue for the 3rd Organizational Conference of Potere Operaio. Almost a thousand delegates came from 57 sections and 108 cells (there was even one in Zurich). The conference tackled what had been described as the crisis of the planner state and gave its blessing to the Leninist shift

in the group's orientation: it was the birth of the "party of insurrection" and the defeat of those who looked to the *Manifesto*, with
its more gradualist line.

At the congress, all had their say amid the usual feverishness of
those years. Two militants in a little room above the auditorium
recorded and transcribed the speeches. Behind them, a strange
character without a mustache was taking notes. When he went
away, discontented, no one noticed. Osvaldo was not convinced
about the equation between the masses in revolt and an army.
Where was the plan? It was all too reliant on spontaneity. Behind
the words there were no concrete facts. The structure they were
creating was too centralized, and it seemed oligarchic and bureau-
cratic. It was also marked by strong personalism: "Many of them
are still petit bourgeois Marxist ideologues." His idea for a common strategy uniting the fighting forces fell on deaf ears. Also, his
relations were not good, especially with Negri. According to
Piperno, the two men really distrusted each other. Negri saw Feltrinelli as the wealthy publisher steeped in the archaic myth of the
Resistance betrayed. Feltrinelli harbored doubts about the ideological myth of the endlessly contentious professor's astuteness.

In October 1971, Feltrinelli prepared a new text, entitled *Lotta di
classe o guerra di classe?* ("Class Struggle or Class War?"). This
fifteen-page collection of warmongering solipsisms written with
cheerful disregard for syntax was handed to Cesare Milanese so
that he could read it and find someone to publish it (under a pseudonym) in some magazine. Feltrinelli and Milanese met in front of
the Parma cathedral and took a stroll through the old city center.
Milanese says that Feltrinelli realized that the situation was not
good. He was disappointed with the failure to apply what everyone
was loudly declaring theoretically and politically. "I had the impression that he wanted to get out from under," said Milanese.

Lotta di classe or guerra di classe? is a text that unfolds in large categories: the state, power, class, and class struggle. A list of definitions provided a more precise picture of the revolution, which was the final measure of both party and state. Feltrinelli was no longer the "rural" GAP member obsessing about the coup d'état: half measures were not admissible. A spade is a spade, revolution is (class) struggle, and struggle is war: the revolution is war.

These statements of principle reveal that Feltrinelli went underground to be more visible, a shift from the implicit to the explicit. Until the winter of 1971, he did not realize that he was out of step with the events going on around him. What he feared most was the failure to follow up in a revolutionary sense the process begun by the movement of 1968: "No appreciable progress has been made. Why this spectacle?" The revolutionary movement lacked "strategic strength, a political, military, and revolutionary counterpower that might confront, wear down, and disarm the political and military power of its adversary." Feltrinelli was afraid that history would decree a no-contest, the dissolution of the revolutionary opportunity.

A one-room apartment, with kitchen and bathroom, in a side street on the edge of Milan. You arrive warily, enter the light-green neon of the stairwell, go up to the first or second floor, to a plywood door. Inside there is a plastic cupboard and two bunks, Italian brandy on the shelf, and a clamp mounted on the table holding a thin steel blade in its jaws: duplicating *spadini** for the purposes of car theft. A crate with "Marlboro" written on it holds stripped-down firearms bought in Switzerland and imported in the chassis of an NSU Prinz. Or maybe they are from Liechtenstein: in the armory in Vaduz, all you have to show is an identity document (but as you may purchase only one item per day, the Blond and Pepito had to stay on for a week).

On Via California, in October 1971, there were four pistols and a

---

*Literally "small swords": a tool for forcing car door locks.

submachine gun. A radio transmitter with a low-frequency feeder stood in place of the television, and there was some canned food beside the stove. For food and company there were the neighborhood eating houses out in the frost, fog, and wind. Other typical hideout materials: newspapers, magazines, pamphlets, bunches of keys, false rubber stamps, document blanks, and clothing. In the cupboard there were explosives, plastic explosive in cigarette packs, a Vietnamese antitank grenade (!), detonators, electrical circuits, and watches. Osvaldo had developed a kind of mania for explosives. Günter said he had bought the watches in a bar for 3,500 lire for three pair. Next to nothing.

In Milan, the GAP had at least four such bases (and the BR were preparing the same number). In 1970, a friend of Lazagna's from Ticino had bought the apartments on Feltrinelli's behalf. "They are not for the revolution, they are for defending ourselves," Feltrinelli told him. They were rented in the names of fronts, who paid the bills regularly by mail. The Milan bases were frequented by two groups: the Giambellino crowd (i.e., Praga, the Blond and his cousin, Pepito, Red Eye, and Sickle Tongue) and a group from the north side of town (Günter, Rooster, Bruno, Napoli, plus a few mavericks from the Italian Maoist outfit). Not everyone knew one another or which outfit they were really from. "You couldn't understand what the fuck was going on," said Cocco Bill, who was one of them. In the bars of Piazza Napoli and Piazza Bolivar it wasn't hard to find men ready for an attack on the state police barracks or to join a quick (armed) anti-Fascist patrol in Brianza. On the fringes appeared characters like Marco Pisetta, a small-time smuggler from Trent imported to Milan by Renato Curcio after a few terrorist attacks in his home area. By the time Curcio introduced Pisetta to his friends at the Bersagliera, Pisetta was already a police informer. He wasn't the only one. It was all very labyrinthine.

Osvaldo trusted four or five of his men, but the others were not allowed to know who he was (and even if they knew, no personal

questions). As for recruitment, there was always the worry of finding new people; there were too many cowboys around.

Giangiacomo got on better with the mixed bag that was the old
PCI: in the fall of 1971, in Milan, he dropped in on Pesce a couple of
times in the dead of night; in Rome, he talked with Aldo Natoli (the
only journalist with the *Manifesto* that he appreciated); one of
Moscatelli's lieutenants was glad to put him up in Romagnano
Sesia; Arnaldo Bera had two hideouts ready near Cremona; and
Lazagna, who was working for the national social security service,
had moved to Turin. Feltrinelli could talk openly with all of them,
and they thought he resembled a hunted animal. Lazagna told a
friend: "His fate is sealed. They will put up with everything, even
supervision in your own backyard, but when you supply arms to
others, you sign your own death sentence." The intelligence services of America, France, Germany, and Israel (the Israelis were
very enterprising in Italy) were keeping tabs on the "chief agent of
Castroism in Europe" on a weekly basis.

At least four people heard Feltrinelli say, "If they find a dead man
under a bridge, that man will be me." When he met Inge, he was
gaunt in the face. It was in the Navigli* in Milan in early October
1971: their first encounter in the city in two years. The street was
dark, and he was dressed too lightly. The talk was again about the
publishing house and the last financing operation: after that, you'll
have to get by on your own. We were already getting by on our own.

November '71

Dear Carlino, So Mama tells me you have to wear glasses? Damn,
you're getting just like your dad, who can't see his own hand in
front of his face! Thanks for your photographs and for your note.
Unfortunately the Fascists are to be feared (never underestimate
your opponent—that's a good rule). They are people who want to
rule by force and to use force to defend the interests of the bosses.

*Old working-class area in Milan.

I'm glad you went to the demonstration. I heard that Enzi got better–you don't know how happy that made me. I've grown a bit of a
beard and you'd hardly recognize me now! You with glasses and I
with a beard! But there's no helping it: if we met on the street, we
would recognize each other right away. Bye Carlino, bye son. Grow
well, grow strong. A big hug and, to the cry of hooray for raising
hell! I send you a thousand kisses.

Your dad.

    I really hope we will be able to see each other around Christmas.
Bye

In the winter of 1971, all the Milanese underground militants
were talking about "attacking the lackeys of power": the bosses,
factory overseers, spies, policemen, and Fascists. The usual thing
was to burn their cars. The pamphlets said that such acts need
not be barbaric: to mock the oppressive structure of power (and
inject the masses with fresh confidence), a little irony was required. The Red Brigades were thinking in terms of symbolic kid-
nappings: you quickly gag the victim, you photograph him, then
you release him. The Blond stalked the German consul for two
weeks, Pepito kept tabs on an executive with the Autobianchi car
firm, and Sickle Tongue knew every move made by Michele Sindona, who was then involved in a takeover bid for the Bastogi
Corporation.

It was only by luck that Feltrinelli was not kidnapped himself.

Martino Siciliano often dined at Endo, the first Japanese restaurant in Milan and the only one in Italy in 1969. Siciliano, a tele-
phonist by trade, was a cog in the very right-wing wheel of Ordine
Nuovo between Milan and his hometown of Mestre, near Venice.
He had become known in that area by sticking up Mao-Nazi
proclamations under fake left-wing acronyms in order to sow confusion (ploys that tickled Federico Umberto D'Amato of the Office
of Confidential Affairs, the Italian intelligence service). At Endo,

Siciliano tackled chopsticks and tempura in the company of his
gang leader, also from Mestre, who was holding forth on the master race and the use of dishwasher timers for bombs. Siciliano listened and learned.

The gelignite he had seen prepared for two missions on Italy's
eastern frontier failed to detonate, but that December the bomb
went off in Piazza Fontana, and twenty-five years later Siciliano
sang. Sure, he said, his group of street thugs had something to do
with it, the "Japanese" gang leader was Delfo Zorzi, and here are
the names of the CIA connections.... A Milanese judge, Guido
Salvini, set to work unraveling the mysteries of the great Italian
garbage dump.

"The name Feltrinelli was a target from the start." Siciliano recalled having taken part in the assault on the Feltrinelli bookstore
on Milan's Corso Europa in 1968, as part of a group that had set out
from the Federation offices of the MSI. In 1971, the target was even
more of a target.

It is not clear who had the idea, but one of the worthies of the
right-wing network in the Veneto area, a person who owns a castle
in Carinthia, had something to do with it. Oberhof is not far from
that castle. Marco Foscari took along his gamekeeper, who was a
former SS member, and Siciliano. The trio had no problem finding
the house; Oberhof is not Tokyo. They had two cars, rifles, binoc-
ulars, ether, ropes, and a trunk for Giangiacomo Feltrinelli once he
was tied up. The plan was to go back into Italy and have him found
by the police. (Alive? Dead?) From the wood, they watched for long
enough to realize that there was no one in the chalet, not even
Sibilla. Mission postponed.

Feltrinelli was now to Italian intelligence what Castro was to the
CIA. D'Amato added something more to the equation. For him it
was a personal matter, it had something to do with a kind of anti-
intellectual hatred, or a different notion of literature, something

toxic. Feltrinelli sold books that were the stuff of dreams; D'Amato had made a career for himself without any need for culture vultures; he was the Italian functionary in control of the room of mysteries, a bon vivant and a gourmand.

The Office for Confidential Affairs commissioned the book *Feltrinelli guerrigliero impotente* ("Feltrinelli the Impotent Guerrilla"). It came out with a khaki-colored dust jacket, publisher unheard of, "printed in April 1971." Giangiacomo bought the booklet in Porta Nuova Railway Station in Turin in November, after Lazagna had told him about it. He went to see Lazagna, who had moved to Turin from Genoa after his promotion. Of late, the two had seen less of each other. In the station bar, Lazagna watched Feltrinelli leaf through the pages with great detachment.

Feltrinelli guerrigliero impotente aimed at showing the world that the man was mentally unstable, a complex-ridden personality with a dash of radical chic. The anonymous author had put together a bundle of press cuttings, divorce decrees, and other scraps. The actual biography is neglected.

At Christmas, I was in Gottingen until the 29th. At Düstere Eichenweg, everything was fine as usual: white berries hanging over the fence, old verandas with merrymaking students, the Max Planck Institute, my grandmother's kindness, and Hans Huffzky, who had come from Hamburg to take me to Austria. Hans and I set off by train. Apart from my father and Sibilla, we found "Camillo" (Stage). On New Year's Eve, the fireworks were reflected by the branches of the trees sagging under the weight of the snow. We also launched a minirocket with a parachute (my father always kept an eye on the toy shops). For 1972 I received a real steel wristwatch, not a toy. The first days of the New Year were one chess match after another. Hans said that when it came to chess my father and I had the same problem: a good attack but a poor defense. He maintained that the match in Reykjavik between Bobby Fischer and Boris Spassky would end the Cold War. Giangiacomo talked politics; you could see that he hadn't changed his mind, but he seemed less obsessed. I showed my father my homework assignment, an essay on the new head of state Giovanni Leone. He said that Leone had been "elected with the votes of the Fascists," but he let me get on with it. When seven years later a Feltrinelli book was to lead to the resignation of an Italian president, Feltrinelli was no longer with us.

Again in January 1972, CIA and FBI dispatches (available under the Freedom of Information Act) pointed to Feltrinelli, "Castro's principal agent in Europe." It would be more accurate to say that he moved alone or with vanguard groups he thought he could count on. The Cubans were not that interested in adventures in the Old World.

In early 1972, Feltrinelli confided in those who met him that he had had to increase his vigilance. He no longer used the car or the plane but traveled exclusively by train, in second class. From his movements it can be deduced that he was spending most of his time between Oberhof, Switzerland, and Milan. But he never let himself be seen in Milan. For three years he had been observing the barbed wire between himself and the world, and it would have been an elementary blunder to emerge from a crowd and say hi to me from underneath a blond wig. Our sole contact was in the Engadine, shortly after my tenth birthday. He had taken a room in a small hotel. I don't have a precise recollection, but he was coughing so badly that the other tourists steered clear of our table. Other people remember that he wasn't well ("He had lost weight." "He was smoking too much"). Sibilla, who lived in Oberhof, mentioned the onset of bronchitis during a hurried visit. This became pneumonia in one of the GAP bases in Milan. Six days in bed. Tina secretly returned to duty to bring him medicines. She was the only person in the world who knew he was there, completely alone.

Around 24 February 1972 Feltrinelli was in Oberhof, his lungs a
little better. He was eating salt for his blood pressure and drinking
hot water for his liver trouble. Robert Amhof, his attorney in Vienna, saw him for an afternoon and found him "normal." They
discussed a few divisions to be made among the Austrian properties and talked about other administrative matters. "Then we took
a stroll in the woods. He was worried. 'You know,' he said to me,
'every time I have my back to the woods, I get the feeling that
someone might shoot me. Let's get this business done quickly. I'm
afraid I won't live much longer.'"

On 27 February, Feltrinelli left Oberhof, leaning out of the train
window to the last minute, waving to Sibilla. He probably stopped
in Switzerland for at least a week. On 4 March he met someone in
the House of the People in Lugano. On 6 March he wrote: "Dear
Ingelein, I suggest that we meet at 1 P.M., Wednesday March the
15th in Caffè Bar Lugano..." The rest of the letter talks of an appointment with a Swiss notary in order to sort out some disposi-
tions by will regarding his son's inheritance. Strange. "Why don't
you bring Carlino along with you or is it too complicated?" the
message ends. On 7 March, Feltrinelli entered Italy by train via
Ponte Chiasso, mingling with a group of commuters.

In Milan the atmosphere was getting very tense. Red Brigades
had kidnapped an executive with the Sit-Siemens group for a few
hours in order to question him about plans for the restructuring
of the plant. It was their first sensational operation. The episode
aroused much comment in the far left: Avanguardia Operaia
thought it was a ploy engineered by the intelligence services, Manifesto said nothing, while Potere Operaio and Lotta Continua ex-
ulted, wanting to emphasize the link between such commando
operations and mass armed struggle. There was a call for a general
mobilization of the extraparliamentary left on 11 March to prevent
MSI leader Giorgio Almirante from speaking in Piazza Castello.
Clashes and aggressive policing were predicted.

On 8 and 9 March, meetings were set up in the suburbs, seven in all. Osvaldo sent Rooster and Bruno, a young worker with the Marelli Corporation, to measure the distance between the girders of an electricity pylon in the countryside near Lecco. The two men carried out their task.

On 9 March, Osvaldo met Oreste Scalzone to talk about the demonstration planned for the 11th. Scalzone recalls: "He asked me if, in my opinion, the movement would accept it if he and some of his comrades came armed to the demonstration, to defend themselves if necessary. It was the first time I had heard the expression 'combat groups.'" Scalzone replied that such a thing was politically untenable. Osvaldo was disappointed.

The demonstration of 11 March resulted in fierce clashes between marchers and police. On Via Verdi, alongside La Scala, a passing pensioner was killed when he was struck by one of the tear-gas canisters fired at eye level by the riot police. Osvaldo had summoned his men to a little villa in San Siro. They listened to the radio news and made ready.

On 12 and 13 March, there were more evening meetings in seedy eating houses far from the usual haunts. Who did Feltrinelli see? Perhaps someone who came from Trent.

On the afternoon of the 14th, after 5 p.m., Günter's brother met Feltrinelli in the hideout just outside Milan. He seemed in a good mood. At 7:30 p.m. Osvaldo had an appointment with Rooster and Bruno in front of the Vox Cinema.

The idea was a real but relaxed operation, almost a rehearsal. It had nothing to do with competition with other groups. Osvaldo had already carried out similar missions, but Rooster and Bruno got to the Vox three minutes late.

Bruno had refused to go, but Rooster insisted. First he asked him as a friend. Then came the confession: "Look, Osvaldo is Feltrinelli!" Then I'll come. If we get busted, someone will look after us." Bruno was euphoric; he had met Osvaldo on various occasions, but he hadn't realized who he was. At 7:35 p.m. on the 14th, they set off with the aim of sabotaging two power pylons along Via Cassanese, near Segrate, a suburb just outside Milan. They were traveling in a Volkswagen minivan. The weather forecast was for intermittent showers.

The chronicle of the hours that followed is the chronicle of another world intruding on mine. Twist was the name of the mutt found wagging its tail frenetically in front of "a corpse of the male sex, lying on the ground, under a power pylon." It was around 3:30 p.m. "A dead man? Are you sure? Couldn't it just be a tramp lying there asleep?" Luigi Stringhetti, Twist's master, who rented a field in the hamlet of Cascina Nuova (Segrate), had to repeat his story to the commander of the local police station. He had seen the man under the four stanchions of the pylon, among the stones, lying on his back with his arms spread, as if on the cross...

At 4 p.m. they informed the police station at Pioltello, while in central headquarters in Milan, on Via Moscova, the new shift had just come on duty. It had been a quiet day, and lots of men were out for the National Congress of the PCI at the Palalido, a large sports complex. The assembly that had witnessed the crowning of Enrico Berlinguer as party leader had opened two days before, with greetings from the foreign delegations. When the station at Pioltello informed headquarters, they sent out the nearest police car. By 4:30 the situation was accelerating fast, and soon photographs of Stringhetti and Twist were all over Italy: portraits with beret, on the bike, with the dog jumping to catch a piece of bread, and the index finger pointing to the misshapen pyramid of the pylon. "Power pylons will never seem the same to me again," writer Vassilikos was to say later. Beneath the pylon in Segrate, at 4:30 on Thursday 15 March 1972, the troops of the bomb squad gathered, along with the "political" squad, the carabinieri, the forensic team, the gravediggers, the journalists (first to arrive were those from

Il Giorno), the photographers, and the spectators. An army of
ghouls beat a path to the scene. Investigators ascertained that the
"terrorist without a name" had used fifteen sticks of dynamite for
the charges at the base of the pylon, but it was impossible to esti-
mate the power of the charge that had exploded on the crossbar
four meters up, and that was presumably the cause of death. On the
edge of a side road, two hundred meters away, they broke into
the sand-colored Volkswagen minivan with the yellow drapes over
the rear window.

Toward evening, after the heat of the moment had passed, investigators examined the evidence in their offices. They had left an
electrical generator at Segrate to illuminate the pylon and to enable
the search for further evidence in the darkness and fog. The body
was in the morgue. It was the corpse of Vincenzo Maggioni, said
the identity card they found in his pocket; born in Novi Ligure on
19 June 1926. The photo was of a face without a mustache. In the
wallet were another couple of photographs, the size of stamps: a
young blond woman running and a portrait of a kid about ten.
They opened the minivan. The insurance was made out in the
name of Carlo Fioroni, and a pack of Senior Service cigarettes lay
on the dashboard.

"Terrorist Dies near Milan While Trying to Blow Up a Pylon.'"
This was the headline in the early edition of the *Corriere*. Below
was a photograph taken from a distance: the man with a beard,
lying among the weeds, seemed to have lost a leg.

At 7:30 on the morning of the 16th, Inspector Calabresi asked the
doorman on Via Andegari to make him a coffee. Calabresi used to
drop by now and then. He waited until Giovanni, the doorman, had
finished shaving. Then he took him down to the morgue. Giovanni
did not make an identification. But he had recognized him.

At least thirty people who had nothing to do with the underground political struggle started with surprise when they saw the

photograph of Vincenzo Maggioni in the papers. The most incredulous tried drawing a mustache on the face. They folded up the papers and then called or dashed off to Via Andegari in person.

Around one, I went into the living room to find the old guard all present: Sergio, Giampiero, Silvio, and Filippo. They were making phone calls, and their expressions were grim. My mother gave me the news. Memories of hugs rose up from deep inside.

On the night of the 16th, my mother had to identify the body. It was Sibilla's turn the following day. The papers were already chorusing, "It's Feltrinelli!"

Milan, September 1999. How's it going? Fine.

I have my sons, Francesca, my friends, rock and roll, my life as a publisher on Via Andegari, my Web site, new bookstores in southern Italy, and the Feltrinelli Foundation. But I still think about that death on 14 March 1972. To die for your ideas is the most radical of fairy tales. But his death did not unleash the power of symbol, it triggered displacement or caricature on both left and right: a life ended by a defective timer that cost no more than a can of beans.

Handling explosives in the night at Segrate was not easy: a sharp movement, a hole in the adhesive tape, and the pin would make contact with the base of the timer. The off-the-record versions don't agree. The case was filed away as an "accident." "But as far as I am concerned, Feltrinelli's death remains a mystery," the magistrate who declared the case closed at the time still says.

Bruno died in a car crash in the early nineties. I tracked down Rooster last spring; it wasn't easy. Pathos is a bubble of hot air, and standing in front of the newsstand in the railway station is no place for pathos: he had been holding a story for me for twenty-seven years. He's no James Bond, and to this day he is brooding over a terrible memory. He didn't know anything about explosives, he told me, and as for the missions, that was his first and last. He did not take part in the preparations. All he had to do was lash a wooden platform to the pylon to support the dynamite. Osvaldo had climbed up, and he asked Bruno to come up and help him: the charge on the central crossbar was to make sure that the pylon would fall in the right direction. An act of sabotage to create a blackout seventeen years before the Fall of the Berlin Wall, one year before the Chilean coup, and one month before the ferocious political elections in Italy.

In San Vito di Gaggiano, the other commando unit decked out its pylon with sticks of dynamite. Nothing happened. The police experts later concluded that the charges 'would never, but never, have exploded.' But, in Segrate, Rooster was hurled several meters backward. Before he noticed the splinter buried in his leg, he was overtaken by the classic split second in which he saw his whole life going by. He could see nothing around him, then he saw Bruno running for the road, one hand clamped over his ear. Bruno had a perforated eardrum.

One was in shock, the other didn't know how to drive, and the keys to the minivan were in Osvaldo's pocket. They ran for it. First on foot, then aboard a local bus.

They could have done nothing to save Feltrinelli.

"Feltrinelli has been murdered" was the immediate conclusion at Via Andegari. Because, on top of the desperation and the not knowing, there came the first slogans from the right: "Feltrinelli, Piazza Fontana, urban guerrilla warfare, and now prison for the accomplices!" For the next ten years, there was scorched earth all around us.

The foreign press entertained the suspicion that the publisher had been taken to Segrate while unconscious. (Poison? A karate blow?) And the suspicion of a "terrible set-up" also resounded in Berlinguer's report to the 13th party congress. The most exact headline: "A Revolutionary Has Fallen" (*Potere Operaio*, 26 March).

L'Unità of 17 March 1972 offered a portrait with the headline "Tragic Symbol of Failure." The PCI's daily was aiming at the big target: "Heir to a colossal fortune, he had a varied career. From the prisons of Bolivia to an appearance in *Vogue*..." They dwelt on the four wives. But the PCI's secret investigation into Feltrinelli's death did not confirm the "accident" theory.

The Monumental Cemetery with the pharaonic family chapel is not the place where I would have liked them to take my father. It is my only regret. Uwe Johnson and Alberto Arbasino have written about his funeral. Some original sequences are preserved in Bellocchio's film *Sbattl il mostro in prima pagina*. Milan was completely militarized: one police officer for every participant. Eight thousand altogether. Helicopters in the crystal-clear light. The coffin was carried on the shoulders of Feltrinelli booksellers.

There were clenched fists and red flags and cries of "Comrade Feltrinelli, you shall be avenged!" Régis Debray used a megaphone to explain that Feltrinelli had friends all over the world. Sibilla was at the cemetery all morning. Shielded by dark glasses and a black veil, Giannalisa issued her statement: "Finally my suffering is over." The student movement leader Mario Capanna (Giangiacomo would have called him a PCI flunky) made a speech. Giulio Einaudi came. There were Feltrinelli's German colleagues Heinrich Maria Ledig Rowohlt and Klaus Wagenbach (who made a brief speech), students missing school for political reasons for the first time, and the tears of those who had shared important moments with him or even just a plate of risotto al salto.

Several years later, a traffic policeman stopped me to give me a ticket. He felt he had to tell me that he had been on duty at the cemetery that day. He recalled seeing the cortège pass by with the red flags and the flowers from Oberhof and Villadeati. He too had raised a clenched fist, and his superiors had made him pay dearly for that. Communism, one of the great themes of the last century, was more than just Ceaușescu overthrown by a crowd in a dreary cement square.

What remains? My father taught me how to get hooks out of fish and now to roast meat, how to walk in the snow, drive fast, and consider that there are not just apples and pears, but fruits that provide nectar in the desert. He taught me to understand the story of the poet who died in his cage and many other things I still don't completely know, or that are part of our secret language.

I saw him overturn tables when they should have remained where they were, "because everything and I mean everything must and will change." I saw him endure the fury of the fever that makes men weak because man is weak. He warned me that life is punctuated by heartbreak, but I didn't see him grow old with cataracts in both eyes. Did the explosion happen because of a sharp movement up on the crossbar (the fabric of the pocket pressing against the timer, the pin making contact), or did someone set the timer with minutes instead of hours? The answer might close the story, but it would not resolve what really matters.

Acknowledgments

The private papers of Giangiacomo Feltrinelli, including the correspondence with Boris Pasternak, are kept in the Feltrinelli Foundation. The Secchia Archives are also there.

The documents from the Office of Confidential Affairs of the Ministry of the Interior come from the files on investigations into right-wing subversion in Lombardy and the Veneto conducted by the investigating magistrate Guido Salvini.

The internal documents of the Italian Communist Party are kept in the Fondazione Istituto Gramsci in Rome.

The papers on my grandfather, Carlo Feltrinelli, are in the state archives.

Archives in Washington, Moscow, Berlin, and Athens were consulted for the purposes of this book.

I wish to thank all the people who gave me their accounts. Many others have not been mentioned in the book but are a part of it: I am thinking, for example, of Irene Panatero, Stella Bossi, Aureliano Casati, Eliseo Campari, and Beniamino Triches.

An affectionate embrace goes to the old guard: Silvio Pozzi, Romano Montroni, Valerio Bertini, Carlo Conticelli, and Tina

Ricaldone. Sadly, Giuseppe Del Bo, Giampiero Brega, Filippo Carpi, and Gaetano Lazzati are no longer with us.

Duccio Bigazzi, who died recently, gave me the courage to finish this book. Bettina Cristiani, Cesare Milanese, Adriano Aldomoreschi, Cecco Bellosi, Oreste Scalzone, Gianfranco Petrillo, Aldo Giannuli, Gianluigi Melega, Luciano Segreto, Chiara Daniele, Peppino Zigaina, Angelo Verga, Alberto Cavallari, Giandomenico Piluso, Giuseppe Saba, Juan C., Margherita Belardetti, and Salvatore Veca were all extremely helpful. None of them is responsible for any shortcomings or errors contained in the text.

The book owes much to many other people, especially at Via Andegari. Every one of them deserves my gratitude.

Finally, the support and encouragement I received from Rodolfo Montuoro was of fundamental importance; and then there is Francesca. Francesca did more than anyone.

Index